AMERICA AMERICA
God Shed His Grace on Thee

MEMOIRS OF CAPTAIN BOB

ROBERT LLOYD SPARE

Written by: Robert Lloyd Spare
Edited by: Lynn Snowden
Cover by: Susan Newman-Harrison
Designed by: Lynn Snowden

Library of Congress Control Number: Pending

ISBN 978-1-7337293-8-3

ROBERT LLOYD SPARE
MEMOIRS OF CAPTAIN BOB

TABLE OF CONTENTS

Dedication

To those who have been most influential in my life:

Judy, my beautiful wife of fifty-four years who taught me
how to love and be loved.

My Lord and Savior who has watched over me and
has been the guiding light of my life.

My adoptive parents, Bob and Lola Spare, who taught me
values to live by and provided opportunities to succeed.

My sons, David and Steven, and my grandchildren,
Sophie, Ali, Matt, and Charlie, all of whom have brought
great joy to my life; and to generations to come.

My genetic siblings, Jim, Barbara, Ray, and Ben,
and to my adopted brother and sister, Tom and Susan.

My many wonderful friends, too many to list,
but each a valued part of my life.

Also dedicated to:

My country, whose Declaration of Independence and Constitution
established a democratic republic, which is a beacon of
freedom for the world.

Our free-market economy, which has created unparalleled prosperity.

Preface

These memoirs are the result of a seminal event in the lives of five siblings. All of us agreed that the traumatic change in our lives at an early age should be chronicled. Jim, the oldest, is a cerebral writer but had no apparent interest in taking on the task. Barbara, the only girl, and Ray, the fourth youngest, did not volunteer to write our "story." Ben, the youngest, was an accomplished writer but tended toward sexually explicit storylines. He passed away prior to taking on this project.

A few years ago, I determined that the event which dramatically changed our lives would not be penned unless I volunteered. In 2011, I leisurely began to write a stream of consciousness on a yellow, legal pad of paper but lost interest after about ninety pages of rambling. In January, 2020, I attended a writing and publishing seminar sponsored by the Stanford Club of Pasadena. Naomi Hirahara (Stanford '83) was the guest speaker. After the meeting, I discussed with her my frustration in developing a format for my memoirs. She suggested I start with a seminal event in my life and then build other storylines around that initial thought.

Coincident with this guidance, the COVID-19 virus started to spread in the United States. With a mandated lockdown on activities, suddenly I had time and significant opportunity to meaningfully pursue my memoirs.

After reading through my memoirs, I thought of other compelling questions. What had life been like for Jim and Ben in the Jennings family? What was it like for Barbara and Ray growing up in the Tripp family? A postscript adds their reflections on the varied and different experiences they had with each of their new families.

My primary motivation in writing and publishing my memoirs was the desire to provide my grandchildren and subsequent generations a glimpse of their heritage. I am grateful to my two sisters (yes, two) for their valuable input of events and dates of which I did not recall. Also, I thank my special friend, Barbara Kirmsse, for her encouragement to continue writing, as well as a first proof reading on each completed chapter. The memoirs would not have been published without the assistance of my dear friend of over fifty years, Lynn Snowden. She performed the final editing and dropped in the photos to create a document ready to be published. Being in the printing business, my good pal, Greg Board, was of great assistance. The final step, publishing, was accomplished by the talented Susan Newman-Harrison.

Introduction

Robert Lloyd Spare

(AKA Captain Bob or Bobby)

Born on April 14, 1935
Monterey Park, California
with the given name of
Duane Lloyd Windham

Chapter One

An Unexpected Reunion

It was a late Friday afternoon in 1988 when I arrived home from work and was greeted by Judy, my wife of 24 years. Our suburban home in San Marino, California was a quiet refuge after a hectic week in the capital markets investment world, and I was looking forward to a relaxing weekend with the family.

Judy informed me we were going to La Posada for dinner with our sons Steven, David, and David's best friend, Jay Dick. Then, Judy did something highly unusual. She handed me a letter and asked, "Aren't you going to open it?" In the obvious handwriting of a woman, I glanced at the letter which had a return address from a B. Martindale in Laguna Beach, California. Then, I knew what had aroused Judy's curiosity. I had no clue who B. Martindale was. Exercising discretion, I took the letter to the bedroom where I changed for dinner-and read the letter.

At dinner, while having an adult beverage, I pulled the letter from my pocket and casually said that I had something important to discuss. Before I could read the letter, David said, "Dad, I bet the letter is from your biological sister." I was blown away by his comment. I had been adopted at the age of six and was aware I had siblings; however, this was not a subject I often discussed. I proceeded to read the letter out loud. It was from Barbara Martindale. She stated that she believed we were related, brother and sister, and asked me to call if I wished to meet her and her husband, Al.

Very soon thereafter, Judy, David, and I drove to Laguna Beach to reunite for the first time in 49 years with Barbara and our oldest brother, Jim. Five of us, four boys and one girl, had been adopted by three different families, and the adoption records had been sealed. Consequently, it had not been possible for my adoptive parents to obtain information about my sister or brothers. Needless to say, our meeting was incredibly emotional, but without tears, for we were filled with joy at the realization we had an entirely new family to celebrate. We had so much catching up to do. At that first meeting, we talked for hours.

Barbara's parents had not told her much about her and her brother Ray's adoption; however, deep in the recesses of her mind, she knew that there had been other siblings in her life. After her parents died, Barbara found her adoption papers. With Al's encouragement, she hired a genealogist to launch a search for her siblings. Finding the first was easy. Our brother Ray had been adopted along with Barbara. They had grown up in Pasadena, California with the Tripp family. The others were not as easy to find. Youngest brother Ben was found in the Village in New York City. That led to Jim, the oldest, who was in Sand Point, Idaho. Ben and Jim had been adopted by the Jennings family and had grown up on a ranch in Red Bluff, California. Lastly, they found me. I was adopted by Bob and Lola Spare of Los Angeles, California. Interestingly, after my adoption, I grew up in the same general vicinity of Pasadena where we as siblings were born and raised in the few early years we were together.

Why were we put up for adoption? Why were we adopted by three different families? This is the story, as I understand it. Our mother, Ellen Harrison Young, had moved to California from North Dakota with her family when she was 9-years-old. Horace Durward Windham, our father, had moved with his family to California from Alabama as a young boy and settled in the San Gabriel Valley. Don, as he was known, attended Alhambra High School. He excelled in track and football, and as a quarterback, he led the team to a league championship. His hopes of competing at the college level were dashed when his father suffered a serious injury, and young Don was required to work full time to help support the family.

Ellen and Don met while painting scenery at the Pasadena Playhouse, fell in love, and were married in 1933 at the age of twenty. What is beyond belief is they produced five children in six years during the worst depression in our nation's history! Ellen later quipped, "Maybe we didn't know any better." In about 1939, our father lost his job. Unlike today, there were no safety nets from the government for the unemployed. He made a tragic mistake when he robbed a store for which he was arrested and went to prison. Without means of support, our mother had no choice but to put the five of us up for adoption. The Children's Home Society took custody of us and began the placement process.

Unfortunately, the placement process was more oriented to the desires of the adoptive parents rather than the needs of the children. Jim, the oldest at seven, was chosen by the Jennings family. He was told to select one other sibling to go with him. This was quite a responsibility for a seven-year-old. Jim chose Ben who was the youngest. Barbara, Ray, and I were selected by the Tripp family. However, around that time, I went to the hospital. When I was released, the Tripps decided I was high risk, so I was sent back to the agency. Soon thereafter, I was adopted by the Spare family. Lola Spare had worked as a volunteer at the agency. Years later, she told me she had inquired about adopting all five of us, but she was told that there were so many families who wished to adopt children that they had to split us up.

Ray   Barbara   Bob

My "new" family truly blessed me with encouragement and opportunities I would not have received with my biological family. The downside, however, was the missed opportunity to grow up together despite sibling competition, fighting, and rivalry. Being split apart, we missed shared experiences that help create life's memories-the highs and lows, successes and failures. Now, we were blessed with a second chance together.

However, there were still pieces of the puzzle missing. In December 1989, the genealogist Barbara had worked with contacted her with a revelation. She had found our mother. She wondered if we would be interested in meeting her. Barbara contacted the brothers. Although Jim was hesitant, we decided it was the right thing to do. Ellen, our mother, was not aware of the genealogist search and, thus, was shocked when she received a letter from Barbara explaining the situation. Barbara invited her to fly to Orange County from Auburn, California. Barbara and Al, being very enthusiastic about their first meeting with Ellen, soon invited all the brothers and their families to a barbeque at their home on the bluffs overlooking Laguna Beach. It was quite a festive but dramatic gathering. Ellen told me that her one wish in life had been to see her children before she died. Barbara and Al's perseverance and generosity made her wish a reality. It was also the first time I had the opportunity to reunite with Ray and Ben, the two youngest brothers. At this gathering, many of the cousins met for the first time, as well.

Al and Barbara Martindale

After half a century of separation, there was a lot of catching up to do. Although dispersed geographically, we arranged several mini-reunions. In 1992, Barbara and Al rented a yacht in Newport Beach, and with many family members in attendance, we celebrated Ellen's 80th birthday. As queen for the day, she was overwhelmed with all of the love and attention. Ten years later, we celebrated Ellen's 90th birthday at an outdoor restaurant overlooking Lake Tahoe.

Still the puzzle was not complete. We had heard our father had worked in Las Vegas. We wondered if he might still be living there. After having met our mother thirteen years prior, Barbara and Al initiated a search for H.D. using the internet. They were able to trace him to Las Vegas. We were enthusiastic about meeting Dur (also known as Don, Papa, or H.D.). At last, in 2003, we finally had closure, and the puzzle was now complete.

Barbara and Al spent six months of the year in Las Vegas. In what must have been an emotional but joyous occasion, they were the first to meet our father. Soon, Judy and I drove to Las Vegas to meet H.D. (my handle for our father). Barbara, being more sentimental, called him Papa. Jim and Ray and Ray's wife, Karen, joined in the reunion. For me it was truly a magical moment. Later, Barbara commented on what a sweet, kind, and loving person Papa was. I agreed! What a joy it was to spend those few days getting acquainted. After our gathering, I could not help but reflect on how life would have been had we survived as a family. What would it have been like to spend those formative years together? At the same time, I could not help but think about my adoptive parents, Bob and Lola Spare, and the foundations of religion and academics they gave me, for which I am eternally grateful.

Sophie with H.D and Ellen

Our parents, Ellen and H.D., were divorced in 1942 after separating in 1939. Subsequently, Ellen married John Butler. They had an idyllic life fishing the lakes and streams in the western United States. Together, they had no children.

World War II erupted when H.D. was in prison. He was approached by a senior army officer who offered to release him from confinement if he joined the United States Army. H.D. was assured his conviction would be expunged from his record if he received an honorable discharge at the end of his service. He jumped at the opportunity and from 1942-1945 proudly served his country in North Africa, Italy, France, and Germany. After discharge, H.D. requested the agreed upon clearing of his record but was told there was no such agreement. I can only imagine his frustration, disappointment, and anger. However, many years later, Ronald Reagan issued a Presidential pardon and cleared his criminal record. Justice at last!

In 1942, H.D. married Evelyn Winters in Jasper County, Missouri. That union did not last long, and in 1946, he married Wilma Meek. They settled in Las Vegas where he worked in the gaming industry. They enjoyed a long, happy marriage but had no children.

By the time we were reunited with our mother and father, their respective spouses had passed away. I'm not sure who's brilliant idea it was, but it was suggested we get Mama and Papa together. Papa was excited about meeting with Ellen, but she was reticent. Eventually, she agreed to the meeting. Barbara and Al flew her to Las Vegas from Auburn. The reunion went well. They appeared happy to be together after nearly a lifetime apart. Barbara sent out a card stating, "Grandma Ellen and Grandpa Dur want to be together again." Unfortunately, the honeymoon did not last long, and Ellen moved back to Auburn. Sadly, "You can't go back."

Ellen was born July 19, 1912 and passed away on June 1, 2005. H.D. was born January 25, 1913 and passed away on May 3, 2006. He was honored with a full military burial at the Nevada Veterans Cemetery in Boulder City, Nevada. God bless them!

Chapter Two

Family Number Two

"For I know the plans I have made for you, declares the Lord, plans to prosper you . . .plans to give you hope."
Jeremiah 29:11

After my adoption at age six until the reunion with my sibling sister and three brothers after forty-nine years, I did have another life with new parents, a new brother, and a new sister.

I have always appreciated the haunting hymn "Amazing Grace" written by John Newton in 1779. The words reflect his traumatic experience as a young man when he was pressed into Naval service then traded to a slave trader before being imprisoned. By pure luck (or divine intervention), he was rescued by a friend of his father's and boarded a ship that was returning home to England. However, on the return voyage they encountered a terrible storm and were lost at sea for 27 days.

Upon sighting land, Newton's faith was renewed. He later became a preacher and wrote his beautiful song, "Amazing Grace."

> "Amazing grace! How sweet the sound,
> That saved a wretch; like me!
> I once was lost, but now I'm found,
> Was blind, but now I see."

These words have always had a special meaning for me. Like Newton, I was given amazing grace and at a very young age entered a bright, new life. I can only speculate what my life would have been like in a dysfunctional family. I am certain that I would not have been provided with the same encouragement, educational opportunities, discipline, church environment, and love. This is not to demean my biological parents, but they did not have the knowledge, resources, or commitment to provide such opportunities for their children. So, I was adopted by Bob and Lola Spare who were wonderful, caring parents. It was as if I had awakened in Disneyland when I entered their home. I remember making my first visit to an ice cream parlor with them where I ordered a double scoop in a cone. Minutes later, while walking across the street, I dropped the ice cream in the middle of the intersection. We turned right around and headed back to the ice cream store. Another first was when Dad took me to Gilmore Field to see the local pro baseball team play. I was so proud of my new, Rawlings baseball glove, and was ready to catch a foul ball, but had no luck.

Lola   Bob

What does every cowboy want for his seventh birthday? A Lone Ranger pearl handled revolver and holster was at the top of the list. I don't remember subsequent birthday gifts, but I will never forget the first with my new family.

Bob

Another first was when I made a friend for the first time. Don Reynard lived in the house behind ours in Leimert Park, a suburb of Los Angeles. There was a gate between our houses. We would meet in his playhouse where he would invite two young ladies to join us in a game of "doctor." Well, Don was the doctor, and I watched his examinations with fascination.

Even better than a first friend was my dog Soxxy who had four white feet. We were inseparable. He ran with me when I roller skated, slept with me under the covers at night, and even stole a boxed apple pie for me from the neighbor's porch. We lived in the hills of West Pasadena with winding streets and no sidewalks. Soxxy had a habit of chasing cars on what he considered his street. One early evening, as we were playing in the street, a car intruded on Soxxy's territory. Sadly, he was killed as he attacked the car's tires.

At this time in our nation's history, the country was slowly recovering from the Great Depression which had devastated the economy and lives of millions of Americans. Also, it was a time of war. Germany had invaded the Scandinavian countries, Poland, and France. Although the United States did not officially declare war until December 7, 1941, we did send aid to England and other western allies. I remember that peaceful, Sunday morning when the Japanese attacked Pearl Harbor, as well as the shock and disbelief of my parents and neighbors.

Today, I think of the abundance of things we enjoy: food, clothing, transportation, and recreation. In reflecting back, many families endured a Spartan existence during the war. At that time, food items, such as meat, sugar, and butter were rationed. Coupons were allotted based on family size. Mom was the keeper of the coupons and had to collect them for several days before she could buy a decent piece of meat. Almost everything was rationed, especially items made with steel, rubber, and aluminum-even nylon stockings. However, cigarettes were plentiful and became a source of barter for rationed items.

We gained an appreciation for the little things we had taken for granted during better times. Resourcefulness, perseverance, cooperation, working as team players, and not being afraid to get our hands dirty were just a few of the many lessons learned during this difficult time. It helped to have faith that God was with us, that He would see us through those dark days, and that there would be better days ahead.

One of the early lessons I was taught was to have a strong "work ethic." I'm not sure I fully understood the meaning of that phrase, but I soon was given a vivid example when my parents helped me launch my first work project-a victory garden. After cultivating and fertilizing the ground, planting the seeds, watering and nurturing the plants, it was time to harvest the crops. I was proud and excited as I picked green beans, zucchini, tomatoes, and green onions. I loaded them into my red wagon, which I hitched to the back of my bike, and went door-to-door selling my produce. This was my first job.

My father was regional manager for Union Oil Co. in Los Angeles. He believed everyone should strive to be the very best at whatever they attempted in life. At his service stations, three men would service a car. One would pump the gas, another would wash the windows, and a third would check the tires, oil, and radiator. The attendants were trained to inform each customer about the "dirty"oil in the engine, cracks in the windshield wipers, and wear and tear on the tires. The restrooms at my dad's stations were the cleanest of any in the area, as they were inspected every several hours. All this service was given for about 25 cents per gallon.

Occasionally, young people do dumb things. Prior to being adopted, my parents had an old fashioned washing machine with rubber wringers which were used to squeeze water from washed clothes before hanging them on the line to dry. As I recall, I climbed on top of the machine to reach into the cookie jar. Unfortunately, as the wringers were spinning, my skinny right hand glided easily into them and did not stop until drawn up to near the elbow. I proudly carry a 3-inch crescent scar from that injury. Over the years, I convinced young ladies I received the scar while bailing out of an airplane at 20,000 feet.

In 1942, my "new" family moved to Pasadena. In those days it was like moving to the countryside. The environment was filled with orange groves and open fields with deer, possums, skunks, snakes, and scorpions. Since it was such a healthy environment, my parents decided to adopt two more children, both orphans like myself. Tom was 3 years my junior. He was a big kid who had been abused in a dysfunctional family. Being emaciated, he needed lots of nourishment and TLC. When Tom was offered for adoption, Mom and Dad took him to the doctor for a checkup. The doctor gave my parents a detailed account of Tom's medical problems and suggested they look for another boy. Dad replied, "Well, it sounds like he needs us. We'll take him home." Enough said about Dad's character. Dad was concerned about Tom's physical condition. The two would get up about 6 a.m. and do "deep breathers" to help Tom develop his chest, as well as a sense of accomplishment. Today, Tom has a large, powerful chest thanks to that regimen.

Susan was adopted at age three, seven years my junior. I was very excited to have a younger sister, perhaps emotionally filling the void I felt with the loss of my sister, Barbara. Susan was a model child, as most girls seem to be. Mom was a most proficient homemaker and taught Sue to cook, sew, set a table, dress properly, and generally "be a lady." Whenever a question of etiquette would arise, Mom would open Emily Post's book for the definitive answer. Next to the Bible, this was Mom's most used book. Susan and I lived under the same roof for only seven years before I was off to college; however, we developed a lifelong relationship. I have always loved her as much as any of my siblings.

Our parents gave Tom, Susan, and me support in an environment in which to succeed. The greatest encouragement and expectations were in academics. Thankfully, their request was that we perform to the best of our abilities, which did not necessarily mean producing all A's.

Prior to adopting three children, Mom was an accomplished seamstress with a special talent for "draping," which I learned was a necessary step in designing clothing. With her talent, she had an opportunity to be a lead designer at a movie studio where she would have dressed many of the movie starlets of the day. This she gave up to raise three orphaned children. However, Mom did receive a patent on an innovative woman's bra. It was the first to be cut on the bias. Manufactured in Los Angeles under the

Tom   Susan   Bob

New Freedom
BRASSIERE

Pat. No. 2087354

"Styled in Hollywood"

by

Tre-Zúr

trade name "Love," Mom received royalties on her bra for 18 years. Whether it was apple, mincemeat, rhubarb, cherry, peach, lemon meringue, or coconut cream, Mom's pies had the flakiest, most delicious crust ever. As a pastry chef, Mom was unexcelled. Her peach or apricot cobblers were a welcome change, especially when served with vanilla ice cream. Just as memorable was the fresh baked bread she served hot out of the oven with lots of butter. This was our treat when we arrived home from our one mile walk from school.

Dad loved children, and he enjoyed providing them with treats. He was in the restaurant business, and at that time he would keep our freezer full of hamburgers and ice cream for bbq parties. When he arrived home on warm, summer evenings, neighborhood children would appear in front of our house. As my sister Susan remembers, they would call for "Mr. Bare, Mr. Bare." Dad would emerge with ice cream bars for each child. Susan also reminded me of an every-Sunday event: "I would watch him fill his pockets with candy coated almonds on Sunday mornings before we all climbed into the car to go to church. During the break between Sunday school and church, everyone would gather outside. All the smallish boys, and occasionally a brave little girl, would approach Dad with very large eyes and simply look up at him. Without a word being said, he would reach in his pocket. They would open their mouths like little birds, and Dad would drop a candy in each as they made a circle around him." We all remember Dad's daily ritual. With a cocktail in hand, he would stand in the dining room and peer out the bay window at the San Rafael Hills and mountains beyond and recite words from the 19th century poet William Wordsworth. Only Susan remembers the words.

> "The shades of night are falling fast,
> And through an Alpine village passed,
> A youth, a mighty man was he,
> With strong and sinewy hands."

We now wish we had asked him what the poem had meant to him.

Church was a central part of our daily life, primarily because of Mom's deep faith and commitment. We attended the Church of Christ, a fundamentalist Christian church. Services were held Sunday morning, Sunday evening, and Wednesday evening. That involvement was supplemented with daily Bible reading. We learned the Ten Commandments and were expected to adhere to them, AND dozens more! The church was very strict and judgmental at that time. I struggled with the doctrine that ONLY members of our denomination would go to Heaven. (Over time the church has moderated some of its positions without compromising its basic values and beliefs.) I had trouble with the words "fear the Lord your God and keep his commandments" until I learned that those were Jesus' words to the devil when being tempted. I found more comfort in Mathew 22:37, "Love the Lord your God with all your heart and with all your soul and with all your mind." Written by the apostle Paul, perhaps my favorite verse learned in Sunday school was 1 Corinthians 13:13, "And now these three remain: faith, hope and love. But the greatest of these is love." What beautiful words to guide our lives.

The Pasadena Church of Christ had a congregation of about 100 or so members. Being small, we became a "family" and developed relationships which have endured to this day. Lloyd Nelson, his wife, Inez, and children, Linda, Coyla, and John, are still close friends after more than seventy years. Lloyd was a professor at U.S.C. and served as Chairman of the Board of Trustees at Pepperdine University, which was founded as a Church of Christ college. Another friend and member of our congregation was Bob Jones. I first met Bob and Jane when they were a young married couple attending U.C.L.A. in the mid 1940's. Bob managed a big-five accounting firm in Los Angeles and followed Lloyd Nelson as Chairman of the Board at Pepperdine.

When I was fifteen, I accepted Jesus Christ as my Lord and Savior and was baptized. Walking down the aisle to confess my commitment and belief was traumatic, not because of a lack of conviction, but because of self-conscientiousness. I wished I had been one of the hundreds of converts who were baptized by John the Baptist in the Sea of Galilee.

Family vacations and travel are such a big part of family life today, but, as I look back on my youth, I remember only one real vacation. We spent a week in a log cabin near June Lake and the Devils Postpile, which is an unusual rock formation in the High Sierras. While at June Lake, we all rowed out into the lake early each morning and caught beautiful, rainbow trout which we cleaned and fried for dinner. As it turned out, Mom was more of a fisherman than Dad.

Several of our other summer "vacations" were spent driving to Arizona in a car with no air conditioning. There, we visited Mom's brothers, Mance and Damon, their wives, and my cousins, Howard and Jackie. Howard was the older of the two and my hero. He took me camping in the desert where we hunted coyotes, which he hated because they had killed one of his dogs. The highlight of the trip was listening to the stories of Grandpa Doodle, a.k.a. Mancel Y. Roberts. Mom's father received his interesting name, I was told, when he was a young boy. He would "doodle" pebbles in water puddles after fresh Spring rains. Grandpa Doodle mesmerized me with stories of his half brother, Dan Roberts, who was a founder of the Texas Rangers and had ridden with Wyatt Earp. As a boy, he recalled standing with a group of soldiers on the banks of the Rio Grande River when one of the soldiers was shot and killed by a member of Pancho Villa's gang on the Mexican side of the river.

In 1908 Grandpa Doodle moved his family in a covered wagon from Texas to Douglas, Arizona where they homesteaded and grew beans. Doodle viewed the move as an adventure to a land of great opportunity; however, the family only saw the harshness of living on the frontier. As a seven-year-old, my mother's responsibility on the trip west was to take care of Mance, her three-year-old brother. Mom never forgave her father for subjecting the family to such a difficult and repressive life.

I cannot even compose two lines of poetry, but Grandpa Doodle, who did not finish high school, wrote a beautiful, insightful poem about his beloved State of Arizona. Entitled "Gold Spot of the West," the poem begins:

"We should thank Our Great Creator,
His precious name be blessed;
He made the mighty oceans,
He made the 'Golden West,'
He made the lofty mountains,
The rivers great and small;
He gave us Arizona,
That I love best of all."

When we moved from Los Angeles to Pasadena in 1942, I was a mid-term student. The Pasadena School District did not have mid-term classes. Consequently, I was required to either repeat a semester or skip ahead half a year. I was a good student academically and could handle the move forward. In retrospect, it was a mistake. I don't know why my parents agreed to the move except for my insistence. I was in need of greater self-esteem and confidence and felt this decision was a positive for me. The negative was that I was a year younger than my classmates. This made it more difficult to compete in sports.

Pasadena had an innovative 6-4-4 school system: K-6th grades in elementary school, 7th-10th grades in junior high school, and 11th and 12th grades on a community college campus. Each school morning Mom would pack a sack lunch with a bologna sandwich and an apple or orange and send us out the door for our one mile walk over the San Rafael Hills to San Rafael Elementary School. It was a pleasant walk through grass fields, which, later, would be filled with new homes. We walked because no parent would waste gasoline during the war. As 6th graders we felt pretty special, but that changed quickly when we started 7th grade at McKinley Junior High School.

McKinley was a melting pot with 50% white, 50% black and Hispanic, and a few Asian students, including upper-middle class families and those living near poverty level. Here, I was introduced to racial strife and students rebelling against authority. Surprisingly, most conflicts were between the blacks and Hispanics. White students were not often involved. The only involvement I had in a racial issue was in defending two students from Beijing, China who were studying in the United States for one year. Leo Love and I were assigned to tutor and help them assimilate. During one lunch period a few Mexican boys harassed them, and we had a brief scuffle. It was encouraging that several other students came to the defense of our guests.

High school years were an age of innocence for me and my close friends. Sex, booze, and drugs were not a part of our life. We were so prudish that we believed "sex" was close dancing and kissing. The good news was, to our knowledge, no one was "doing it," so there was no peer pressure to be sexually active.

During the first three years of high school, I had few dates and certainly no one I could call a "girlfriend." But, that changed when first I saw Barbara Thomas. She worked as a salesperson at the old Broadway Department Store in Pasadena. With medium length black hair, dark eyes which sparkled when she smiled, and a peaches and cream complexion, I thought she was the most beautiful girl I had ever seen. I did not know she was a classmate in school, but I was anxious to meet her. Finally, I bought something I didn't need from the beautiful salesgirl, and we met. We started dating, and although I didn't know what "love" was, I had very warm affection for her. We were inseparable that school year but faced the inevitable upon graduation. Barbara attended Occidental College, and I went off to Stanford. Receiving my diploma in cap n' gown, attending the formal dance with my girlfriend, and ending the magical evening at the local drive-in restaurant with friends, Jim Farmer and Ann Metten (who I recently visited in San Luis Obispo), high school graduation was everything a young person could hope for.

During high school I was involved in many activities, including Key Club (Kiwanis), sports, tutoring Chinese students, and the Letterman's Club of which I was elected president. This was a shock, because I was anything but an outstanding athlete.

BULLPUP LETTER CLUB

The Bullpup Lettermen's Club supplies a strong fellowship and good sportsmanship at all lower division athletes.

ROW ONE Bob Spare, President II; Bob Powers, Jack Mullen, Dan Shoemaker, Vice-president I, Secretary II; Joe Wel Richard DeNek, Treasurer II; James Edmondson, Vice-president II.
ROW TWO Joseph Hall, Adviser; Frank Reinhart, Mike Dorrance, Mickie Downs, Charles Crain, John Werle, James Faree
ROW THREE Dave Stubbs, Terry Smith, Sergeant-at-Arms II; Chuck Gelfond, Lee Conover, Roger MacGregor, Jerry Gova
ADDITIONAL MEMBERS: Eddie Askew, Martin Posner, Tom Ryan, Roger Taylor, Sergeant-at-Arms I; Dirk T

A DAY OFF for Police Chief Clarence Morris came about yesterda when Bob Spare from a local city college took over the chief' duties as part of Youth Day in Pasadena. Here Morris shows hi youthful replacement where to flip the switch which will put hi on the air and enable him to talk to his entire force on a two way broadcast relay.

Before I leave my relationship with Barbara Thomas, I must relate a story that unfolded years later. After I was reunited with my siblings, my sister, Barbara Martindale, told me about her growing up in Altadena and attending Eliot Junior High before going to the Pasadena City College campus for her final two years of high school. Her best male friend was Ladd Thomas. Ladd played the organ at Barbara and Al Martindale's wedding. Amazingly, Ladd was my girlfriend Barbara's younger brother. My sister and I would not have crossed paths on campus, as she arrived at the high school campus after I had graduated; however, we could have met at Barbara Thomas' house. Small world!

Previously, I wrote about my first job growing and selling vegetables and how that was a lesson in "work ethic." My parents gave me an allowance, but I wanted to earn my own money. Thus, I had many jobs, including delivering newspapers, gardening for neighbors, working as a box boy in our nearby market, and as a bus boy in a local restaurant. My best paying job was working for the Los Angeles County Road Department the summer after high school graduation and during the summer breaks while at Stanford. To me "work" was not work, if that makes sense.

Chapter Three

From the Farm to Paradise

Before heading to Stanford, Don Hausman (a high school and church friend) and I took a one week vacation to Sequoia National Park and Lake Tahoe. The national park is home to majestic sequoias, which are some of the largest and oldest trees in the world. Some can live over 3,000 years. On July 21, 1952, while we were on the ground in our sleeping bags, the 7.3 magnitude Tehachapi earthquake hit at 4:52 a.m. As we stared into the star-lit sky above, we could see the giant trees rolling with the shock waves. With nowhere to run or hide, we waited until the major shock waves subsided to pack up the car and head for Lake Tahoe.

In September, Mom, Dad, and I drove to Stanford with my clothes, typewriter, desk lamp, alarm clock, and radio. Cell phones and computers would not be essential equipment for many years. Stanford was affectionately referred to as the "Farm." It was located in the hills above the southern end of the San Francisco Bay and was surrounded by vast expanses of open fields and farmland. We were known as the Stanford Indians. Our mascot was a proud, full-blooded Indian, and at athletic events Prince Lightfoot would ride around the stadium on his pony with headdress, war paint, and spear held high in the air.

I shared a room in Toyon Hall with three other freshmen. Roger Nye was from Alhambra, a town not far from my hometown of Pasadena. Bill Coffee was from Missoula, Montana. Ned Avery was an American who lived in Argentina where his father was a commercial airline pilot. We all got along exceptionally well, probably because we were so occupied trying to survive academically and did not have time for dissension. Our home for the next nine months was a small room with

22

four desks for studying and a smaller room with two bunk beds for sleeping. We did have a wash-basin in the room, but the showers and toilets were down the hall.

Even though I had excelled academically in high school, I had not attended a school district with a high academic rating. Consequently, I was not as well prepared to compete against the older, brighter students, many of whom had attended prep schools. As if school wasn't difficult enough, my friends talked me into running for freshman class president. Mercifully, I lost the election.

Fraternity rushing was a big event and an exciting time. I had offers from several fraternities but decided, along with my friends, Jerry Fuller, Jiggs Davis, and Bill Coffee, that Theta Xi was the best choice. We had a dynamic group of pledges with diverse interests, backgrounds, and talents. The fraternity allowed for a healthy balance between academics and extra-curricular activities.

Freshman year was difficult socially for us males, because there were so few women in our class. The ratio was two men for every woman, many preferring to date upperclassmen. Through my buddy, Jerry Fuller, I was fortunate to have a few dates with Bobbie Carter. Jerry had known her at Punahou High School in Hawaii. However, our relationship was fleeting, as she was swept off her feet by Stanford's star pitcher.

After my freshman year, I again worked for the County Road Department and lived at home for the summer. This allowed me to earn much needed cash for the next school year. Stanford was on the quarter system, which was in contrast to the traditional two-semester system. Back at Stanford, fall quarter began with Hell Week or initiation into

Theta Xi. All of us survived except one pledge who complained about being "humiliated." Needless to say, he was "de-pledged." The worst event of initiation week was when all the pledges were herded into a small, dark room and forced to listen to Chinese happy birthday music all night. It was not long before the pledges were able to get even with the "active" members. One Saturday night after several members dropped their dates off at the dorms, we kidnapped them and drove to a deserted barn across the bay in Hayward. We chained them together with leg irons and left. Sunday morning, the police picked them up walking as a chain gang down a lonely, country road.

Bob during Hell Week

Academics became more challenging during sophomore year. This was partly due to my spending too much time engaged in fraternity activities, as well as "hashing" in the girls' dorm, playing soccer, and having an occasional date. If "hashing" is a new word to you, it means working in the kitchen either washing and drying dishes or serving meals and busing the dishes. My parents paid my room and board and tuition, but I needed to supplement their assistance. Hashing allowed me to receive free meals.

My grades suffered. After not passing a geology final when I was sick with the flu, I was put on academic probation for a quarter. I was embarrassed but able to obtain a job on campus doing construction work. Instead of "hashing," I was able to make good money and get into excellent physical shape at the same time.

I returned to Stanford for winter, spring, and summer quarters. Summer school allowed me the opportunity to take the classes I missed while on probation. I resided at the Kappa Alpha Fraternity house where I developed a life long friendship with Bill Russ with whom I would play rugby the next year. During the summer, I also had an operation to remove bone chips from my ankle. After surgery, the Stanford orthopedic surgeon put a non-walking cast on my leg, because he didn't want me to put weight on my ankle. I had the best of intentions of staying off the cast, but the volleyball court was too enticing. Bill and I played the game almost every day. When I went to the doctor for the follow-up appointment, the cast under my foot was worn off. Needless to say, the doctor was furious. I blamed him for not initially putting on a "walking" cast. Fortunately, the ankle healed completely.

Junior year was upbeat. My academics improved. I enjoyed fraternity life, as well as playing soccer and rugby. Early in the first quarter, the fraternity invited potential pledges to an open house. Al Hilton was responsible for inviting attractive, young coeds to help host. There, I met freshman coed Karen Shearer. Before any of my "brothers" could make a move, I asked her for a date. After that first date, we were inseparable and dated only one another for the rest of the year. I knew I was in love. It was the "real thing." Whether studying alone or involved with a group, I wanted to be with Karen every moment. The feeling was not one I had experienced, and it felt good. Our romance grew. As the end of the school year approached, I planned on our seeing each other over the summer and looked forward to a wonderful senior year together. Suddenly, my world came crashing down when Karen informed me she was going to transfer to the University of California at Santa Barbara to be with her former high school boyfriend. She had told me about this dude but had led me to believe I was the only one for her. I was devastated. We did have a "goodbye" date that summer. My fraternity brother, John Clark, and his girlfriend joined Karen and me for an evening of refreshments on the cliffs overlooking Santa Monica Bay. We threw blankets on the grassy hillside and drank beer as the sun set over the horizon of the Pacific Ocean. As the sky darkened and stars began to brighten the sky, Karen and I reminisced about the wonderful year we had spent together. I saw tears rolling down her cheeks. My buddy, John, told Karen she was making a terrible mistake, but her decision had been made. I gave her a hug and a kiss. As I departed, I wondered how two people could be in love and then have it vanish so quickly. This was a painful lesson in "love."

That summer my father bought property in Ojai, California. Ojai is an old town sitting in a valley surrounded by orange, lemon, and avocado groves where delicious fruits and vegetables abound. Located in the mountains east of Ventura, he built a motel near the exclusive Ojai Valley Inn and golf course. I was given the opportunity to dig ditches for the sewer lines. This got me in great shape for the upcoming soccer and rugby seasons. I dated a few gals from nearby Santa Barbara and Carpinteria, but my heart was not ready for a new relationship.

Bob

Tom   Sue

Senior year arrived. Important decisions needed to be made, but the furthest I could project my life was nine months, graduation time. At this time, there was a military draft in effect. I had been given an exemption while attending college. The prospect of being drafted by the Army was not appealing. Along with my fraternity brothers, Peter Brink, Mike McGinnis, Jerry Fuller, and Chet Bjerke, I applied and was accepted into the Naval Officer Candidate School (O.C.S.) in Newport, Rhode Island. I then knew the path for the next four years.

With academics, social life, two varsity sports, and several paying jobs, senior year was almost too busy. George Priddle was my soccer coach and a senior administrator at the main library. When Coach knew I was looking for work, he got me a job delivering books from the main library to satellite libraries around campus: medical, business, law, and others. My hours of work were flexible. I was paid $60 a month which was a lot of money when you consider tuition was only $220 a quarter. Tuition did not increase during my four years on the "Farm." I also gardened for a lady in Palo Alto each Saturday morning, worked for the Student Police at athletic events, and was a lifeguard at the women's swimming pool- my easiest and favorite job. I mentioned my hashing job at the fraternity house; senior year I was the dish washer and Jim Morrow was the drier. We worked with the house cook, Jimmy Perkins. As graduation approached, Jimmy asked me, in all sincerity, "Spares, what's 'yo last name?" I responded, "Spare." To which he quizzically replied, "'Yo name is Spare Spares?" A side note: Jimmy was fired the following year when it was discovered that he ran a restaurant in town and much of our food was going to support that enterprise.

Just before the beginning of senior year while at home in Arcadia, I met Sonya Davison at a reception sponsored by Stanford. The purpose of the gathering was to allow incoming freshmen the opportunity to meet with and ask questions of a few of us who were upperclassmen. Sonya lived in Arcadia a few blocks from my parents. My parents had recently moved there from Ojai. I also met Mike Cory, an Arcadia High School graduate with Sonya. A year later Mike pledged Theta Xi.

Shortly after arriving back at Stanford senior year, I made a date with Sonya. I was not looking for a serious relationship. However, after a few dates, I was hooked. She was an outstanding swimmer and skier and was selected to become a cheerleader, otherwise known as a "Dolly Girl" on the "Farm." Sonya had medium length black hair, dark eyes, stood 5' 4", and had a girlish, athletic build. Her sparkling, expressive eyes lit up any room. Sonya was gregarious and fun loving but, also, sensitive and studious. Truly, we were inseparable. We went to sporting events, picnics, the beach, and fraternity parties together. On most Wednesday evenings, we could be found in the quiet solace of the chapel service at Memorial Church on campus. It was one of the few times during the week we could meditate and commune with God.

The year passed much too quickly. Even though Sonya was my girlfriend, I did have time to enjoy my pals, many of whom have been lifetime friends: Jerry Fuller, Jiggs Davis,

Chet Bjerke, Pete Brink, Chuck Arledge, Mike Cory, Jim Morrow, Nate Topol and Dick Babb. I left Dick's name for last, because I wanted to comment on our friendship. Dick was my roommate in the fraternity house during junior year and again senior year when five of us rented a house close to campus in Palo Alto. I must confess that Dick gave me an inferiority complex; however, one filled with admiration and amazement. He was slight of build weighing about 135 pounds, but he started on the varsity soccer team and was an intra-mural wrestling champion in his weight class. Dick took an overload of classes, dated bright, attractive coeds, played in a classic Dixieland band, and read two novels every quarter to keep his mind active. As if we weren't busy enough, Dick and I decided to attend a different church each Sunday to learn more about different religious teachings. After one Sunday outing, evidently Dick was moved by the Spirit and gave most of his clothes to the needy. Not surprising, Dick went on to become a medical doctor.

As the school year progressed, the emotional feelings between Sonya and me flourished and blossomed into a deep love. We knew we wanted to be together forever. However, the reality was that she was a freshman, and I was soon to depart for Officer Candidate School and then serve a three-year commitment in the Navy.

Meanwhile, it was graduation time. Sonya and I were blissfully enjoying parties and festivities surrounding that event. It was a time of satisfaction and relief, as well as a time of uncertainty and mixed emotions. As seniors, we were ready to conquer the world and could feel the excitement and energy as graduation approached. The only sadness was parting from friends with whom we had shared agonies and victories for four years. We had shared "life" and would remain friends until our paths crossed again. The graduation ceremony was held at the outdoor Frost Amphitheater. The commencement speaker was former President Herbert Hoover who had attended Stanford University and founded the Hoover Institution. Mom and Dad attended the ceremony and took Sonya and me to dinner after the graduation. I don't think everyone was happy about the seriousness of our relationship.

Sonya and I returned to our homes in Arcadia where we had an opportunity to solidify our love away from the campus scene. Before leaving for O.C.S., I worked for the County Road Department one more time. On September 13, 1956, I departed for the Navy, confident our love would endure throughout our separation.

After graduating from O.C.S., I had a two week leave over the Christmas holidays, which I spent at my parent's home in Arcadia. Sonya was home from school, and we enjoyed being together and reinforcing our commitment to each other. My parents invited Sonya's parents, Rudy and Elsa, to dinner at our house. They wanted to meet the parents of this girl with whom I was "infatuated." The event was anything but festive. The talk was pleasant, but there was no support or enthusiasm for our relationship. This was an issue we should have addressed at that time.

Susan   Tom   Sonya

The holidays ended much too soon. Sonya returned to school, and I flew to Jacksonville, Florida to attend Naval Air Ground Officer's School for two months. Sonya and I did not know when we would be together again, but the Navy and God were on our side. From Jacksonville, I was sent to Hawaii to join my first active duty airplane squadron which would be relocated to Guam. There were no cell phones, e-mails, texts, or Facebook in the 1950's. This meant communication was by landline telephone, which was very expensive, or by mail.

Sonya faithfully sent letters and cards, often with her own poetic verses. Her poetry was personal, sensitive, and always romantic. The verse was sometimes a little suggestive, although we had never been intimate. Her poetry was beautiful, professional, and should have been published.

To my surprise and delight, I was selected to attend Air Intelligence School at the Naval Air Station in Alameda, California beginning in January 1958. This would allow me to take leave prior to reporting for school, and Sonya and I could spend the holidays together after being apart for only one year. The bonus was that Alameda was only forty-five minutes from Stanford. For three months, we would be able to spend weekends together. During this time we were able to enjoy a memorable ski trip to Lake Tahoe where my friend Bill Weinberg broke his leg.

During the holidays, we discussed marriage. Sonya's wish was for us to marry as soon as possible. I offered the wisdom of waiting two years until she graduated, and I completed active duty. Not surprisingly, emotion prevailed over logic, and we announced our engagement. Our parents responded to our joy and excitement with half-hearted congratulations. Sonya may have been right in wanting to start our life together away from external pressures and enjoy new experiences in foreign lands.

Six months later, I returned home on two weeks leave. Sonya and I were married in the Episcopal Church in San Marino. It was a small wedding with family and friends. Sonya looked gorgeous in her long, white gown and pearl necklace I had given her as a wedding gift. Rudy walked her down the aisle. We said our vows, "For richer or poorer, 'till death do us part." We honeymooned in Santa Barbara before I returned to Guam. Sonya then awaited transportation by ship to our tropical home in the

South Pacific. It was nearly six months before she walked down the gangplank in Agana. That day, I was the happiest sailor in Guam, maybe even the entire Navy.

The day she arrived was a typical day filled with sunshine: temperature 86 degrees, humidity 86%, and a trace of rain. The scenery was beautiful with coconut palms covering the hillsides and towering white, cumulus clouds on the ocean's horizon. The environment was similar to Hawaii's but without the trade winds to stifle the heat. We drove to the Naval Base where I had arranged for housing in the married officers quarters. Sonya was pleasantly surprised at the quality of our housing. We had a new two-story, two bedroom duplex located about two minutes from one of the most magnificent ocean diving areas in the world. We looked at each other and thought, "Are we really here, married, and ready to begin our life together?" It was a feeling of total ecstasy.

About 30% of the time, I was deployed to the detachments in Japan, Okinawa, and the Philippines. Sonya was hired as an assistant to the fire chief at the Naval Base, and we settled in developing friendships with other married couples. Our closest friends were John and Louise Dorcak, Ron and Maureen Castle, and Larry and Sylvia Conn. Larry was a fraternity brother and was the Supply Officer at the Naval Base. Every weekend, when I was not deployed, Sonya and I would dive with the Castles and the Conns.

On the occasion of our first wedding anniversary, June 28, 1959, Sonya presented me with a poem entitled, "Life's Dream of Love."

'Twas the night of Kalua,
Stars danced over head,
Sweet music, fruit, and flowers,
A king-sized bed.

California summer,
We stayed in many a town,
Our dreams now realized,
Love bore us her crown.

Storms blackened our pink clouds,
Our seas pitched and tossed,
Our love boat of dreams,
Seemed hopelessly lost.

The goddess of Love,
Snatched back her crown,
"You shall not defile it,
Though your dreams you let drown."

Now life without love,
Is not 'living' at all,
An existence merely . . .
An assent to The Fall.

And love dreams composed,
Of a misty pink cloud,
Are transient and lost,
When the thunder gets loud.

But all dreams aren't nebulous,
Though they soar very high,
They never will vanish,
If love is kept nigh.

There is something akin,
To Hope and a dream,
Secure in the future,
The Promise to redeem.

With the vanishing cloud,
We did not despair,
We salvaged our dream boat,
With love did repair.

She sails now most boldly,
On tropical sea,
The crown now restored,
To thee and to me.

God bless our smooth sailing,
In waters more cold,
To north seas departing,
To a future untold.

The weather and water,
Are beyond our control,
But the safety of "dream boat"',
Is kept in each soul.

One year has proven,
Sea-worthy our craft,
Through life we will man her,
You forward, me aft.

For the dream of a life,
With you to create,
Is a ship well worth sailing,
A sin to forsake."

One of the side benefits of being in the squadron was that Sonya and I could fly, space-available, on one of the aircraft. In the year that Sonya was in Guam, we flew to Japan for a vacation with our friends John and Louise Dorcak. We landed at the Naval Air Station in Atsugi, From there, we rode a train to Hakone National Park which had a magnificent view of Mount Fuji, a mountain 12,000 feet above sea level. We then trained to Nara where they have ancient temples, one with more than three thousand lanterns; it is known for the 1,000 deer that roam the park. Another hour ride took us to Kyoto, my favorite city in Japan. We visited Kinkaku-ji which, in my eyes, is the most beautiful temple in the world.

A week was not enough to fully appreciate the simple elegance of Japan, but I was happy Sonya had experienced exotic foods, slept on a tatami mat in a futon with hot rocks to keep her feet warm on a cold night, and watched a Kabuki stage play.

John and Louise Dorcak

Mt. Fuji

Kinkaku-ji

Another vacation was to Hong Kong-a vibrant city with one of the most picturesque harbors anywhere. We visited just fourteen years after World War II had ended. It appeared that the entire city was under construction. The Chinese Communists had overthrown the Kuomintang, or Nationalist Party, on the mainland in 1949. Three million people then fled across the border into Hong Kong. Many were sleeping in cardboard boxes on the sidewalks. The human misery was sobering, but the sightseeing and delicious food made the trip rewarding. The highlight of the trip was being rowed in a sampan out to a floating restaurant in Aberdeen, a town on the harbor. As we dined in the gently rocking boat lit by hundreds of colorful paper lanterns, we enjoyed the lovely, moonlit evening. What a romantic ending to our trip to Hong Kong.

During the last year on Guam, John Dorcak and I spent significant time identifying quality products we might import to the United States after our completed military obligation. We identified the finest wood carvings in the Philippines, the highest quality lacquer wooden bowls in Okinawa, and many other products in Japan. The most important was Noritake China, which was unknown in the United States at the time.

Our year in Guam went by much too quickly. In December we returned to the United States for my release from active duty. It had been an idyllic year. Sonya and I had played together, worked together, laughed and loved together, and now it was time to plan our future.

We flew to San Francisco where we spent two weeks as the Navy processed my release. We planned to relocate near Stanford, so Sonya could finish her senior year of college. Christmas was nearing. We decided to visit our families for the holidays. This turned out to be a major mistake. Over the holidays, our parents' lack of support for our marriage was evident. It began to negatively affect Sonya's and my relationship. I recall only one argument we had previously, but now we were arguing almost daily about things unimportant.

The day before we were to drive back to Northern California, Sonya told me she wanted to separate: no tears, no drama, just a factual statement. Through my shock, I simply asked, "Why?" She replied she wanted to date Stan Lamb, her high school boyfriend, as well as continue to date me. My response was not gentlemanly, but to which I have no regrets. "For richer or poorer, 'till death do us part."

Obviously, we did not drive north together. Sonya stayed with her parents and I with mine. Shortly after separating, I took some of Sonya's belongings to her house and encountered Rudy working in his garage. We talked civilly until he stated that he and Elsa did not believe I could provide for their daughter "in the manner in which she was accustomed." I told him I was a hard working guy and confident I could adequately provide for Sonya, especially with a degree from Stanford and honorable service in the Navy. With their interference, I was not given the opportunity to prove myself.

One of the fallouts of our separation was that John Dorcak opted out of our import business plans. This was due to his wife's insistence. She felt John should not do business with a divorcee.

As I reflected on our year in Guam, I remember teasing Sonya about her psychoanalysis of people. She did not accept a person's words or actions at face value and believed there was a secondary or tertiary reason for their actions. Years later, I was not surprised to learn that Sonya had completed her undergraduate schooling and went on to receive her PhD in, you guessed it, psychology.

The good news is that Sonya and I had no children. The divorce was not contentious and, happily, I have not needed psychological treatment!

A second lesson in "love."

Chapter Four

Sports

My first memory of playing a sport was when I played baseball with neighborhood kids in front of our house on a winding asphalt street in the San Rafael Hills of Pasadena at about the age of eight. The excitement of batting or catching a long fly ball was exhilarating. Since then, I have never lost the love of competing or camaraderie with others through sports. Over the years, I have played many sports and enjoyed every occasion whether in a sandlot or college stadium.

My favorite friend to play ball with was Karen Ehrenclou, a neighbor. She had a great arm and could hit the ball as well as any of the guys. Karen was fearless. She played tackle football with the boys in a grassy vacant lot, dove out of the treehouse in our large oak tree to a one inch rope, and slid down a steep canyon covered with wet, Spring grass in an old Ford fender. Although Karen was three years older than I, we were inseparable and remained friends for a lifetime.

Like most young boys, I had visions of becoming a professional baseball player and began the odyssey as a third baseman at McKinley Junior High School in Pasadena. I was a pretty good glove man and hit about 300, but the curve ball was my nemesis. I wanted to play football in the ninth grade but was too small and had to wait a year to be eligible. I would rate my performance as a football player as "undistinguished."

Pasadena had an unusual educational system. After junior high school, we spent our junior and senior years at Pasadena City College. My parents placed more emphasis on education than on sports. Consequently, they informed me that I could play only one sport during the last two years of high school. I selected football. Since I was a better baseball player, this was much more of a "macho" decision than an intelligent one. Football turned out to be a bad decision, as I never made the starting lineup. However, my grades were good enough to be accepted at Stanford University.

I did not play basketball in high school, but in my freshman year at Stanford, I decided to try out for the basketball team. I don't know where the impulse originated. Not surprisingly, with no experience and no concept of the fundamentals of the game, I was cut. It was time to hang up the jockstrap and hit the books.

I pledged Theta Xi fraternity. During my sophomore year, I was anxious to move beyond intramural sports. Dick Babb, one of the "brothers," suggested I try out for the varsity soccer team on which he played. I had never seen or played soccer; however, that did not deter me from a new adventure. To my surprise, when Coach Priddle posted the starting lineup for the first game, I was penciled in as the starting left fullback. At the conclusion of our senior year, I was selected as co-MVP fullback in the conference. I credit that honor to Charles Annicq who played directly in front of me as left halfback. Charles was a graduate transfer from Belgium and had played on the Belgium national team. Needless to say, he made my job easier. The biggest surprise of my soccer adventure was when I was selected to attend the Western Regional tryouts for the 1956 Olympic team. Tryouts were held at San Francisco State on a cold, rainy morning in December of 1955. Regrettably, I did not make the cut.

Dick Babb

SOCCER

FIRST ROW, left to right: Charles Annice, Jill Wren, Dick Babb, Total Jones, Steve Welch, Werner Henry, Bill Abbott, Gary Childress, Eduardo Maal, Peter Hanna, Jim Bowditch. SECOND ROW: Hank Palk, Tim Scheck, Peter Meck, Dan Yates, Bob Spare, Steve Griffith, Kirk Mariscol, John Leonard, Dan Whittier, Lennie Gamble. THIRD ROW: Tim Ward, Dave Wrexler, Skip Lord, Art Harlow, Dave Olendorf, Paul Dogbe, Bob Hedrick, Jerry Lith, Ned Avery. FOURTH ROW: Atif Atlor, Roe Faum, Geoffrey Gregory, Scott Krag, Murray Innes, Dick Vinett, Nick Phillips. FIFTH ROW: Mr. Priddle, Jim Montgomery, Tim Condor, Bill White.

Derek Waldeck   Bob

In 2019, I visited my alma mater and was anxious to spend time at a soccer practice and attend a game. It was such a pleasure and honor to meet the head coach, Jeremy Gunn, as well as his assistants and some of the players. Coach Gunn had taken an average soccer program and built it into a championship team winning the NCAA title three consecutive years, 2015-2017. It was astounding how far the team had come in the 65 years since I had last played for Stanford. After two years of correspondence, I was finally able to meet Derek Waldeck. I also had the opportunity to speak with some of the players, and I told them how proud I was of them. Today, there is no way someone could "walk on" and compete without soccer experience. These young men are truly outstanding athletes, many of whom are now playing in Major League Soccer, including Derek Waldeck.

During my junior year at Stanford, I ran into my freshman roommate, Ned Avery. Ned was on the varsity rugby team. Stating that rugby was a

40

"man's" sport, he encouraged me to tryout for the team. Since soccer was played in the Fall and rugby in the Spring, I realized there would be no seasonal conflict. So, I said "ok." I made the team that season but was not on the starting roster for the first game against the University of the Pacific on their field. About ten minutes into the game, as I was sitting on the bench enjoying the action, Coach Pete Kmetovic hollered, "Spare go in at fullback." I was shocked and not certain he had really called my name. There was no time to hesitate, as substitution can only be done when the ball goes out of bounds. I jumped up and pulled down my sweatpants along with my rugby shorts. That elicited probably the greatest applause of my sports career. The only other vivid memory of the game was when Dick Bass, who later became an all-pro running back for the L.A. Rams, ran by me like I was standing still. Thus, began my two-year experience in rugby. This was another sport I had not seen played before I "walked on." The only interruption to my playing was when I had a shoulder separation, minor concussion, and torn ACL-no, not all at once!

The highlight of my rugby days at Stanford was when a rugby side representing Oxford and Cambridge traveled from England to the United States. They toured the country playing matches against several American university teams. The scrum half from Oxford and fullback from Cambridge were guests at my fraternity house. We were much more hospitable to them than they were to us on the pitch (field). They toyed with us the first half and ultimately thrashed us 48 to 8. To add to the insult, their fullback made a running dropkick of nearly 60 yards. I stood watching in awe. If that was the highlight, the low point was playing Cal at Strawberry Canyon, their home field. Cal had the best college team in the country at the time, but we felt we had a good chance of knocking them off. I was involved in a pileup, and while on the ground, a player's cleats caught the back of my head. Later, when the ball went out of bounds, I was ready to throw it back into play when I heard Johnny Wilson, a running back for Cal, yell, "Hey Spare, your head is bleeding." (Johnny and I had grown up together). I reached behind my head, and sure enough, my hand was bloody. Today, a player would be taken out of the game in such a situation, but in those days the rules were more lenient. I finished the game and was taken to the dispensary for stitches. The worst part was that I missed the beer party. On the bus ride back to Stanford that night, Coach Kmetovic, the backfield coach for the football team, asked me to try out for the football team. I was honored but explained that I had been a lousy player in my football playing days. Plus, I felt there really wasn't a position I could play. I was too slow for running back, too short for receiver, and too small for the line. He dismissed my comments and said I would play guard. At 175 pounds I was 40 pounds lighter than most guards. I politely said, "No."

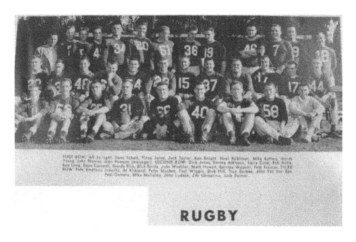

RUGBY

I loved the much more civilized sport of volleyball. It was a favorite recreational and intramural sport at Stanford. When time could have been better spent studying, I played way too much volleyball ball both at the frat house and beach. Later, at my first duty station at Naval Air Station, Barber's Point, Hawaii, I had an opportunity to play competitively with the base volleyball team. By coincidence, there were three of us from Stanford on the team: Cookie Barbeau, Rabbit Miller, and me. Because the team won the all-islands military tournament, we were sent to Memphis, Tennessee for the national tournament. We did well finishing fifth. Regrettably, I was not allowed to travel with the team. I was in navigation school, and my Commanding Officer would not approve my absence.

I have always enjoyed the ocean. During high school and college, I loved to bodysurf. At Barber's Point, I found a new love, board surfing. The day I arrived, my friend and fraternity brother, Pete Brink, took me under his wing and said, "Grab your bathing suit. We're going surfing." Pete joined his squadron two months prior to my arrival, and he had become an avid surfer. I caught the first wave as it crested and rode it as it crashed toward the beach. I was hooked. During my brief three months in Hawaii, we surfed every evening, as well as all day Saturday and Sunday.

When our squadron was moved to Agana, Guam, the romance of surfing was over, for there were no surfable waves on Guam.

The Navy encouraged sports participation, and all bases had teams representing many sports. In 1957, when the squadron moved to Guam, we had a Naval Air Station Agana baseball team that competed with all the other military bases on the island. The baseball team provided me with an opportunity to again play the sport which had been my first love. At 22 years of age, I was the oldest player/coach on the team, and, yes, we did win the all-island military tournament.

Although there was no surfing on Guam, there was some of the finest underwater diving in the world. In ensuing years, I dived in the United States, Hawaii, Philippines, and Caribbean; however, nothing compared to the beauty of the fish and coral in Guam. The island sits atop a tall landmass that drops off 35,000 feet into the "Challenge Deep" in the Marianas Trench, which is the deepest part of the ocean in the world. The island is surrounded by a coral reef. The best diving is within the reef where the water is about 60 feet deep. The water is crystal clear, and you could see a shell on the sandy bottom from the surface. Typically, we would snorkel, but occasionally we would put on tanks and dive outside the reef where the environment was inhospitable with an ocean floor that dropped off rapidly into a dark abyss. The best diving was early in the morning when the fish were out "feeding." The number and variety of fish were amazing and their beauty breathtaking. The only fish we avoided were sharks, manta rays, and eels. The tropical fish swam in schools of hundreds, all with gorgeous colors of blue, green, yellow, black, red, and colors I cannot even describe. It was quiet, peaceful, and serene as we floated with the underwater currents and watched these beautiful creatures living their lives. Occasionally, we would spearfish and sell our catch at the local market. White fish brought 50 cents per pound, eel $2.00, and grouper zero! Today, you can find grouper on the menu of many fine restaurants in the United States.

Diving can be dangerous if you do not follow a few simple rules with number one being "never dive alone." A young pilot on base often violated that rule. On Guam the garbage trucks dumped their load over a cliff into a deep bay where sharks would gather daily to feed. Prior to the dumping, our squadron mate would dive to the bottom of the bay with a camera and film the feeding frenzy. On another occasion we flew to Kwajalein Island. Landing during a severe tropical storm, the waves were breaking over the end of the runway. This same officer asked me to go dive with him once we landed, to which I responded, "You're nuts." The visibility under water had to be close to zero that day. Undaunted, he dove with his spear gun and returned 30 minutes later with a three foot eel he had shot. However, his third daring dive was the unlucky charm. Our squadron mate dove alone in the "hole" off of Guam. He ran out of air at 180 feet. A buddy was in a boat on the surface, but he did not have a team diver with whom to share oxygen. He surfaced too rapidly, got the bends and, after a day in the decompression chamber, was paralyzed from the waist down.

After release from active duty, I returned to civilian life. Even before being gainfully employed, I joined the Eagle Rock Athletic Club rugby team. It was good to get back into some serious competition with a semi-pro team. Few of the players had significant experience playing rugby. Many had been hot-shot community college football players who had not progressed further in the sport and had found rugby. But, there were a handful of excellent players who had competed at the college level. I volunteered to help coach the team while playing fullback, my old position. Many of the players were tough, macho guys with a chip on their shoulder. However, I enjoyed the Sunday afternoon games, as well as the beer parties after each game. Rugby is a violent and exhausting game, running continuously while tackling and being tackled with no blocking allowed. Players receive many bruises but get far fewer serious injuries than in football. At one post-game gathering, one of our more confrontational players left the party with another player, because they wanted to find a bar that served hard liquor. The next day we heard that our teammate, upon ordering a drink, was told by the bartender to "wait your turn." Not being a man of patience, our player climbed over the bar to get his own drink and was tragically shot and killed by the bartender.

All good things must come to an end. My last game of this rough but wonderful sport was in the California Senior Olympics when our Southern California team beat the Northern California side. After the game, although I was only 36 years-old, my wife threw my cleats away. With that, my rugby career ended. To quote W.C. Fields, "And, I never had the courtesy to thank her."

Eagle Rock Rugby Club

The days of playing organized, competitive sports were over. The ensuing years were occupied with more gentlemanly activities: volleyball, softball, golf, and backpacking with the Boy Scouts. Some of the more enjoyable times were spent as a coach or spectator at our sons' sporting events: swimming, baseball, and soccer. At San Marino High School, David ran cross-country and Steven was an all-league tackle on the football team.

Although not an Olympic sport, white-water rafting is as exhilarating, thrilling, and challenging as any in which I have participated. Rapids are rated by size and speed with five being the most difficult. My first experience was on a trip to the Rogue River on the California/Oregon border with my great pals George Miller and John Coleman. Both had their own Avon boats and were seasoned rafters. George also organized trips to Idaho through Idaho River Journeys, which was owned by his longtime friend, Bob Volpert. Typically, we would raft the Middle Fork of the Salmon or the Main Salmon in six-man Avon inflatable boats. On one trip, George wanted more of a challenge, so he reserved Torpedo boats. These were basically single-person, inflatable kayaks with our backpacks used as backrests. Utilizing Torpedos versus Avons doubled the fun but, also, the trouble.

My last trip to the Salmon River was in 2009 when George convinced Volpert to combine the Middle and Main Forks into one ten day trip. I invited my friend, Monte Ross, to join us. Each day, two from the group would take turns riding on the "pig boat." This boat carried the food, as well as the camping and cooking equipment. Late in the trip, Monte and I took a respite from rowing in the Avons and rode on the "pig boat." While steering the boat, the guide proudly proclaimed that he had only flipped one boat in twenty-six years on the river. This was a bad omen. At first, the ride was quite enjoyable. We sat high above the water and gazed at the sculptured canyons and magnificent pines. As we approached each rapid, mostly with a rating of four or five, the guide would relate his strategy for running the rapid. All went smoothly until we approached a particularly large, fast, and steep rapid. Calmly, our guide explained that he would enter the rapid on the right side and slide off a large rock. This would propel us to another huge boulder on our left. We would then bounce off a wall and glide through to calmer waters. He executed the maneuver perfectly until we hit the second boulder. The boat flipped sending Monte and the guide into the river. I ended up under the boat. It was difficult to pop out from under the boat because of the buoyancy of the life vest. On the second attempt, I was successful. After swimming to the shoreline, I was picked up by an Avon crew. I don't think Monte has ever forgiven me for our crazy adventure. At least at the end of each day being beat up on the rapids, George would share with us a sip from "Old Red"-a dented, metal bottle filled with George Dickel bourbon.

Lunch at Big Creek - Middle Fork of the Salmon
Idaho River Journeys   1-888-997-8399

George Miller

My sons and I enjoyed a rafting trip on the Kern River in California. Subsequently, Dave and Steve have introduced rafting to their families. What other sport allows you to participate and have such fun in the beauty and magnificence of the great outdoors?

For many years friends asked me why I didn't play golf. I always answered, "Golf is a sport for old people." Well, I did get older, and I learned that golf could be fun, as well as an asset in business. Quickly, I found out how very difficult this new sport was to play. I like to describe it as the only sport that is more difficult than pole-vaulting, which is impossible.

In my business life there were many conferences. Most included a golf tournament. During the fifteen years prior to retirement, I played in nearly 100 tournaments in some 20 states, as well as internationally. After Judy retired from teaching, she accompanied me to many of the conferences. She fell in love with the game of golf, and we were blessed to be able to play many of the great courses in the country. Golf became an integral and enjoyable part of our lives. We enjoyed golfing so much we joined San Gabriel Country Club near our home in San Marino. We purchased a large second home at Lake Arrowhead. After being guests at Lake Arrowhead Country Club a few times, we decided to join. It is a beautiful course with small lakes and lush, green fairways meandering through valleys covered with huge ponderosa pines. While playing this course, you could not spend a more beautiful day in nature.

Steve Andrews

I retired in 2000 and quickly realized that one of the downsides was having too much time to dream. Judy had always wanted a "little getaway" in the desert. Being a Michigan girl, she disliked cold weather. The desert was certainly not cold. We found a nice three-bedroom condo across from the 14th green on the Arnold Palmer course at PGA West in La Quinta, California. The condo came equipped with a golf cart. The cart was worthless unless we joined the club, so we did. Palm Desert was a golf mecca, and we were fortunate to be able to play on five excellent and challenging golf courses. There was no shortage of friends in the area, as well. Two former business associates had condos nearby. Longtime friends, Al and Sue Williams, lived in the neighborhood year-round. My Navy pal, Woody Clum, and his wife, Lu, had a condo three doors away from us. Also, we had streams of friends who would visit for a few days of golf. The yearly highlight was the Bob Hope Pro-Am golf tournament when the course was graced with notable celebrities and professional golfers.

PGA West

When we sold our family home in San Marino and moved to Pasadena, we resigned our membership at San Gabriel. We then joined Annandale Golf Club for which I had a sentimental attachment, as it is located in the neighborhood where I grew up as a child.

Chapter Five

Military

"Duty, honor, country, those three hallowed words reverently dictate what you ought to be, what you can be, what you will be. They are your rallying point to build courage when courage seems to fail, to regain faith when there seems to be little cause for faith, to create hope when hope becomes forlorn."

These memorable words were delivered by General Douglas MacArthur in a speech to the cadets at the United States Military Academy on 12 May 1962. For some Americans today, these words do not resonate, but for me they are profound and have had an impact on my life. Duty is not a legal obligation but more a moral imperative, a commitment to someone or something. I find it incomprehensible any American would choose to dishonor those who have made immeasurable sacrifices in order to insure our precious freedoms.

When I was in high school and college, the United States had a mandatory military draft. All men 18 years and older were subject to being called into service. There was an academic exemption for men in college, but this was only applicable until graduation. At the end of my junior year at Stanford, four fraternity brothers and I applied for Naval Officer Candidate School. We began after we graduated.

On 13 September 1956, I flew on United Airlines from Los Angeles to New York City. Then, traveling by train to Providence, R.I. and by bus to Newport, I finally arrived at my destination. On that flight, I met two men who would become lifetime friends, Mickey McIntyre and Dick Sowby. Mickey later became a business associate and Dick, my optometrist for fifty years.

The school and barracks were located on the coast, but there were no ships or harbor. Upon arrival, we received our enlisted uniforms and were assigned to our barracks, M4. Our group numbered about forty, and we were in the Class of 29. We lined up alphabetically and were assigned bunks. Richard Lamont Sowby's initials were identical to mine, so we became bunkmates with Dick on the bottom and me on top.

Several years later, after completing our active duty, Dick introduced me to his new girlfriend stating, "Phyllis, this is my friend Bob. He slept on top of me in the Navy." Dick was Mormon and did not drink or swear, but he did have a sense of humor.

The program was heavily oriented toward academics, especially engineering. This left little time for physical fitness, except for marching to all activities. The program was intense. The only free time we had was from early Saturday afternoon until 2100 hours Sunday evening. This liberty did not begin until we had been confined on the base for the first four weeks.

Dick Sowby   Bob

Jerry Fuller

Every minute of every day was programmed-reveille at 0530 hours until "lights out" at 2200 hours. We marched to breakfast, attended classes all day, marched to dinner, showered and shined shoes, and prepared for the next day's classes. We had a special group of guys who decided early on that we would need to share each other's academic knowledge, so we set up a tutoring program where a student who was struggling in a class could get assistance. My weakness was engineering. I would not have passed that phase of the curriculum without help. Even today I cannot explain how to convert seawater into drinking water.

Graduation was a time of celebration, and M4 was especially proud. Our group was the only unit that graduated all candidates. This was unprecedented. At the ceremony, we were saluted by Chief Miller and declared, "Officers and gentlemen by Act of Congress!" This was a lot to live up to.

Prior to graduation, we were asked to choose a preference for active duty. The choices were east or west coast, large or small combatant ship, submarine, supply corp, flight school, Underwater Demolition Team, explosive ordinance disposal, and a few others. We had many laughs when our orders arrived. Jack Simms requested large combatant on the west coast and was assigned to a destroyer on the east coast. Interestingly, I ran into Jack several years later. He ended up being elated with his duty. As it turned out, he had loved the small ship where he was able to do two cruises to the Mediterranean. Go figure!

I requested flight school; however, it was not available at the time because of the backlog of students waiting to train in Pensacola. Lieutenant Echert, our company officer, suggested I attend Air Ground Officers School in Jacksonville, Florida. This would facilitate my getting into flight school.

We were given two weeks leave before reporting for duty at Naval Air Station in Jacksonville, Florida. After the intensive regimen at Officer Candidate School, this duty was like being assigned to a country club. My fraternity brothers, Jerry Fuller and Chet Bjerke, as well as my bunkmate, Dick Sowby, also attended the school. Consequently, it was a pleasant time, because we had more free time to spend as we desired.

This was my first travel to a Southern state. I was surprised and offended by the separation of blacks and whites with the blacks being considered second-class citizens. Having gone to a fully integrated primary school, I was not prepared for the reality of the south.

On a beautiful Sunday morning, Dick Sowby and I got on a city bus to travel from the base to downtown Jax to attend church. The bus was full up front, so we moved to the rear and sat down. The driver informed us that we were not allowed to sit in the back, because the area was reserved for Negroes. Dick and I refused to move. There was a stand off for several minutes before the driver relented and drove on. I don't believe in special treatment for any race or group of people, but I do believe in equal treatment and respect for all people.

The curriculum at Air Ground Officers School was an orientation into the air arm of the Navy. In addition to classroom study, we were given an unexpected invitation to board the aircraft carrier, Franklin D. Roosevelt, CVA 42. We spent a week at sea while the air squadrons conducted CARQUALS (carrier landing qualifications). There was a squadron of A3D Sky Warriors on board. They would be the first to qualify in the Sixth Fleet (the Atlantic). The A3D was a new Naval aircraft, the largest plane to land on an aircraft carrier. Its mission was to deliver nuclear weapons. Seeming choreographed, it was fascinating to watch the deck crew position, launch, and recover the aircraft. Watching flight operations up close renewed my desire to attend flight school. Having passed the physical and written exams, I applied once again. I was again denied. Upon graduation from Air Ground Officers School, I received orders to go to San Diego and attend Bombardier Navigator School.

Because his wife was with him, I did not see much of Chet Bjerke during the two months we were in Jacksonville. I did spend time with Jerry Fuller, my closest friend from Stanford. He was dating an attractive young lady from Jacksonville. It was evident that this cute, Southern belle was more serious about Jerry than he about her. When we finished our class and were ready to move on to our next duty station, Jerry insisted that I be with him for his "goodbyes."

On the way to report to my new duty station in San Diego, I was able to spend one night with my family in Arcadia. My orders were to report to Naval Air Station North Island. This would allow me to qualify to fly in the second seat in the A3D. I was very excited. I believed being put in the catbird seat would give me the experience necessary to qualify for flight school. When I presented my orders to the Duty Officer at the air station, I was informed that the Bombardier Navigator School was already in transit to Whidbey Island, Washington and would not be operational for several months. You can imagine my shock and confusion. It appeared as if God and the Navy were telling me something.

After waiting around for two days, three of us were told we were going to Barber's Point, Hawaii to join VW-1. Upon arrival at our new squadron, the Duty Officer did not know why we were there. Evidently, the Naval Bureau of Personnel had neglected to apprise Barber's Point of our assignment to the squadron. To further complicate the situation, the squadron was in the process of moving to Agana, Guam. They had no idea what to do with us for three months. But, we were not to worry, for the Navy always had schools where they could park people.

During the three months before the squadron moved, I attended navigation, survival training, and escape and evasion courses. Classes finished about 15:30 each day. It was then off to the beach to board surf until about 18:00. After surfing, we played volleyball at the station gym.

Jacksonville had been a nice respite after Officer Candidate School, but this was paradise!

On the first Friday of our first week in Hawaii, the squadron had a softball game followed by adult beverages on the patio of the Officers' Club. Executive Officer (X.O.) Commander Montgomery asked Jack Egan, another new arrival, and me if he could buy us a drink. I ordered a beer and Jack requested a gin and tonic. The conversation went something like this.

> "Bartender, give Ensign Egan a gin and tonic," ordered Commander Montgomery. He then asked, "Bartender, WHAT are you doing?"
>
> The bartender stated, "Sir, I'm making a gin and tonic."
>
> Commander Montgomery then said, "Bartender, we drink only Beefeaters in this squadron."
>
> With that, the bartender poured out the bar gin and substituted Beefeaters, as instructed.
>
> "Bartender, what are you doing NOW?" asked Commander Montgomery.
>
> By now the bartender was frustrated and curtly answered, "Sir, I'm making a gin and tonic with Beefeaters as you requested."
>
> Commander Montgomery said, "Not on ice which has had that other gin on it!"

This was our introduction to Commander Montgomery, a man we would be working with for the next few years.

Earlier, I described the reunion with my siblings after forty-nine years. The five of us discussed our growing up in separate families, as well as the experiences we had in our adult lives up until our meeting. Jim, my older brother, was a Naval aviator. In the Spring of 1957, his ship, the Bonhomme Richard, CVA 31, sailed from San Francisco to Hawaii where an ORI (Operational Readiness Inspection) was required before proceeding to the Western Pacific where they would operate for six months. Jim flew with VA-56, flying F9F-8 Cougars which had a nuclear weapons capability. While the carrier was in Hawaii, Jim's squadron off-loaded at Barber's Point for the inspection. At the same time, I was stationed at Barber's Point with VW-1. Because we were not operational at the time, we became part of the team conducting the ORI on the Bonhomme Richard. Jim and I had not seen each other since we were six or seven years-old and would not have recognized one another. However, there was a high probability that we hoisted a cold, refreshing beer together at the Officers' Club.

On 1 July 1957, we flew our planes to Guam. At this time I was given my first opportunity to navigate. It was a fifteen-hour flight with a refueling stop in Kwajalein. John Landon and Lowell Earl were part of the crew. In Guam we would become roommates in a Quonset hut that had survived since W.W. II. Lowell's dachshund accompanied us on the flight. While standing on the navigation chart, he would put his nose on the map. Lowell claimed that the dog had a better idea of where we were than I did. It was sad leaving the country club life of surfing and volleyball in Hawaii, but it was exciting to look forward to operating in the south Pacific and Far East.

The mean average temperature and humidity in Guam was 86, a bit higher than Hawaii but without the refreshing trade winds in the islands. Cockroaches and mosquitos were prevalent. The base sprayed for cockroaches, but it was highly ineffective. Upon our return to the hut after a few beers at the Club, we would hear the cockroaches scurry across the floor. Our solution in eradicating them was to see how many we could stomp on and kill in the dark. Geckos were prevalent, too, but we were grateful for their feasting on flying pests. For mosquitos, the base would spray the outdoor movie theatre with DDT before the evening show. The mosquitos disappeared, but the obnoxious smell lingered over the audience.

The climate and living conditions were noticeably different, and the change in food was quite dramatic. Guam was a lush, fertile island filled mostly with coconut and papaya trees. There were few fresh vegetables or eggs, and there was no fresh milk. At the BOQ (bachelor quarters) and Officers' Club, we were served powdered eggs and sterilized or powdered milk. Vegetables were frozen except when a ship from the United States would deliver a fresh load of brussel sprouts. The cook, not chef, would prepare them in a huge vat and cook them until they were flavorless mush. It was a treat when we deployed to Japan where we would gorge ourselves with fresh milk, fruits, and vegetables.

It was not long until the squadron was ready to fulfill its mission. This was to provide early warnings for the attack carriers (CVA's) when they were on six month deployment in the Far East. The CVA's operated from Russia's Sakhalin in the north to China's Hainan Island in the south. They were primarily in the Sea of Japan and the East and South China Seas. To accomplish the mission, we maintained detachments in Japan at Atsugi, Naha on Okinawa, as well as Cubi Point in the Philippines. These bases were nearly equidistant from our home base in Agana, approximately 1350 miles.

The squadron had ten Lockheed Super Constellation aircraft configured with long-range search and height finder radar. The plane was equipped with electronic counter measure (ECM) equipment to jam enemy radar and electronic signals. What the aircraft did not have was a weapon system, which rendered us highly vulnerable. Also, it didn't help to cruise at 210 knots. The Super Connie had a Navy designation of WV (W for early warning and V for fixed wing). Thus, we were VW-1 flying WV's and our call sign was "Red Devil." Although there were some tense moments, the aircraft was very dependable, and the squadron had a perfect safety record.

Shortly after arriving in Guam, I had another interesting encounter with Commander Montgomery. At about 0100 hours I was awaked by a telephone call in my Bachelor Officer Quarters room. I was ordered to meet immediately with the X.O. and other senior officers in the X.O's Quonset hut. Upon entering the hut, it was apparent the commander and several of the senior officers had been partying. These officers were married, but their wives had not yet arrived from Hawaii. Commander Montgomery asked me if I liked sports, to which I replied, "Yes, sir." He then requested that I develop a multi-sport athletic program for the squadron's 500 enlisted men and 125 officers. He wanted it on his desk at 0800 that morning. I didn't mind the assignment but thought the deadline was a bit aggressive. However, I suspect it led to greater opportunities and increased responsibilities later on.

In the fall of 1957, I was chosen to replace our squadron air intelligence officer. This required that I attend AI school in Alameda, California. Since I was going to be in the states, the squadron added orders to UCMJ school (Uniform Code of Military Justice). This training would later allow me to serve as prosecutor or defense counsel in military court-martials.

I mentioned tense moments while flying. There was one such event that occurred when I was on the mainland attending Navy schools. Commander Bill Dunham commanded our plane's crew of eighteen. They took off from Agana on a routine flight at about midnight. Shortly after takeoff, the plane lost its # 1 engine at about 1,000 feet and moments later had a fire warning in the #2 engine. It was a four engine aircraft. The manual said the plane will lose 700 feet per minute when two engines were out on one side of the aircraft. The flight engineer frantically attempted to restart the engines as the altitude gauge read "0." The plane was literally held up by the ground effect created when flying close to the water which creates lift with less drag on the wings. There was great relief when the flight engineer restarted one of the engines and Commander Dunham was able to return and land safely back at the air station.

Our sister squadron on the island, VW-3, did lose an aircraft. This was strictly due to pilot error. While on a flight, the plane was directed to a sinking ship and asked to vector a rescue vessel to the distressed ship. The plane's commander ignored the advice of the flight engineer when advised to depart. Returning to home base, the plane experienced fuel exhaust, and the pilot made a beautiful wheels-up landing 60 miles short of the runway. Luckily, the crew climbed out and sat on the wing until a Navy ship could rescue them.

Captain Game, our Commanding Officer, was the senior aviator on the island. As such, he was entitled to a staff separate and apart from the squadron staff. He selected John Dorcak and me to serve on his two-man team. John, a brilliant and creative strategist, was on a second tour with VW-1. The Commander of the Seventh Fleet invited our skipper to a 7th Fleet conference in Pearl Harbor, Hawaii. Captain Game had a conflict in scheduling, so he sent John and me to represent him. What was he thinking? Admiral Arleigh Burke was Commander Seventh Fleet and a legend. He was known as "31 knot Burke" for exceeding standard sailing speed when he transited from the west coast to the battlefields of the Pacific. John and I, two very junior officers, were seated around a huge, highly polished oval table face to face with many men who had helped win the second great war. We were both quiet as mice until a Captain informed us that the Admiral wanted VW-1 to radar photograph the coast of China from Sakhalin to Hainan Island. Our response was respectful but firm, "Captain Game would strenuously oppose this assignment." When questioned, we explained that our aircraft had no weapon system, and we would not proceed 100 miles down the coast before a MIG would eliminate us. To the Admiral's credit, he withdrew the request.

John and I had questioned the current strategy for providing early warning for the carriers. Our aircraft would fly a 150-mile barrier between the CVA and expected direction of attack. It seemed logical that the enemy knew this and could easily determine the location of the ship. We had a simple solution; we proposed that the GCI (ground control intercept) sites located on the island chain, including Okinawa, Japan and the Philippines, be integrated into an area-wide warning system. Captain Game agreed. With concurrence from Seventh Fleet, a new operational doctrine was adopted.

To my surprise, I received orders to report to flight school to begin in January 1959. I was married, so this became a family decision. Sonya, my wife, was not keen on the idea. I responded to the Navy stating I would gladly accept the orders if they guaranteed advanced jet training upon my completion of pre-flight. I wanted to fly jet aircraft and did not want to make a career decision that would cause me to come back to a multi-engine squadron like VW-1. Not surprisingly, my request was denied, and my dream of becoming a Naval Aviator was history .

One of the benefits of being the squadron AI was that I flew aboard a carrier when it arrived in the operating area. In 1959 I flew aboard the USS Ranger, CVA 61, and spent three days briefing the staff on how VW-1 would operate with the ship. Dick Sowby, my Officer Candidate School bunkmate, was the air intelligence officer for VAH-4, a heavy attack squadron flying A3D Sky Warriors. Before I left the ship, Dick arranged for me to ride in the second seat on a flight. The thrill of launching and recovering on the pitching, yawing deck of an aircraft carrier was beyond description.

With mixed emotions, coupled with great memories and unimaginable experiences, I returned to the United States in December 1959 for release from active duty. My commitment had been fulfilled and I was once again a civilian. After completing my active duty service, I wanted to join the Naval Air Reserve program at Los Alamitos, California. Because I had a work conflict, I could not drill on weekends. The Naval Security Group in Pasadena met each Wednesday evening, so I joined the unit for about a year. When my work schedule changed, I transferred to an Air Intelligence Reserve Unit (NAIRU) at Los Alamitos. There I drilled one weekend a month. A secret clearance was required; therefore, I had to wait for the FBI to update my background investigation before I could participate as an analyst.

For most of the 1960's, we were tasked with creating target folders on North Vietnamese military facilities. Our carrier based squadrons would review these folders prior to flying to the assigned target. Although we were not in the forward theatre, we had a sense of pride believing that our work could help a pilot successfully complete a mission and safely return to the carrier.

In the early 1970's the Viet Nam War was winding down and several officers from the reserve intelligence units were trained to debrief Navy and Marine prisoners of war, most of whom were aviators. However, the Navy decided to use only active duty officers to conduct the debriefs. We reservists were disappointed. Later, we were allowed to read the documents, all of which were classified. There were two things I learned. First, John McCain was a hero while a P.O.W. His captors offered to release him early, but he refused to go until prisoners who had been in captivity longer than he were released. Second, Jane Fonda and her traitorous acts while visiting the P.O.W.'s in Viet Nam were mentioned in every debrief I read.

During my 29 years in the Reserve program, I was promoted in normal sequence. With each advancement I would have additional responsibilities. After promotion to Commander, I served as Commanding Officer of several units at Los Alamitos and San Diego.

After selection to Captain, I served as Commanding Officer of an Operational Intelligence Unit at Naval Air Station North Island in San Diego. We met in the Commander Naval Air Forces Pacific headquarters and provided direct support to the Admiral's staff. The Admiral commanded all the active duty air assets in the Pacific region, which extended to the Indian Ocean. My unit consisted of a highly skilled, motivated, and dedicated group of men and women who were enlisted, as well as officers. I was proud to serve with them.

Change of Command

With the rank of Captain, I was eligible to apply to attend the Naval War College senior reserve seminar. During the twelve months prior to attending the school, each candidate was required to successfully complete an intensive correspondence course. The two-week course was held at the Newport, Rhode Island Naval Base where I had begun my naval career thirty years prior. The weather was abysmally hot and humid. The classrooms had no air conditioning. Even with the windows open, there was no breeze. Despite this inconvenience, the war game we "played" was topical and challenging. We were presented with the following scenario. Iranian naval ships had blockaded the Straits of Hormuz. To sail out of the Persian Gulf and into the Arabian Sea, ships had to pass through this strategic point. Much of the world was dependent on oil from Saudi Arabia, Iran, and Iraq. It was essential that their oil tankers be allowed to pass safely through the Straits. The research we did prior to beginning the class was applicable in developing a strategy to meet the operational situation. The class was divided into several groups. Each competed to develop the best strategic plan to resolve the problem. The "game" was very realistic. The solutions had to be practical and achievable. There was no "right" answer to the scenario. Consequently, there was no group winner. We all learned there are no easy solutions to difficult problems.

All the projects we were tasked with on our monthly weekend drills were in support of the active duty Navy. Many of the required annual two weeks of duty were performed working side-by-side with active duty personnel at their command. A side benefit was that we had access to current operational intelligence

As I have mentioned, the Navy believes in continuing education. This is a list of some of the schools I attended as a reservist:

*Anti-submarine Warfare
*Survival, Evasion, Resistance and Escape (SERE)
*Photo Intelligence
*Radar/Multi Sensor Analyst
*Naval Amphibious Warfare
*Nuclear Weapons
*Computer and Communications

There are few reserve commands available for Captains. After being passed over for selection to Admiral, I retired. The retirement ceremony was at Naval Air Station North Island on a beautiful, 75 degree day with towering cumulous clouds over the ocean. Our proud American Flag whipped in the breeze. I was pleased to have Judy and a few friends attend. It was a special day for Judy, too. She was driven to the ceremony in a navy vehicle and then presented with an armful of roses which she carried while being escorted down a long, red carpet. It was a well-deserved tribute for my wife and all the others who had stayed home to raise families for decades while their "warriors" had been off playing war games. It was very emotional, as my former Unit was in attendance looking very military in their dress whites.

During thirty-two years of Navy service, I was never shot at in anger. For those who died in service to our great country, I dedicate these words from the Navy Hymn.

"Eternal Father, strong to save,
Whose arm hath bound the restless wave,
Who bidd'st the mighty ocean deep
Its own appointed limits deep;
O, hear us when we cry to Thee,
For those in peril on the sea!"

Chapter Six

And, Family Number Three

My plans for the future had included Sonya. Now that I was single again, I had to refocus and establish goals and aspirations for myself. This was a new challenge. However, I felt a new sense of freedom, because I no longer had to consider another person's wishes when making decisions. In the Navy, I had turned down orders to attend flight school, because Sonya had not been in favor of my extending past the required service to become an aviator. Now, I seriously considered re-applying for flight school but knew I was not emotionally prepared to make such a commitment. This was probably a fortuitous decision, because three years later I might have been flying F-4 Phantoms in Vietnam. God works in mysterious ways!

Shortly after Sonya and I separated, I met with Mickey McIntyre, a Navy friend, to discuss how we might make a living. We saw lots of opportunities in the business world, including IBM, insurance, and banking. But, Mickey had a better idea. He had met a men's clothing store owner who wanted to expand. This idea appealed to me. My mother had been a fashion designer, and I had grown up around the business.

In January 1960, I went to work at Bill Winn's men's store in San Marino to learn the retail merchandising business. Six months later, Mickey and I became partners with Bob LaMarche, owner of Hackett's Men's Store on South Lake Avenue in Pasadena. Mickey opened a store in Arcadia, George Johnson (a Navy buddy of Mickey's) opened a store in Glendale, and I opened a men's shop in Alhambra. We sold only traditional clothes, mostly to young businessmen and college students. We built a solid, loyal customer base, and the business grew substantially. However, after eighteen months, I was bored. After being inside the store sixty hours a week, I decided to sell my interest in the partnership and switch to a different career path. I had become interested in the stock market and decided to join Eastman Dillon Union Securities in San Marino.

Upon my return to Pasadena after the Navy, I lived at home with my parents for a short time. I was anxious to move out for several reasons. I did not want to hear Mom comment on how Sonya had never been "right" for me. However, my parents were of greater concern. They had drifted apart during the years I had been away at school and then in the Navy. Dad had retired from his many business ventures and spent afternoons with his pals at the Costa Grill near Chinatown, a favorite watering hole of mine, also. There was a great deal of friction between Mom and Dad. I do believe Dad retreated with his friends to avoid confrontation. Mom objected to his lifestyle which exasperated a situation that became untenable.

At this time, my brother, Thomas Eric Spare, was away in the Air Force after having graduated from Arcadia High School and Pasadena City College. In the Air Force, he found his niche as a medical technician. He fell in love with Ginny, a wonderful Christian gal, who was also in the military. In the 1970's they were transferred to Anchorage, Alaska where they enjoyed the rugged lifestyle and beauty of the state. After he left the Air Force, Tom worked at the local BMW and Mercedes dealerships in town. He always enjoyed working on cars. This job offered him the opportunity to work on some of the finest automobiles in the world. Together, he and Ginny settled in Anchorage and raised terrific twins, James and Katrina, and a second son, Michael. I loved their Alaskan spirit of adventure. After a few years of living in the big city of 250,000 people (half the State's population), they believed Anchorage was getting too crowded and too busy, so they built a home in Chugiak, located 32 miles outside of Anchorage. Tom was the Boy Scout troop leader, and his group's favorite outing was to hike into the wilderness in the winter and dig ice caves where they would spend the weekend.

Tom James Virginia Michael Katrina

I was away during my sister Susan's important developmental years between 10 to 18. These years had not been tranquil for Tom or Sue, as there was often a contentious atmosphere at home of which I had not been aware. Tom never discussed his feelings about our parents, but Susie clearly sided with Dad with whom she had a warm, loving relationship. When I returned home from the Navy, Sue was a coed at the University of Southern California (USC). She had grown into a lovely young lady during the years I had been away. I enjoyed spending time with her when she came home for the weekend. I also visited her at the Alpha Phi Sorority house on campus. She boasts that her "sisters" would argue as to whether I looked more like Paul Newman or Marlon Brando. I would not have included this tidbit of information, but Sue insisted that it be included in my memoir. Candidly, I thought Brando was an insufferable jerk!

George Johnson and Susan

Sue introduced me to Judy Wheelhouse, a former high school friend from Arcadia, who had been married briefly and had a very young baby. She was a gorgeous gal. We dated briefly but had little in common. A few years later Judy moved to New York. On a business trip to NYC, I invited Judy and Charlie Hale to dinner. Charlie was a Stanford friend who had moved from Pasadena to New York and was working in the City. We had an enjoyable evening together. The next day Charlie asked if I was dating Judy, to which I replied, "no." Charlie wasted no time in asking her out. Over the Christmas holidays, Charlie and Judy visited his parents in Pasadena. Charlie's mom and dad hosted a festive party where Mrs. Hale cornered me and sternly asked, "Are you the one who introduced Charles to that woman?"

Frank Shine III and I attended Naval Reserve meetings each Wednesday. Afterwards, we visited the Coventry Inn for a few beers. Because of their surfing, skiing, and auto racing movies, the Coventry was a magnet for young people, not to mention free beer for the ladies every Tuesday evening. Al Williams was the proprietor. The two of us developed a friendship and are still friends sixty years later.

Through Al I met Barbara Huffa. She was a good-looking, fun loving young lady. We dated for more than a year and became close friends with Al and his girlfriend, Jan Williams. Eventually, Al and Jan were married, despite Al having pushed Jan into the swimming pool during a party at my apartment. Normally that would not be a "cause célèbre," but Jan had on a Sebastian knit dress which shrunk to the size of a children's sweater. Barbara and I had a great relationship. However, we drifted apart. She grew tired of my not being willing to make a commitment. Dick Sowby, my Officer Candidate School roommate and optometrist, was more disappointed than I, because we had enjoyed many double-dates together.

Mickey McIntyre   Barbara Huffa

Dick Sowby and I had intelligence billets in the Navy, and our area of interest was Asia, China in particular. We decided to write a thirteen-week series for television on the communist takeover of sovereign governments around the world. We wrote the first of the series on China and an outline for the remaining twelve segments. Surprisingly, CBS reviewed our project and asked if we would be available to work full-time to produce the series. Both of us had jobs which we were not prepared to leave. We were disappointed not to be able to follow through on the project but felt some pride when a series with a similar concept was produced several years later.

In 1963 I was awakened at 4 a.m. by a telephone call from Gene Rouse, my manager at Eastman Dillon. His voice was trembling, for he had received a call from the Yucaipa Police Department stating my adoptive father had been found dead from a self-inflicted head wound. Nothing had ever jolted me as hard as that news; it was like a sucker-punch to the gut. I had the unpleasant task of sharing the news with my mother, Tom, and Sue. I made most of the arrangements for the funeral. We had a small church service prior to the burial at Rose Hills Cemetery. Dad did not leave a note explaining his action, but Mom believed he may have had an inoperable brain tumor for which he became despondent. He could not have known how devastating his decision was, especially for family and friends. I am eternally grateful to the folks at church who were incredibly supportive during that painful time. For me, the early sixties was a time of healing and recovery from my divorce and adoptive father's death. Putting my focus on a new career path in the investment world helped. I recall an old saying, "To get knocked down is not failure; to not get up is."

I moved into an apartment in South Pasadena on Raymond Hill (A.K.A. "orgy hill") with Dave Cashion and Gary Holland, two USC grads. The area was a cluster of apartment buildings filled with young, single men and women who partied around the swimming pools during warm Southern California weather. There were four ladies living in the apartment below ours. I became friendly with Sienna Mondavi. She was one of the wackiest gals I ever dated. Her family owned Charles Krug Winery in St. Helena, California, one of the oldest wineries in the Napa Valley. Sienna skied Vale, Colorado for four or five months during the year and then returned to Southern California after ski season. Back on Raymond Hill, we laughed and played together but never let romance get in the way of our friendship.

I dated many interesting women but none seemed to light a spark. Fortunately, my world changed in September, 1963 when I was introduced to a young lady who had just arrived from Michigan. Judith

Ann Jay's college friends came to California the prior year. They convinced Judy to come west to teach and enjoy the sunshine. Her new roommates, Betsy Hanna, Merle Creighton, and Jackie Kroenke, wanted Judy to meet all of their friends on the hill, so one evening they took her door-to-door introducing her to friends and neighbors. Hot, dirty, and sweaty, I had just returned from a rugby practice and was sitting on the coach drinking a beer when the doorbell rang. I was too tired to get up, so I yelled, "The door is open." In walked a bevy of beauties. It was then I was introduced to Judy Jay. I offered the ladies a beer; however, they declined, as they were off on their appointed rounds.

A few days after Judy and I met, I drove home from work to my apartment at lunchtime. As I parked the car on the street, Judy came walking down the sidewalk. I said "hello" and asked her if she was enjoying her new environment. She replied that everything was going well and mentioned she needed to pick up her trunk full of clothes at the Greyhound bus depot in Los Angeles. After we determined the trunk would not fit in her Chevy II, I offered to drive her to Los Angeles to retrieve her goods. After lunch time, we arrived in Los Angeles and decided to get two Italian submarine sandwiches with the best salami this side of Genoa at Dario's Deli. From there we found the Greyhound depot and Judy's trunk. The afternoon stretched into "happy hour" at the Costa Grill. We enjoyed getting to know one another and had much to talk about, as I had not been to Michigan and this was Judy's first trip to California. The next few hours passed quickly as we enjoyed our adult beverages, fried scallop appetizer, and turkey tetrazzini dinner. I delivered Judy and her trunk back to her apartment and had only a half a block to drive to my residence.

A week passed. I couldn't get Judy out of my mind, so I called and invited her to join me for dinner at the Green Lake Restaurant. It was the "in" spot in Pasadena. I told her I would pick her up at 6:30. She asked if I could make it 7:30, as she had a date for an afternoon Dodger baseball game. Wow, I thought, "This lady doesn't let any grass grow under her feet." We had a delightful evening. The spark which had been missing for so long, slowly began to glow. From that night forward, we had a whirlwind romance.

Life on Raymond Hill was a continuous party interspersed with work. My fraternity brothers, Chuck Arledge, Mike Cory, Bill Harsell, and

Berkeley Johnston, lived in nearby apartments. I don't know why, but I became friends with John Bitzer, Dean Hawley, and Dan Redden, all USC grads. Over the holidays, my roommates and I invited friends to our ever popular New Year's Eve party. To everyone's shock and amazement, Judy and I announced our engagement. We had only known one another for three months, but we were confident in our love and saw no point in waiting to be married. Through our many conversations we realized we shared the same moral, ethical, political, and religious values, which was a good base on which to start a life together. I must admit, I thought long and hard about my two previous love affairs, but I felt confident I was making the right decision.

Judy

John and Mimi Bitzer had become our close friends. They offered to host an engagement party at their home in Pasadena. At Harvard University, John had made a bet with several of his classmates that he could pass all of his classes without attending one. Needless to say, he was forced to drop out when he lost the bet. He married Mimi Adams, and they headed west where John earned his BA and Masters of Business degrees at U.S.C.

Mimi   John Bitzer

Upon our engagement, Judy and I called her parents, Elden and Priscilla Jay, in Grosse Pointe, Michigan to ask her Dad's permission for the marriage and seek their blessing on our union. Although I had not met Judy's parents, they could not have been more cordial. Deep down I knew they must have had their doubts about Judy marrying a cowboy from California, one who was divorced and five years older than their daughter.

Our wedding was six months later, on July 11, 1964 in Judy's hometown of Grosse Pointe. I flew to Michigan a week before the wedding and spent time getting to know Judy's parents, her brother, John, and sister, Mary. Elden could not have been more hospitable. Together, we spent a day in Detroit having lunch at Joe Muer's and then at several of Elden's favorite watering holes. He introduced me to some of his friends, as well as the "perfect Manhattan" with a twist of lemon and no cherry.

John Bitzer was my best man. He and John Jay organized a surprisingly civil bachelor party at Sinbad's on the Detroit River. The next night I hosted the rehearsal dinner which my friend Charlie Hale failed to attend; he and my old friend, Judy Wheelhouse, were "delayed" in route. We narrowly avoided a disaster at dinner. I was seated next to one of Judy's bridesmaids who was extremely liberal politically. Barry Goldwater was the Republican presidential candidate. This young lady insisted Goldwater would start a nuclear war if elected. I held my tongue through two perfect Manhattans and then told her to shut up. Judy ran to the bathroom in tears. Sweet Priscilla calmed things down, and we enjoyed the rest of the evening. Later, Judy apologized for seating me next to that bridesmaid. She had not realized her political convictions. No harm, no foul!

On our wedding day the weather was beautiful with white cumulus clouds and a slight breeze, but very humid. The wedding was held at the Congregational Church which had a tall bell tower, picturesque against the azure sky. Elden beamed proudly as he walked his daughter down the aisle. Judy was incredibly beautiful in her white, trailing dress. The ceremony was solemn but sealed with a kiss that said, "Forever." This time I believed it would be "until death do us part." We had a brief reception at the War Memorial, a historic building in Grosse Pointe, followed by another at the Jay's home where I was able to get to know many of Judy's friends and family in a relaxed atmosphere.

Mr. and Mrs. Elden B. Jay
announce the marriage
of their daughter
Judith Ann
to
Mr. Robert Lloyd Spare
on Saturday, the eleventh of July
nineteen hundred and sixty-four
at
Grosse Pointe Farms, Michigan

Reception
immediately following ceremony
Grosse Pointe War Memorial
Fries Ballroom
32 Lake Shore Road

Please respond
831 Lincoln Road
Grosse Pointe, Michigan

P.J. Elden

Lola

That evening we flew to Chicago and stayed overnight before flying to Mexico for our honeymoon. After a few days of sightseeing and outstanding food in Mexico City, we flew to Puerto Vallarta where we stayed at the newest and most prestigious hotel. The hotel had advertised air conditioned rooms; however, when we arrived the air was not working. I learned that Judy looked really cute with curly hair.

Judy's brother, John, and his girlfriend, Barbara, whom he had known since grade school, were married one week after our ceremony. We were disappointed not to be able to be in attendance, but John Bitzer represented us in our absence. What a true friend!

Barbara and John Jay

After our honeymoon, Judy and I returned to our small, rented house in Pasadena. Judy began teaching first grade at Holly Avenue School in Arcadia, and I returned to my job as a stock broker. We hosted our first party during the Christmas holidays. We decorated a fresh cut tree, put out Christmas decorations, and hung mistletoe in conspicuous places. We requested men dress in coat and tie, something unheard of today. Judy invited Grace, one of the teachers at her school, and I invited Dave Cashion, my former roommate. Much to our surprise and delight, they spent the evening talking only to each other, and then extended the evening at the Tahitian Restaurant. They have been married for more than fifty years, and we all continue to remain friends.

Judy did not want to wait to have children. To fulfill her wish, she became pregnant during that Christmas holiday. (It had been a great party!) Just before our first son's birth, we bought a house in Arcadia for the exorbitant price of $25,000. After eight hours of labor, Dr. Nanniga performed a caesarian section, and David J. Spare was born on September 29, 1965. We agreed Judy would not return to teaching, as we believed it was important for our children to have a full-time mother. David was a type "A," hyper-active, risk-taking child. Judy had second thoughts about being a stay-at-home mom, especially after one particular incident. One evening around 9 p.m. our doorbell rang, and there stood our neighbor with David, in his pajamas. David had crawled out of his bedroom window and gone next door to play with his buddy, Jimmy.

Sue and Willy Hahn and Judy and Don Fickas were a few of our terrific neighbors. The Fickases hosted a beautiful Christmas party every year. Judy Fickas, who was a gourmet cook, spent weeks making cookies and other goodies for the party. Because Don had a sweet tooth, she had to hide the cookies prior to the party. One year, she didn't hide the bourbon balls. When it was time to serve them, she found the jar empty. I often prepared the liquid refreshments for a party and would mix a smooth, but potent, "Wapatula" punch. It was served in a plastic turret from a B-29. Late in the evening when the punch bowl was nearly empty, we found a white athletic sock at the bottom of the turret-never did find the culprit. Steven Spare and Jill Fickas were born a week apart in September, 1967. I suspect the two Judys became pregnant after a fantastic, Fickas Christmas party.

Steven Lloyd Spare was delivered by caesarian on September 15, 1967. Steve was the polar opposite of David; he was quiet, big and strong, never cried, and loved to eat. After two C-section births, the doctor recommended we not have more children. We were disappointed, because we wanted a third child, preferably a girl, whose name would have been Jennifer.

Grandma Spare

With an expanding family, our 1250 square foot house was getting crowded, so we started looking for a new home. My business was growing, and although our house had not appreciated in value, we felt we could afford a larger home. The move became more compelling when I decided to leave Eastman Dillon and take a position in institutional sales with W.E. Hutton and Company in Los Angeles.

We searched for a home in La Canada, San Marino, South Pasadena, and Southwest Pasadena. Judy did most of the footwork. She found a house at 1723 Kaweah Drive, located in the hills of Pasadena. In my youth, I had done gardening at this house for the Bergers. They had built the home and were now selling the property. We fell in love with the total package. The well-maintained home was located high on a hill with an unobstructed view of downtown Los Angeles. The property was surrounded by open fields and few homes. Coincidentally, it was located just a block from where I had been raised at 1632 Kaweah Drive. We purchased the three bedroom, 2 ½ bath home for $35,000 in 1968. We were excited about our life: new home, new job, and two boys to raise in a healthy environment.

What is a family without a dog? We were in a new home with acres of open fields. The boys were old enough to care for a dog. We found a black lab, Sweetie, who was young but not a puppy. Even though the garden was fenced, he still found a way to escape. His favorite escape route was jumping from the staircase off the kitchen onto the garage roof and into the front yard. When Steve was about four years old, he took Sweetie for a walk. When they didn't return, I went looking for them and found Steve flat on his stomach. Even though the dog had dragged him through the field, Steve was still holding the leash. The boys were heartbroken when we gave their dog to a family who owned a ranch where Sweetie could chase chickens and run with the horses. We replaced Sweetie with Angel. She was of mixed breed but mostly Cocker Spaniel. Playful but not hyper, she was the perfect dog. Angel was a member of our family for a dozen years and brought us immense pleasure.

Judy was settling in as a wife and mother. She attended Bible study classes and sang with the Arroyo Singers. This group consisted of women only, all of whom had outstanding voices. They had a paid, professional conductor. The group performed throughout the San Gabriel Valley, especially during the Christmas holidays. Judy had not sung on stage since her college days when a group from Western Michigan performed the play, "The Tender Trap," on a U.S.O. tour to Greenland, Iceland, and Newfoundland. She was happy to meet new friends who shared her passion for singing.

Wednesday, October 11, 1961

Will Appear Overseas In 'Tender Trap'

Judith Jay, daughter of Mr. and Mrs. Elden Jay, 831 Lincoln Rd., is one of ten from Western Michigan University to fly from New York to Thule, Greenland Air Force Base, Oct. 16 for the first stop on their tour of overseas Northest Command armed-force bases. They will present the play "The Tender Trap" and a variety show.

The troup will have approximately n i n e t e e n performances starting in Greenland and going as far into the Scandanavian countries as the weather permits. The tour extends from Oct. 16 until Nov. 13, at which time they will return to Kalamazoo.

This play is sponsored by the U.S.O., the American Educa-

JUDITH JAY

tional Association and Western Michigan University.

Miss Jay is a junior in the elementary education curriculum. She was a 1958 graduate of Grosse Pointe High School. She will play the part of "Julie Gillis."

Shortly after moving to Pasadena, David began kindergarten at San Rafael Elementary School. This was the elementary school I attended in my youth. His tenure lasted about a week before Judy pulled him out and registered him at Pasadena Christian School. Correctly, she realized the students in the Pasadena Unified School District were being "dumbed down." Steven followed his brother at Pasadena Christian School two years later. The boys received an excellent education both academically and spiritually.

We were blessed with truly great neighbors: Bob and Shirley Griffith and daughter, Karen; Marlin and Irene Espe and son, John; and Gary and Marilyn Hudson and son, Sherman. We barbequed on weekends and celebrated birthdays and holidays together. I think the parents had more fun than the boys, especially on Halloween when the dads would "trick or treat" for refills in their adult beverage glasses.

The boys were young, energetic, and adventuresome. Seldom did they get into serious trouble, except for one very hot summer day when they "mooned" the unfriendly, old-maid school teacher next door. Judy and I quietly chuckled. On Steve's fifth birthday, we took all the neighbor boys to Disneyland. Everything went well until we arrived at the Haunted House. Sherman wouldn't go on the ride, because he was afraid and believed the house was truly haunted. I stayed with Sherman while Judy and the other boys rode through the house filled with ghosts. When the train returned, Judy and the boys were not on it. Sherman screamed, "See, I told you. The ghosts got them." Somehow, my gang had gotten off the train at a stop inside the house.

Sherman   Dave   John

Judy grew up in the Christian Science religion. She was not attending church when we met. I had grown up in the Church of Christ, attended church regularly, and invited her to join me during Sunday services. The exposure to a "fundamentalist" approach led her to begin attending Bible study classes with her friends Grace Cashion, Sally MacLeod, Dina Roberts, Anita Lewis, and many other devout Christian women. The study of God's "Word" changed Judy's lifestyle and outlook on life.

The 1970's were challenging but a happy and rewarding time for our family. Much of our time and activities were centered around David and Steven. The boys were involved in Little League baseball and AYSO soccer. I enjoyed coaching some of the teams. Equally enjoyable was our participation in the Boy Scouts, Troop 358. It was a backpacking troop. Most of the fathers, known as the "old goats," packed and carried their own gear and food on weekend outings in the local mountains. With the troop, we visited the Colorado River and Joshua Tree in the desert. The highlight of one year was a weeklong trip to the High Sierras. We hiked in the mountains above 10,000 feet, swam and fished in crystal clear lakes, cooked over a campfire, and slept under the stars. David received his Eagle Scout designation. Steven completed his Eagle Scout project. It was sent to the regional headquarters where it was lost. Steve was asked to redo his project, but he declined. Steven learned the lesson that life is not always fair. Through high school, the boys continued to learn life lessons. As a young teenager, David suffered a compound fracture in the upper arm, caused by a cancer in the bone. The arm healed and the cancer was removed. Not able to play a contact sport for more than a year, he started running cross-country. Steven was an all-star third baseman until his coach moved him to catcher to make room for his son.

At year-end, Steve quit baseball to focus on football where he was named to the First Team in the Rio Hondo League. As a 225-pound tackle, he also played in the post-season, all-star game.

EAGLE SCOUTS RECEIVE HONORS. Lew Coppersmith, scoutmaster of Troop #358 from San Marino Community Church and Arnold Soderberg (far right), assistant scoutmaster flank the following boys who have just been elevated to Eagle Scout rank: John Giddings, Mike Mehterian, Ken McBride, David Spare, Jay Dick and Ian Smith.

When the boys were growing up, we had different vacation experiences from most of our friends. We did the usual trips to the mountains, desert, and beaches; however, we also "vacationed" when I served my annual two weeks Naval active duty. Our first Navy vacation was in Hawaii when Dave and Steve were about four and six years old. I worked at the Fleet Intelligence Center at Pearl Harbor, but our housing was in the old, WW II quarters at Fort DeRussey on Waikiki. The accommodations were less than even Spartan-a one room wooden structure with a bathroom and shower. We had a wonderful experience on that trip. A few years later, we made the same trip, but the accommodations were quite different. The military had built Hale Koa, a high-rise hotel on the beach at Waikiki. It had excellent restaurants and access to many beach activities. The hotel was built as a refuge for military personnel on leave from the war in Viet Nam. Judy and the boys explored all of Waikiki, swam, and listened to music in the garden at the Hilton Hawaiian Village. I generously gave them a five-dollar bill each day for lunch. Evidently, Emily, the lady cashier at the sandwich stand on the beach, was not able to determine the cost of their lunch, so David would tell her how much change to return. That was before calculators were available. On the weekends we rented a car and toured Oahu visiting the Polynesian Cultural Center, Dole Plantation, and all of the famous scenic beaches. It was a perfect vacation.

Perhaps the family's favorite Naval reserve vacation was spent on Ford Island, located in Pearl Harbor. Access to the island was by ferry. Transportation on the island was on a WW II Navy bus. Our housing was in the bachelor officers' quarters (BOQ), which was a large cement building dating to pre-WW II. We had a large room with four beds, a refrigerator, and a bathroom. With few people around, it was like being on "Gilligan's Island." Each evening, when I returned from work, we went to the bar in the BOQ for "happy hour." Often, we were the only patrons in the bar. We became well acquainted with John, the bartender, who had arrived on a destroyer the day after Pearl Harbor was bombed by the Japanese. John completed his Navy tour and retired in Hawaii as the bartender at the Ford Island BOQ. John is now deceased, but his memory remains. The bar now carries his legacy, "John's Place."

The U.S.S. Arizona lay at rest about 100 yards offshore. Sunk on December 7, 1941 by Japanese airplanes, it is the final resting place for 1,102 sailors and marines. The boys were excited to find the U.S.S. Utah, which rested just a few yards off the shore of the island. The boys wondered why this ship didn't have a memorial similar to the beautiful monument built for the Arizona. I did not have an answer. Today, a bridge connects the island to Pearl Harbor. It has become a tourist destination with tours of the Battleship Missouri and the Pacific Aviation Museum, which displays a historic collection of WW II airplanes. However, you may only cross the bridge on a tour or with military I.D.

As much as we enjoyed vacationing in Hawaii, we also loved camping on the Kern River, three hours north of Pasadena. Our friends, Al and Jan Williams, introduced us to Camp James where we pitched tents in the shade of trees on the river's edge. Jan enjoyed cooking breakfast which consisted of bacon and eggs and her famous "swamp" toast fried in bacon grease. Al and I prepared creative dinners each evening. We found watercress in a tributary of the river and cooked it with potatoes and onions to make a delicious soup. One year, Al was in a full leg cast because of a knee injury suffered from a dirt bike accident. The rest of us floated down the small rapids in car and truck tire inner tubes, while Al was relegated to sitting in the stream in a camp chair with his leg elevated. The Williams children, Ginny, Brett, and Amy, still talk about the wonderful times the two families shared at the river.

Jan   Al   Judy

When David graduated from seventh grade at Pasadena Christian, we moved from our beautiful home with a magnificent view to a smaller home in the flatlands. For only $165,000, we found a well kept, three bedroom, 2 1/2 bath residence in San Marino in 1980. The San Marino school district was ranked as one of the best in the country. This made the move a good decision for the boys and the family. The demographics were changing in San Marino. Asians from Japan, Hong Kong, and Taiwan were moving into the city because of its quality education. The Asian students were dedicated and set a standard of achievement which challenged the American students. This caused some tension but no overt hostility. Dave and Steve still socialize with high school friends and tell of their exploits, which I am glad I didn't know about. One such incident Steve recalls was when he and his football pals would jump the fence at the Huntington Library and Botanical Gardens and run to the Japanese Garden to ring the huge gong. Luckily, they never got caught.

The most interesting and enjoyable Naval Reserve vacation was to Washington, D.C. The boys were old enough to be able to appreciate the museums, monuments, and historic sites. It was extra enjoyable, because we stayed with Judy's brother, John, his wife, Barbara, and their sons, Mike and Rob. Mike and Rob were the same age as our boys. I could not join the family for their sightseeing tours. I was busy working side-by-side with regular Navy intelligence officers on highly sensitive projects. I was able to visit my Los Alamitos Navy buddy, Commander Bill Poteet, at the Pentagon. From Washington, D.C. we traveled to Gettysburg and hired a Park Ranger to describe the battles in great detail as we drove through the National Military Park. The boys still say that our weekend tour of the Gettysburg battlefields was the best of their lives.

Steve Dave Rob Mike

We then drove to Boston, stopping on the way at the John Jay Homestead. Judy's father told his children they were related to John Jay, the first Chief Justice of the Supreme Court. We met Linus Lapinski, the curator, who was writing a book on the Chief Justice. He broke Judy's heart when he informed her that she was not related to John Jay. He said perhaps she was related to his stepbrother who went to France and became an admiral in the French Navy. Judy called her dad that evening with the distressing news to which he replied, "Linus Lapinski doesn't know what he is talking about." The story served its purpose; when Judy was in school, she had received an "A" on a term paper about her ancestor, John Jay.

We continued to Boston where we walked the Freedom Trail and ate so much seafood I thought we might grow fins. From Boston, it was a short ferry ride to Martha's Vineyard. There we spent a few days with our dear friends, John and Mimi Bitzer, and their children, Polly, Charlie, and John.

When Judy and I married, I had only one week to develop a relationship with her parents. Consequently, I felt it important to take the family to Michigan as often as possible. Our Christmas trips to Michigan were especially exciting for the boys. It was cold, and they had an opportunity to have a "white" Christmas and play in the snow. Over the years, I drew closer to Judy's family and enjoyed each time we were together. One of our favorite trips was to the Upper Peninsula of Michigan where the entire family vacationed at Little Glen Lake. The accommodations were rustic and the scenery beautiful. The swimming, boating, and exploring kept the children well occupied. We took a side trip to Sleeping Bear Dunes which was a huge, high sand dune on the shore of Lake Michigan. Both the children and adults enjoyed climbing the dunes and then rolling back down.

Judy's sister, Mary, went to Michigan State University. There she met Larry Epstein. After dating for several years they were married in a Jewish ceremony. Mary converted to the Jewish faith. Together, they raised their children, Lainie and Josh, in the Jewish religion. Judy's family was always respectful of Mary's decision despite their worshiping in the Christian Science Church. It was a tribute to both families who had warm, loving relationships.

Mary and Larry Epstein

My Mother, Lola (Grandma Spare to the boys), was an important part of the boys' life and development. She loved boys and had less affinity for girls. This caused problems in her relationship with my sister, Susan, and some women in my life. Lola was an exceptional pastry chef, especially with fruit pies. Steven's favorite was lemon meringue. We dined together on most Sunday evenings and were always hungriest when Lola made tamale pie or chili rellenos. The only rellenos that rivaled Mom's were found at a shack near the Mexican border when Judy and I visited Susan in Sonoita, Arizona. I don't like heavy egg batter on a relleno, so Abel, at El Portal Mexican Restaurant in Pasadena, makes mine without batter-delicious! If Judy and I had plans to be out for an evening or away for a weekend, Grandma Spare was always anxious to stay with the boys. When the boys were young, she was in her 70's and healthy physically and mentally. We felt comfortable leaving the boys with her. She was a valuable mentor and focused on the greatness of our country, as well as the many opportunities available to the boys through hard work and education. Her knowledge of the Bible was immense, and she always had a pertinent story for the boys. She stressed Christian values, integrity, honesty, and the truth. She liked the quote, "The truth shall make you free." She taught the boys table manners, as well as the proper behavior a man should observe, especially with women.

When the boys were in their mid-teens, Judy saw an advertisement for cheap airfare to the Bahamas. With a myriad of activities, including parasailing, we thought it would be a great holiday for the boys. Especially enjoyable for the three men was watching the young women waterskiing topless! Other than Steven being bitten on the back by a scorpion, it was a fun, relaxing vacation.

In 1980, the boys were in high school, so Judy decided to continue her teaching career and secured a position teaching kindergarten at Valentine Elementary School in San Marino. It was a match made in heaven. Judy loved children and teaching. Judy was always upbeat, positive, and loved her family and friends, but being back in the classroom, interacting with students and faculty, really rejuvenated her. The boys were doing well in school. My job was stable. Spiritually, we were active in church. We had wonderful friends. Life was good. At the beginning of each school year, Judy invited me to meet her new students. One memorable morning, I entered the classroom and Judy announced, "Children, I want to introduce you to Mr. Spare," to which one child raised his hand and asked, "Mrs. Spare, is he your father?"

David graduated from San Marino High School in 1983 and decided to attend Claremont McKenna College. (CMC was formerly a men's college.) He and many students in his high school class had applied to Stanford. Only an Asian female and Asian male were accepted. CMC was a wonderful environment for David. The classes were small, and the professors were involved with the students and their learning. Often the professors would invite students into their homes for dinner or small discussion groups. Claremont was only an hour drive from our house. Occasionally, David would come home for dinner on a Friday evening. At home one weekend, David shared with me that he and his buddies were going sky diving the next day. He said, "Don't tell Mom." I wondered why anyone would jump out of a perfectly good airplane unless it was on fire. During David's junior year of college, he and several friends spent a semester at Franklyn College in Lugano, Switzerland. It is a miracle that he passed any of his classes, as most days were spent drinking beer at the piazza or skiing in the magnificent Swiss Alps, especially at Zermatt.

Judy had two students who were very special to her, and to me. When Judy had Cameron Smith in her class, he was a five-year-old undergoing treatments for cancer. He had endured several operations prior to entering kindergarten. Patti Smith, his mother, met with Judy and the class to explain Cameron's condition. She told them Cameron was bloated, had no hair and difficulty walking because he had an illness. From that day on the boys in the class took turns playing with him at recess. Sharing life with Cameron was a beautiful lesson in humanity and compassion for those young children.

One Sunday, Judy and I stayed with Cameron so Patti could attend church. We had fun playing games and talking with Cameron. I gave him a pair of my Navy wings. He was so excited you would have thought he had just completed flight training. Cameron successfully completed kindergarten and moved to first grade. He completed a few more years of school before God had other plans for Cameron. In 1988, the year Cameron died, Patti wrote in her Christmas letter, "My faith was faltering. I missed Cameron and walked through my days in constant prayer: 'I need a sign, Father, to let me know he is okay. I know I should trust that You are caring for him, but I can't stop being his mother. Please, just let me know that he is okay.' I was half afraid to acknowledge these feelings were in my heart. Fearful I would be conditional with God, I was scared He might not answer me. I would lose touch with my faith. But a friend urged me on and encouraged me to be open to His answer. And, so I prayed. No vision came to me. No voice. No light. I continued to pray. Then, one evening, I had reason to call a friend whom I had not seen in months. My friend had also been close to Cameron, but my call that night had nothing to do with him. We talked for a while, and then she paused, and her tone became very serious. She said she had something to share with me, and that it was incredible I had called her. Cameron had been on her mind all day. She told me she had had a dream the night before. I held my breath, knowing that this was going to be important. In her dream she was alone in her classroom (my friend was a teacher) when suddenly her door burst open, and Cameron, healthy, bright, and smiling as he was in life, walked in the room. She asked, 'Hi Cameron, what can I do for you?' And he replied, 'Oh nothing. I JUST WANTED TO LET YOU KNOW I'M OKAY.'" That friend and teacher was Judy.

Cameron

The other student special to Judy was J.P. Blecksmith. He was a natural leader, smart, and athletic. One day in class a student was struggling with the Pledge of Allegiance. J.P. jumped up and said, " It goes like this." In high school, J.P. attended Flintridge Prep and was both an outstanding student and football player. His father, Ed, served in the Marine Corp and was elated when J.P. was accepted at the Naval Academy in Annapolis, Maryland. J.P. played football for Navy and graduated in 2003. He elected to serve his duty as a Marine and led his patrol in Fallujah, Iran as part of Operation Phantom Fury when he was killed by a sniper's bullet. I wonder what he would do today if he saw a rioter burning our flag in the streets of America. His Dad is still a close friend. When we talk about J.P., he still tears up. What a great loss to his family, friends, and country.

2nd Lieutenant JP Blecksmith, 24

Handsome, talented, and privileged, JP Blecksmith joined the military possessed by a burning desire to serve his country. He died on a rooftop in Fallujah in November 2004.

By Jeff Gordinier

PERFECTTEN Blecksmith addressing his men before they entered Fallujah, and (below) playing with receiver for the Navy football team.

ON THE NIGHT BEFORE 2ND LIEUTENANT JP BLECKSMITH SHIPPED OUT TO IRAQ, after his family took him out for dinner in Newport Beach, California, his older brother, Alex, picked up a pair of clippers and shaved JP's head. When that was done and JP looked ready for combat, Alex gave his brother a hug. Then Alex climbed into JP's green Ford Expedition and drove it north, back to the family's house in San Marino, weeping part of the way. He had a feeling. So did his parents. A premonition. They didn't talk about it much, but two months later, in November 2004, when JP joined a wave of U.S. Marines roaring into the city of Fallujah as part of Operation Phantom Fury, the feeling intensified. ¶ On the night of November 10, Blecksmith and his closest friend in Iraq, Lieutenant Sven Jensen, slept on a rooftop in Fallujah. It was, miraculously, a quiet night, and chilly. They got a decent night's sleep. They awoke just before sunrise and were amused to find a

DETAILS.COM ¶HOLIDAY 2007 DETAILS 95

Overall, Judy's years at Valentine School were fulfilling and enjoyable. She team taught kindergarten with Janice Board. Those gals should have paid the school district for all the fun they had teaching. The photos of them with their students whether costumed for Halloween or singing for Christmas, are still memorable today. After ten years of teaching, Judy damaged her vocal chords, probably from playing the piano and singing with two classes each day. The doctor suggested she rest her voice for a year. Reluctantly, she took a leave of absence for a year in 1994.

91

Janice & Judy

At the time, Steven was ready to begin college at Cal Poly, San Luis Obispo. We drove Steve to school, found his dorm room, and then toured the campus. Cal Poly is a fine school academically with well regarded schools in business and agriculture. The beautiful hills surrounding the campus, as well as the nearby beaches at Avila and Pismo, were idyllic for a college student. Steve had a busy freshman year playing football, pledging Sigma Chi, and taking classes in his major, political science. Steve went to Cal Poly to play football. He had a good freshman year, but at year-end, he decided to quit football. The coach wanted him to bulk up from 225 pounds to 265 pounds. There was only one way he could gain that much weight. He was not willing to do so. I was grateful and proud of his resolve in a difficult decision, because he loved football.

Just prior to leaving Eastman Dillon, my associate, Parker Williams, and I learned the American Basketball Association (ABA) was being organized, and they were looking for people to establish franchises. Having no money, and perhaps fewer brains, we expressed an interest. We were invited to an organizational meeting in New Orleans. Shockingly, we were granted the last franchise, which we elected to place in Louisville, Kentucky. At the meeting, we elected George Mika, a Hall of Fame player, as commissioner of the league. Each team was required to post a bond of $300,000 for operations the first year. "No problem," said Parker. "We'll raise the money." Unfortunately, we were unable to raise the money and sold our interest to a young lady who was a member of the Reynolds Tobacco family. Along with her dog-trainer husband, they bought the franchise for their young son. In turn, they sold to John Y. Brown, the man who built the Kentucky Fried Chicken Company. Later, he was elected governor of Kentucky. When the ABA merged with the National Basketball Association (NBA), Brown chose to fold the franchise for $3 million and purchase the Buffalo Braves, a NBA team. Through this experience, I learned too many lessons to enumerate.

In 1967, I began to transition into new responsibilities at W.E. Hutton and developed friendships with my associates. Institutional sales were quite different from a retail broker's responsibilities. Our institutional department was comprised of Dennis Becker, George Weintz, and our assistant, Donna Johnson. I looked forward to learning from my new partners, but they had no more experience than I. It was somewhat like "the blind leading the blind," except we were young and highly motivated. We worked hard and built a respectable book of business. During my seven years at Hutton, Judy and I enjoyed social relationships with Dennis and Pam Becker, George Weintz and his girlfriend, and John and Linda Seiter. Following the Reagan gubernatorial campaign, Judy and I arranged a "blind" date for George with Maureen Reagan, Governor Reagan's daughter from his first marriage to Jane Wyman. Maureen was as gregarious as George was reserved, but they enjoyed each other, and it was obvious they would date again. Not surprising, conversation during that evening focused on politics. George and Maureen were comfortable with each other. Judy and I felt proud to have played "cupid." George and Maureen did date for a year or so and had what I would consider a "serious" relationship. I hoped Governor Reagan would run for President. Kiddingly, I told George not to screw up his affair with Maureen, because I wanted to be appointed as Secretary of Defense. Unfortunately, their romance ended, as did my chance for a cabinet appointment.

During my seven years at Hutton, I learned a great deal about the institutional market place and worked with clients, such as Capital Guardian, Capital Research, Security Pacific Bank, Transamerica, United California Bank, and Farmers Insurance. I developed a special relationship with Charles Hale, father of my Stanford pal, Charlie Hale. Mr. Hale was Chairman of Great Lakes Chemical Corp, headquartered in West Lafayette, Indiana, but he and his wife Carmen lived in Pasadena. Mr. Hale and I met for lunch every month, either at his Petroleum Club or at my University Club. He had become wealthy trading stocks on the floor of the New York Stock Exchange in the 1930's and had then moved to London. While in England, he and Carmen were entertained at Winston Churchill's summer mansion. One evening in 1939 over brandy and cigars, Mr. Churchill said, "Charles, you and Carmen should leave London and return to the United States, because we are going to war!" They did return home and England did go to war against Germany. Mr. Hale was reserved, soft spoken, and brilliant. I considered him somewhat of a second father.

While at Hutton, my old Navy buddy, John Dorcak, asked me to meet with his friends at Microseal in San Jose. The company had a proprietary process for impinging a graphite compound into metal substrates to reduce friction. Short story, I sold the company to Great Lakes. In an unusual arrangement, I represented both companies in the negotiations. Because of a potential conflict of interest, I should not have represented Great Lakes; however, Mr. Hale insisted I be the representative. It was a huge compliment and show of trust that I would act fairly. I received shares of Great Lakes stock as a finder's fee. That stock paid for David and Steven's college education.

Through the Bitzers and Charlie Hale, we were introduced to new friends, Andy and Albie Vollero, and Albie's sister and husband, Marian and Chuck Rogers. Those friendships have lasted a lifetime, except Andy. Judy put it best, "He is not a nice man."

The years at Hutton had been satisfying, but I felt it was time to explore other opportunities. Morgan Stanley and First Boston (FBC) were two premier institutional brokerage and investment banking firms. I flew to New York to talk with Buzz McCoy, a fraternity brother, who was working at Morgan Stanley. They did not have an office in Los Angeles and did not plan to open in California for five years. However, in 1974, First Boston opened an office in Los Angeles. I was offered a position as the first equity salesman. It was an offer I could not refuse. It was an opportunity to assist the firm in developing a major presence in Southern California, Arizona, and Nevada. The work regimen was more rigorous and expansive than at Hutton. The initial team consisted of Dick Waldron, office manager; Ben Noll, corporate bonds; Joe Patterson, cash management; and me. My day began with a conference call between the six offices at 6 a.m. and usually ended about 5 p.m., except when an investment-banking client was in town. We would take the client to dinner at the California Club. On those evenings, it was home at about 11 p.m.

First Boston had a highly respected and nationally renowned economist, Al Wojnilower. Al spoke to the sales force at 6 a.m. every Monday morning. I took notes and messengered them to our most important client, Capital Research. The rest of the day was spent talking with client research analysts and portfolio managers about an industry or a company specific research report. Each of the sales representatives had a great deal of freedom in their job, because Waldron would spend most of the day in his office with the door closed. Occasionally, he would pop his head out and ask Ben if he had shown a block of bonds to Transamerica, or if I had called Capital Research with our research report on J.C. Penney. Later, I was appointed Deputy Manager for the office. When Dick was in New York for management meetings, it was my responsibility to manage the office. Upon Dick's return we would review what had transpired in his absence. Because he did not like my management style, he stated, "You need to lead by fear." I promptly respond that I was resigning my position as Deputy Manager. He then asked Al DeSpirito to be Deputy Manager. Al declined the offer, as well. Thereafter, we operated very well with no backup in management.

Although I got along well with others in the office, social friendships were not developed as they had been at Hutton. Most of my business social friends were clients: Randy Finefrock at United California Bank, Mike Papworth at Loomis Sayles, Bob Sandroni at Security Pacific N.B., and George Miller at Capital Research. George was, and is today, one of my closest friends. George is brilliant and irreverent. When George was selected to lead the research department at Capital Research, he had a shaggy, Willy Nelson looking beard. Even though there was no dress code, one of Capital's senior officers suggested that George think about his appearance. The next morning George walked into his associate's office and said, "I've decided to meet you half way." He had shaved off half of his beard.

George was a bow tie man. At one business Christmas party I observed a young lady talking with George about his tie. She didn't believe George could tie a bow. She then pulled his tie, which to her embarrassment, untied. She recovered her composure and asked him how he tied the bow. He replied, "You just lay on the floor and pretend you're a shoe."

In 1983, after ten years at First Boston, I was bored and felt I could do my job blindfolded. Even though compensation was adequate, I was anxious for a new challenge. Frustration led me to make a poor decision. This was the only unpleasant period in my business career. Don Crowell, a fellow Stanford classmate, headed Crowell Weedon. It was a respected, local retail brokerage firm in Los Angeles. He asked me to join the firm to establish an institutional research and sales department. The time was right, and I accepted the challenge. I hired my old friend, Dennis Becker, two additional salesmen, and two securities analysts: one to follow the motion picture and cable industries and the other to research regional hi-tech companies. While at Crowell Weedon, Al Williams called to ask if I would assist him in selling BioClinic, the medical products company he and Bob Downer had founded. I solicited Jason Pilalas, the health care analyst at Capital Research, to help find a buyer. We signed an agreement whereby the finder's fee, if any, would be shared by Crowell, Capital, and me. Meanwhile, Crowell was not living up to the terms of our agreement, and they were over-allocating costs to the institutional department. BioClinic was not sold, and there were no negotiations with a potential buyer; however, Crowell thought they were owed part of a non-existent fee. After a year, it was clear to me that the firm did not understand the institutional business. My "marriage" with the firm was not going to improve. I remained until all my people found other jobs. I then departed. It had been a bad experience; however, it quickly turned into the best opportunity and experience of my working career.

I had maintained contact with several of my former VW-1 friends, and we were excited to have a squadron reunion in San Diego. Our friends, John and Louise Dorcak attended, as well as my old roommates "Dapper" Dayton Daberkow, Norman Sollie, and Jack Eagan. It was fun meeting the wives of the latter three who were single on Guam. Judy was unhappy, but laughed, when she was presented with a lapel pin, "NGW"- Not Guam Wife!

Dayton   John & Louise

Chapter Seven

The Glory Years, 1985-1999

On April 14, 1985, my 50th birthday, Judy hosted a party around the swimming pool in our backyard. The party was attended by loving family, long-time friends, business associates, and military buddies. The party was more memorable due to the people in attendance than for the occasion. Each person had been special to me in various ways at different times in my life. It was also memorable, because I was making a major career change and joining The Capital Group (CG) the next day.

I have a simple philosophy-be ethical, intellectually honest, hard working, and let the chips fall where they may. Capital was greatly respected within the investment industry for their high moral and ethical standards, so our values were well aligned. This was the beginning of what I consider the "golden years" of my business career.

I was hired to work with Capital Research and Management, a subsidiary of CG. I endured a short, disciplined orientation on how to tell the Capital "story." My first assignment was to determine if major pension funds would purchase mutual fund shares in their defined benefit plans. Additionally, would they consider using our mutual funds as investment options for their defined contribution plans (i.e. 401[k], IRA).

I visited major corporations and public pension funds from California to New York. After nine months, I concluded that most plan sponsors would not use any mutual funds in their defined benefit plans, because they would not receive the same service as they did with separately managed accounts. However, they would consider our fund shares as investment options IF we could provide the administration of the plan. Capital did not possess that capability and was not prepared to develop that service at that time. I was left wondering what I would do next in my young, new career.

My friend, John Seiter, with whom I had worked at Hutton, had been hired as a consultant to develop a marketing plan for Capital Guardian Trust Company's (CGTC) institutional services. After a year, John was hired with responsibility for sales, marketing, and client service in the United States. It was clear that his job was too big for one person, and he convinced the Company to bring me over from the mutual fund side of the business to assist him. Many of the folks at CGTC were former clients from my time at First Boston, so the transfer was quickly approved.

The institutional market was huge and fertile ground for CGTC products, especially for non-U.S. equity and emerging markets mandates. We were a pioneer in developing a research capability outside the United States, opening our first overseas office in Geneva in 1961.

John and I divided responsibility by type of institution; he focused on corporate accounts, and I targeted public funds, both nationwide. After a year, we hired Merle Robertson and Fred Betts to augment the team. Merle had worked at Eastman Dillon and was an outstanding institutional salesman. As a side note, Judy and I introduced Merle to his wife, Linda, a dozen years prior. Although they had not worked together, John and Fred knew each other in business. We worked as a team for fifteen years, and with our wives, continued our friendship into retirement.

In 1987, David graduated from Claremont McKenna College and was hired by Ogilvy & Mather, an excellent advertising firm. As an advertising manager, he was responsible for developing an advertising program for clients. With generous "perks," his favorite client was Hilton, Las Vegas. They approved every advertising proposal David presented to them, without objection.

David

Steve graduated from Cal Poly, San Luis Obispo two years later and joined my friend, Larry Stone, in his insurance agency in Pasadena. Steve quickly obtained his Certified Life Underwriters designation and worked with Larry and his son, Bruce, for a few years before deciding the insurance industry was not for him. He packed a few clothes and headed to Chicago to find a job in the investment world. Soon, he was trading commodities and currencies on the floor of the Mercantile Exchange.

Steven

During the first six years at Capital, I was the only sales person in the public funds group. I called on plan sponsors in all fifty states (or attempted to). The corporate market was large; therefore, John, Fred, and Merle were focused there. Phil Swan was in a support role in my group, and I trained him to take on some initial sales responsibilities. He was bright, energetic and had great potential, but to my disappointment, he decided to make his mark in the corporate world. CGTC was well known in the corporate market, but almost unknown to public fund

100

sponsors, which meant that our selling cycle was much longer. Also, typically there was one decision maker at a corporate sponsor. At the public funds, the consultant, administrator, CIO, and trustees were all involved in the selection of investment managers, with many people to get to know.

CGTC sponsored an investment conference every two years, either in the United States or overseas. The first one Judy and I attended was in London. It was an important opportunity for us to meet many of my new associates and clients. Judy met the other spouses in attendance. We had one evening with no scheduled events and were able to have dinner at the renowned Langan's Brasserie with my associate Jason Pilalas and his wife, Rena, as well as Stanford friend Charlie Hale and wife, Kaaren. When Kaaren had trouble deciding what to order as an entrée, Jason picked a rose out of the centerpiece, ate it, and said, "Try these, they're delicious."

In 1988, Capital offered me a membership in the San Gabriel Country Club. The club was near our home, and I was able to use it for business entertaining, as well as personally. The year after joining, we celebrated Judy's parents 50th anniversary, her brother John's 25th and our 25th wedding anniversaries at the Club. It was a beautiful evening, dining on the outdoor patio with a small but lively band, delicious food, and wonderful friends of the three families. Judy had never played golf, but she took lessons and became proficient enough to play eighteen holes of golf on our challenging course. The club was not far from our home, so we enjoyed going out late in the afternoon, when the weather was warm, and playing nine holes of golf before dinner. What a nice life!

Through our friends Berkeley and Maria Johnston, we learned about the Harambee School in Pasadena. This Christian school educated at-risk children. In Swahili Harambee means "Let's push together." The children wore uniforms, were well-behaved, and thrived in this loving environment. We supported the program for decades. It was exciting to watch the children grow and progress. One young lady became a medical doctor. Judy and I preferred to support charities that provided health and educational services to children who otherwise might not receive such needed assistance.

As a family, we vacationed at Lake Arrowhead in the San Bernardino Mountains. This mountain getaway was less than a two-hour drive from our home. In 1989, we bought a three-bedroom condominium on Meadow Bay at the lake. It was large enough for our family, but not many more. It came fully furnished and included an old Century ski boat. Several of our friends owned homes at the lake. With them, we spent many weekends water skiing, swimming, and playing volleyball on the beach at the condo. Despite being a community of 125 condo units, it was a tranquil, beautiful place to escape to for a few days. The Fourth of July was the biggest celebration of the year when fireworks were shot from a barge in the middle of the lake. Residents in their boats enjoyed the spectacular show.

Kate Martin   Judy

In 1988, I retired from the Navy after thirty-two years of service. The boys had graduated from college. It was time for a memorable adventure with the family. We flew to Vienna, a city of magnificent palaces, classical art and music, and home of Beethoven and Mozart. We believed the Schonbrunn, the summer home of the Hapsburgs, was the most beautiful edifice in the city. The first evening in Vienna, Dave and Steve chose not to dine with Judy and me and ventured out on a "people to people" mission. Mark Gibello had travelled to Vienna many times and recommended we have dinner at the oldest restaurant in the city. The food was excellent, but the waiter was surly and slow in responding to our glass of wine and menu requests. When he failed to bring the bill, we got up and left the table. I paid the bill when the owner caught up to us at the exit. However, for the first time, I left no gratuity. The boys had a successful outing, because it was difficult for them to rise the next morning for our scheduled tour.

From Vienna, we drove to Salzburg where Judy had one objective. She wanted to find the von Trapp home as featured in the classic movie "The Sound of Music." After much detective work, we were directed to the home, which had been converted into a girl's school.

Next, we drove to Munich, home of the world-famous Octoberfest and the Hofbrauhaus, founded in 1589. Judy's mother was of German descent (the Wildes). We enjoyed savoring the excellent sauerbraten, wienerschnitzel, red cabbage, and potato pancakes. Judy didn't drink beer, which was fine with the guys. It left more for us.

We took a side trip to Dachau, the infamous German prison where the Nazi's murdered several hundred thousand Jews during W.W. II. It was a cold, rainy day fitting for such an experience. We visited the barracks where the prisoners (men, women and children) had

been kept until they were taken to the showers, gassed, and then cremated. It was hard to imagine such inhumanity. Sadly, Dachau was only part of a vast network of camps that had exterminated an estimated six million Jews during the war. I think of the verse in the Good Book, in Heaven "the first shall be last, and the last shall be first."

Back on the autobahn, we headed to Lugano in the Italian-speaking region of Switzerland. David had attended a semester abroad when he was at Claremont. It was a miracle he passed any of his classes, because most of his days were spent socializing with the town's people in the plaza. He proudly took us to the scene of the crime and introduced us to his favorite restaurant, Gambrinus. Today, we enjoy Steve's rendition of "penne Gambrinus with vodka." The highlight for Steve was water skiing behind a vintage, "woody" ski boat on Lake Lugano. Prior to arriving in Lugano, the boys detoured to David's favorite ski resort, Zermatt. This village lies below the iconic Matterhorn mountain and is known as one of the most beautiful in the Swiss Alps.

We continued to Florence in the Tuscany region of Italy. It is known for art and culture, as well as the finest wine in Italy, Brunello di Montalcino. We visited the Uffizi Gallery to view da Vinci's "Annunciation" and Botticelli's "Birth of Venus." We saw Michelangelo's magnificent statue of David. We walked across the medieval Ponte Vecchio stone bridge with its numerous vendors selling gold and silver jewelry; I escaped without a purchase.

We spent a wonderful unplanned day in Siena and dined on the Piazza del Campo. The Torre del Mangia, a 14th century tower, reflected the golden light of the afternoon sun and was spectacular. The "Palio" horse races were run twice a year around this Piazza. We could only imagine the excitement of the crowd as the horses challenged each other in close proximity to the people.

We loved Tuscany and could have spent more time there, but it was time to head to Rome, one of our favorite cities in the world. By coincidence, our guide there was the same fabulous, young man who had shown us Rome six years prior. This was the first visit for the boys, so we visited all the "must see" sites: the Colosseum, Vatican, ancient palaces, ruins, and the ubiquitous, ornate waterfalls and fountains. We had a surprise lunch with our friend, Albie Booth, who was touring Rome with her college friend, Ernestine Gianelli. Over some of the best pasta in Italy at Il Matriciano near the Spanish Steps, we had a good time together with pleasant conversation. Every meal in Rome was a gourmet's delight. The single best dish I was introduced to was lightly battered, fried zucchini blossoms. When I can find the blossoms, I enjoy preparing them at home. Delizioso!

Rome never disappoints. Judy and I enjoyed our third visit as much as the boys enjoyed their first. We were then off to the last leg of our trip, the Amalfi Coast. We visited Positano and Sorrento, both scenic towns with vivid, colorful houses perched on steep cliffs. Out of Sorrento, we boarded a tour boat to the island of Capri for a day tour. Dave and Steve rented a boat and toured the island from the water. Judy and I were invited to join a small group of Belgian tourists who were on a private tour. At the top of the island, we were given thirty minutes to explore. One of the Belgian men asked if I had ever visited Belgium. I told him I had not. He then asked if I knew anyone from his country to which I answered, "Yes, Charles Annicq, a Stanford soccer friend." As it turned out, Charles and his wife, Gabbi, were best friends of his in Brussels. Charles had played on the Belgium National team before attending Stanford. Needless to say, he was the best player on Stanford's team. We drove back to Rome to catch our flight home. We had never had so much quality time together as a family. Although we were sad to leave, we had created memories to last a lifetime.

David returned to Ann Arbor to complete his M.B.A. at the University of Michigan. There, he met Rosemary DeGange who was doing graduate work in Russian studies. After graduation, David worked for S.C. Johnson Company in Racine, Wisconsin. On October 10, 1991 he and Rosemary were married in Hanover, New Hampshire. Judy was familiar with the changing colors of the fall foliage during her childhood in Michigan, but I had never had the opportunity to see this miracle of nature with leaves of vivid yellow, orange, and red-colors which I could not capture in photos. Rosemary's parents, Jack and Jane, were very hospitable and considerate of our family and many friends who attended the wedding. Judy and I hosted the rehearsal dinner for the wedding party, family, and many friends. It was a Catholic wedding, long but beautiful. Rosemary sparkled in her long, white gown. One of the highlights at the reception was when Rosemary's brother, John, sang, "What a Wonderful World." What a bright future awaited the newlyweds!

Judy loved art, especially beautiful paintings. Thus, when she was asked to become a docent at the Huntington Gallery in San Marino, she quickly accepted. The learning program lasted a year and consisted of lectures and extensive reading. Judy's teacher was an outstanding art historian. The gallery at the Huntington houses one of the finest collections of 17th and 18th century European art in the world. Her duty was to escort elementary students through the gallery and make the paintings come to life for them. Two of the most famous pieces in the gallery are "Pinkie," by Thomas Lawrence, and "Blue Boy," created by Thomas Gainsborough. If you had been on Judy's tour, you would have learned it was the custom, at the time these paintings were

created, for women to wear blue and men to wear pink or a faded red. No one knows why each artist painted their subject's clothing in the opposite colors typical of the day.

After covering the public funds nationally for eight years, Capital realized the potential for this rapidly growing sector of the market. Mike Nyeholt was working in the mutual fund accounting department and wanted to transfer into sales and client services. Some of my associates questioned whether he could stand the rigors of travel, because Mike was a paraplegic. He was injured in a dirt bike accident a year after graduating from U.S.C. where he had been an All-American swimmer. After the accident, Mike and his swim buddies started a foundation, "Swim With Mike," to raise money for other disabled athletes. Mike was bright, persevering, optimistic, and had a contagious personality, which convinced me he could do the job. In 1991, he joined the team.

Mara Redden

Sophie

Tommy Lasorda   Melinda Gordon

Joe Kay   Mike Nyeholt

At the same time, I was interviewing a high-profile, black female marketer who had earned a M.B.A. from Harvard and had worked at Goldman Sachs. Her referrals were excellent. She was highly recommended by my friend, Cody Ferguson, a trustee for the Los Angeles County Employees Retirement Association (LACERA). Pam joined our team with the primary responsibility of working with plan sponsors on the East coast.

We had a dynamite team in place and were able to penetrate the public fund market in the 1990's in a major way. I give some credit to our group, but success was primarily due to Capital's outstanding equity products, which we were able to offer to plan sponsors. Our international equity and emerging markets portfolios were some of the best in the industry. They were asset classes which public funds were building in their portfolios. It is always best to be humble when times are good, because there will be times where investment returns are disappointing. As my associate George Miller said, "Don't confuse brains with a bull market." Our Chairman, Bob Kirby, told the trustees for the Oklahoma Public Funds, "We are never as smart as we appear in a bull market, and we are never as dumb as we appear in a bear market."

In 1992, Lafayette Barnes, a strategic analyst in our Washington, D.C. office, and I spent ten days in South Africa to determine if Capital should invest in their capital markets. Apartheid was about to end, and it was clear that the African National Congress (ANC), headed by Nelson Mandela, would be governing the country. We met with government officials, the ANC, Communist labor leaders, professors, industrialists, the Central Bank in Pretoria, and owners and workers in small businesses. The culture was clearly changing because a few years earlier Lafayette, a black man, and I would not have been able to operate as a team in many venues. We concluded that it was too early to invest in South Africa. We were quite concerned about the level of crime, as well as tribal warfare that had persisted for generations.

Judy's parents, Elden and Priscilla (P.J.), moved from Michigan to Sun City, Arizona. Because there was never snow on the ground, Judy especially enjoyed visiting her parents in Arizona. We spent Christmas there with Judy's brother, John, her sister, Mary, their families, her cousin, Jan, husband Bob Meyerott and family, and Aunt Marge, who lived in nearby Glendale. It was a special time because we seldom had the opportunity to get the four families together.

We took advantage of the children's Spring break to, once again, meet in Arizona. P.J. organized a BBQ breakfast in the nearby rocky hills where the kids had a great time hiking and exploring while John, Larry, and I cooked. It was truly a ranch breakfast with bacon, sausage, potatoes, eggs, sweet rolls, toast, fruit, cowboy coffee, and well-spiced Bloody Marys for the cooks. It was wonderful for the cousins to spend time together, because Mike and Rob Jay lived in New York, Lainie and Josh in Michigan, and Dave and Steve in California.

In 1993, Elden died suddenly from a heart attack. P.J. sold the house in Sun City and moved into a nice apartment in an adult community. She had a small kitchen but, also, had the option of meals in a community dining room. It was a difficult adjustment for P.J., although Marge did live nearby.

The public funds held many conferences sponsored by the Teachers, Fire, State Treasurers, and others. The meetings presented an opportunity to meet the staff and trustees of the pension funds.

Additionally, several investment managers jointly sponsored overseas conferences to which we would invite our public fund clients and prospects, all expenses paid. These meetings were organized and executed by Phil Shaefer and Joanne Svensgaard of Pensions 2000.

John Wooden

There was a group of institutional sales people who represented their investment management firms, and we all attended the same conferences. A typical conference would last two to three days with meetings in the morning, planned activities or a golf tournament in the afternoon, and a sit-down banquet dinner in the evening. On a "free" evening when no dinner was scheduled, Bankers Trust or another large manager, would host a dinner, by invitation only, for a large number of the attendees. However, there were a few attendees who were not invited, and others who had no interest in hearing a sales pitch at a dinner. Two of my competitors, Melinda Gordon and Bill Nurre, and I decided to invite a small number of plan sponsors to a more intimate dinner where there would be no "selling." The clients and prospects liked the idea of being with a small number of other plan sponsors and managers with the opportunity to get to know one another on a more personal basis. Our events came to be known as the "orphan's dinners." Other managers started asking if they

Mike Nyeholt

could join the group. Melinda, Bill, and I hosted dozens of "orphan" dinners across the United States. They became a successful marketing tool. I should mention that Mike Nyeholt participated in most of the dinners, as well.

We had more fun than any person should have and were paid to do so. At a Treasurer's conference in New Hampshire, we had a few free hours one afternoon, so Melinda, Bill, and I, along with a few clients, decided to try to find where the movie "On Golden Pond" had been filmed. We drove around asking locals as to the location of the pond. Receiving little help and about to give up our search, we stopped at an ice cream stand. Half kidding, we asked the lady if she knew where Squam Lake (the pond) was located. She said, "Sure, it's on the other side of that grove of trees," about fifty yards away. I have dozens of wonderful memories like that of "Golden Pond;" however, I can no longer share them with Melinda and Bill, as they have both passed away. God bless!

When Judy retired from her teaching position, she became a valuable asset to me when we attended Pension 2000 conferences around the world. Attendees typically took their spouses to the gatherings. As a team, Judy and I were able to get to know people on a personal and business basis. The purpose of the conferences was to educate plan sponsors on the investment opportunities in emerging markets, globally.

In 1993, Judy accompanied me at her first Pension 2000 conference in Beijing, Shanghai, and Hong Kong. I had been to Hong Kong several times, but the Navy would not allow me to travel to a Communist country for five years after I retired from the Navy in 1988. I had done significant intelligence work on China. Therefore, visiting China was a special occasion for me. Half kidding, I said to Judy that I never thought I would be on the ground in mainland China unless it was as a P.O.W.

Asian cultures are fascinating, because they are so different from our Western culture. Pensions 2000 gave us an opportunity to interface with indigenous peoples at many levels of society and learn about their lifestyles and customs. The entire program was first class with outstanding speakers, hotels, banquets, entertainment, and tours. We visited the Forbidden City, which was built in the 15th century and was the state residence for the Emperor of China. When attending a dinner at the Great Hall of the People, we were almost lost in a small corner of the second floor hall. We were a group of 125 in a room that could accommodate 10,000 people for dinner. Adjacent to the Great Hall was Tiananmen Square where tens of thousands of people demonstrated against the government in 1989. The Communist Party does not tolerate dissension, and the People's Republic of China (P.R.C.) military fired on the crowd killing, according to various accounts, several hundred to several thousand protesters. We had an interesting tour to the Great

Great Hall

Tiananmen Square

Forbidden City

Bicycles

Wall of China, which is 13,000 miles long and extends across the historical northern border of China. We had box lunches outside, under a few sparse trees. Judy and I were seated with Stanley and Edwina Siu.

He was the Executive Director of the State of Hawaii pension fund. Many of the dishes we were served at dinners in China were of suspicious origin. Stanley became an invaluable source giving us either a thumbs-up or down. We met the Sius at several other conferences and became close friends.

We spent two days in Shanghai, which was a letdown after the vibrant atmosphere of Beijing. We did visit the stock exchange and toured the massive manufacturing plants and adjacent apartment developments, which were replacing state-run farms. As a consequence, the farmers and their families were moved, but no one seemed to know or care what happened to them.

Being one of my favorite cities in the world, I looked forward to sharing the sites of Hong Kong with Judy. Unfortunately, there was a typhoon near the city, and we were not allowed to leave the hotel for more than a day. We did have time to walk around the city, ride the Star Ferry, and shop for irresistible bargains.

Our children had a plethora of weddings in the 1990's. Steve was "Best Man" and Mari was "Maid of Honor" for Chris Atkinson and Jill Fickas. Jill had tried to get Steve and Mari together despite Mari having a boyfriend at U.S.C. I believe the time Steve and Mari spent together before and during the wedding lit the flame of what was to come. Judy and I enjoyed attending the weddings of the young people we had watched grow-up and mature. The weddings of Rod MacLeod, Tim Mucillo, Mark Ross, Dave Hathaway, Cam Rueff, Drew Vollero and his sister, Susan, were opportunities for us to celebrate happy occasions with our friends. Susan's wedding was special to me because it was in the Chapel at the Naval Academy in Annapolis, Maryland. The only drama was when Judy's suitcase did not arrive with our flight, and she had to shop for an appropriate dress for the occasion.

Chris and Jill

John McIlwraith and I traveled to Sioux Falls, South Dakota to review the State Pension Fund portfolio which Capital managed. We met with the staff and trustees. On one trip, I took Judy with me, so we could visit Mt. Rushmore after the meeting. We drove through the Black Hills and saw herds of magnificent buffalo roaming the stark but beautiful hills. We drove through sparsely forested, rock mountains. Finally, we arrived at Mt. Rushmore where we looked up at sixty-foot high facial carvings of Presidents Washington, Jefferson, Teddy Roosevelt, and Lincoln; it was inspiring and breathtaking. Judy wanted to see where "Dances With Wolves," starring Kevin Costner, had been filmed, so we drove to Deadwood and environs.

That same year Judy and I went to Johannesburg and Cape Town, South Africa as one of twelve sponsors of the Pensions 2000 conference. Our fifty guests and spouses represented the largest public pension funds in the United States. Cape Town is a beautiful city on a peninsula beneath the imposing Table Mountain, with cable car access to the top of the mountain. The city is near the confluence of the Indian and Atlantic Oceans. One of the pleasant walks was among the penguins along the shoreline. The highlight of the conference was meeting Nelson Mandela, who had been elected recently as the first president of South Africa after the end of apartheid, which was a system of institutionalized segregation. At the completion of the conference, several in our group flew to Mala Mala Game Reserve where we landed on a dirt strip and spent two days viewing the animals in the wild. Our guides took us out in open Land Rovers early in the morning and again in the evening when the animals were out hunting. It was a great experience, and we wish we could have spent more time exploring the reserve. The trip did not end well for Judy. She became dehydrated and was put on an intravenous solution by a veterinarian. In two days she was back to normal and we returned home.

Nelson Mandela

After too many years as a bachelor, our friend Dan Redden married the beautiful Mara who was instrumental in managing the "Swim With Mike" program at U.S.C. The wedding was in Ojai. We guests spent three glorious days at the Ojai Valley Inn, played golf, and celebrated the occasion in style. It was even more special, because John and Mimi Bitzer came out from Pennsylvania. John was "Best Man."

Mara   John Bitzer   Dan Redden

The year 1996 had extreme highs and lows, interspersed with several exciting events. My friend George Miller retired from Capital. Generously, he invited Judy and me to join a group of nine on a trip to Bali, with travel and hotels provided by George. His girlfriend, (now wife) Janet, made most of the reservations and was a wonderful hostess. George had been to Bali many times and was a proud guide. His favorite venue was the market place with spices, fruit, vegetables, strange animal meats, clothing, and other things too numerous to mention. George would have spent the entire day visiting every stall, but we were saved by a rainstorm. We stayed at a four-star hotel, and at the King's Palace with two cots for beds, one forty-watt light bulb, and an army of ants. However, in the evening the Palace presented, reportedly, the finest Balinese dancers and band in the islands. The mornings were not as enjoyable, because the chickens arose at 5:00 a.m., and all the birds on the island began singing, "Good morning." For a week, George talked about the Tanah Lot Temple and the "death march" required to reach the site. The weather was very hot and humid as we began the seven-mile hike on the sand at waters' edge. It was an adventure, stopping to help fishermen pull their wooden boats up onto the sand. As we neared the temple, George described the deep religious feeling we would experience. As we rounded a rocky outcrop, George stopped and shouted, "Oh, no! This is awful." There was the majestic Tanah Lot with construction crews building a modern hotel and golf course nearby. To George, Bali had been desecrated. No one could leave Bali without purchasing one of their intricate wood carvings. Judy named our selection "Romeo and Juliet," a man and woman carved out of a single piece of wood.

The family was growing, so we began looking for a larger condo at Meadow Bay. We did not find a unit to meet our needs, so the realtor

asked if we would be interested in a house, to which we said "no." Two days later we bought a six-bedroom, five-bath house on the water with a dock. Being within a two-hour drive for all the families, it is the retreat where our children and grandchildren have grown up, and where we could all vacation together.

It was a busy year. Our first grandchild, Sophie Wilde Spare, was born to Rosemary and David on July 18, 1996, in Racine, Wisconsin. Mother and daughter were well, and Judy and I were anxious to visit them; however, we were not able to do so until after Steve and Mari's impending wedding.

Grandma Spare moved to Villa Gardens when she was no longer able to live alone. She adjusted well to her new environment. Giving up her independence was made easier because of the attentive and loving caregivers. Mom was elated when we showed her photos of Sophie, her first great-grandchild.

Another highlight was Steve and Mari's wedding. We were excited they had finally gotten together. Judy called them, "The love birds." They were

and still are. Jill had worked her magic and convinced Steve and Mari they were meant for each other, although I suspect they knew that early in their relationship. The marriage ceremony was at Church of Our Savior and the reception at San Gabriel Country Club. We loved our new in-laws, Mike and Dani Rueff. They must have been excellent parents, because they had raised a lovely, charming, intelligent, Christian lady. We soon had another wedding when Mari's brother, Cameron, married his longtime girlfriend, Pam.

Grandma Spare was unable to attend the wedding, but was excited that Steven had found a wonderful companion and doubly pleased when Dave and Rosemary took baby Sophie to see her. Mom's heart was full of joy holding her first great-grandchild. She peacefully passed away two days after the wedding. Lola had spent a lifetime studying the Bible, believed that Jesus had gone to prepare a place for her, and looked forward to being reunited with family and friends.

Judy and Bob   Dani and Mike Rueff

The frantic pace of 1996 slowed. Prior to a conference in South America, we traveled to Machu Picchu to see one of the Seven Wonders of the World. Before ascending the ruins, we spent one night in Cuzco acclimating to the elevation. We took a train to the base of the mountain and stayed at a modest but clean hotel. Early the next morning we boarded an old school bus with bald tires and began our venture to the historic site. We traveled five miles on a gravel road with no rails on the cliff side of the mountain. The all-day tour by our excellent guide was educational. We were able to view the incredible construction genius of the Peruvian Incas who had built Machu Picchu six hundred years earlier.

From Peru we traveled to Buenos Aires for another Pensions 2000 conference. After three days of investment meetings, we spent an afternoon at a cattle ranch where the vaqueros treated us to their horsemanship skills and a BBQ featuring their renowned Augustine beef. Although the ambiance and aroma from the large slabs of meat on a glowing grill wetted our appetites, the meat was tough to chew and a disappointment. Buenos Aires is known as the Paris of South America and is a lovely city to explore and enjoy.

We arranged a post-conference tour to Iguazú Falls, located on the Argentine/Brazilian border. One of the Seven Wonders of the World, it is the largest waterfall in the world. Judy had been to Niagara Falls and indicated the size of it was a fraction of Iguazú. The falls were spectacular. We ventured to the end of the catwalks jutting out into the falls. It was a wonderful trip until Judy's bracelet watch was stolen at the airport. Actually, it turned out to be more of a loss to me. I bought her an exquisite, black sapphire watch from H. Stern in Brazil, as a replacement.

I was fortunate to work with the finest group of investment professionals anywhere, including men and women of intelligence, intellectual honesty, integrity, and dedication to the interests of the firm, shareholders, and clients. The Capital organization was founded by Jonathan Bell Lovelace in 1931. His philosophy and values were perpetuated through the years. Today, Capital manages more than $2 billion in assets and has 7,500 employees worldwide.

Bob Kirby was part of a small group of Capital professionals who founded Capital Guardian Trust Company (CGTC). This group provided investment management services to large pension funds. Until that time, Capital managed only mutual funds. Bob was a giant in the industry and a delight to travel with. He completed flight training just as W.W. II ended but never pursued flying. He had a passion for auto racing which led him to found the Kirby Racing Team. He drove in Le Mans and many other challenging races internationally. When we did portfolio reviews with clients, my favorite portfolio manager to travel with was Robert Ronus. Educated at Oxford, he was a Brit who was serious regarding business, but he enjoyed life and people. For a Brit, Robert was informal and humble despite his achievements. He was a voracious reader, and when traveling by air, he would leave behind a pile of newspapers, magazines, and research reports on his seat. Robert boarded one flight carrying clothes on hangers, fresh from the laundry. He was definitely unpretentious and made me laugh.

Capital hired bright, inquisitive people for specific positions, but encouraged employees to create their own career path in order to be productive and satisfied. A great example was Shaw Waggoner who worked on the trading desk. Capital recognized his potential and allowed him to transition to the research department. Shaw was bright and ambitious and, eventually, headed the emerging markets product team. All of us worked long hours. We loved our work, but we had a lot of fun along the way. Shaw and I were invited to make an emerging markets final presentation to the Hawaii Employees Retirement System at 1:00 p.m. at the Princeville Hotel on Kauai. Shaw was an excellent golfer and suggested we play the long, windy, and difficult Prince Course prior to our presentation. In warp speed, we played the course in three hours, showered, put on our aloha shirts, made the presentation, and won the assignment. I thanked my friend, Stanley Siu, who was pleased that Capital was finally an investment manager for the pension fund.

After the dissolution of the USSR, many of the eastern European countries started developing free market economies, stable governments, and potential markets in which to invest. Pension 2000 arranged a trip to Prague, Czech Republic and Warsaw, Poland. Prague, with the hundreds of majestic towers, was beautiful, especially at night. The mood of the people in adjacent countries was interesting. The people in Prague appeared to be somewhat depressed and unsure about their future. In contrast, the Polish people were happy and excited about the direction of their country. Much of their positive attitude was a result of Lech Walesa. He was the combative leader of the Solidarity Party which demanded the Communist Party allow free elections. Walesa addressed our conference. Three years later he was elected president of a free and independent Poland.

Lech Walesa

Hawaii was our vacation of choice during the 1990's. We traveled to several islands but our favorite venue was the Kapalua Bay Hotel, north of Lahaina, on the island of Maui. My associate, Fred Betts, and wife Bettye, owned a condo at Napili Kai that was a nine iron shot from our hotel. We arranged a golf outing with the Betts, Stanley and Edwina Siu, Woody and Lulu Clum, and Judy and me. That evening we gathered in the lounge for refreshments and convinced Edwina to sing the "Hawaiian Wedding Song." She had a professional soprano voice. As a younger woman, she was the lead singer at the Kahala Hilton Hotel near Waikiki. After finishing the song, the hotel entertainment manager offered Edwina a job.

Judy and I enjoyed collecting paintings. We were delighted to meet Guy Buffet at his studio in Lahaina. He was a Frenchman who painted whimsical Hawaiian people and colorful landscapes. Over the years, we collected several of his works. We had other trips to Mauna Kea on the Big Island of Hawaii and to the island of Lanai. There we spent a few days playing golf with the Sius at Manele Bay and Koeli golf courses. Until the industry became unprofitable due to costs associated with the longshoremen's union contracts, Lanai was a major growing area for pineapple. Today, the only pineapple grown on the island is for local consumption. Efforts to make Lanai a vacation destination have been mostly unsuccessful. The only attractions today are two lovely hotels with their golf courses and scuba diving boats.

1998 was another hyperactive year beginning with a Pensions 2000 trip to Australia and New Zealand. Our meetings started in Sydney. We cruised around the beautiful harbor while dining on delicious roasted rack of lamb, assorted salads, vegetables, and desserts. Our closing banquet was at the spectacular Opera House on the Bay. After traveling

so far, it was unfortunate we were not able to spend more time in the country and meet the people.

We flew to Christchurch on the South Island of New Zealand for what would be a wonderful adventure. Our meetings and golf tournament were at a quiet and pleasant resort. The conference agenda had many interesting and exciting events planned. We panned for gold in a river, rode in air-cushioned boats over swamplands, and went to a bunji jumping bridge. Several in our group took the plunge to the river below. Mike Nyeholt wanted to jump with his police and fire buddies, but, after a call to his doctor, he was convinced

it was a bad idea. After a morning business meeting, we flew to Milford Sound in single engine, private aircraft and landed on a dirt runway. There, we enjoyed a gourmet lunch by the water's edge. The flight to Milford was over the Sound. We flew at a low level near steep, heavily forested mountains with dozens of large, dramatic, cascading waterfalls.

At the conclusion of the conference, Judy and I planned to drive to the North Island with our friends, Stanley and Edwina Siu; however, Stanley was called back to Hawaii for an important meeting. They were not able to join us. Judy and I drove north to Mount Cook where we saw Chuck and Barbara Arledge. I booked a helicopter flight to the glacier but was not able to convince Judy to accompany me. Judy and I spent a week touring the North Island with a stop in Rotorua, home of the Māori people who had traveled from Polynesia one thousand years earlier. A thatched, wooden structure housed the largest and most beautiful carved outrigger canoe in the world. In the northern reaches of the island, we visited Waitangi. This is where a treaty between the British Crown and Maori chiefs became New Zealand's founding document. We stayed in a small, friendly B&B in the Bay of Islands. It was every bit as delightful as our friends Fred and Bettye Betts had described. They had visited the prior year. We found time for a round of golf before flying out of Auckland back to the United States.

It was unusual to have two Pension 2000 conferences in one year. But, it was not long after returning from New Zealand that we were off to Scandinavia and Russia. We made plans with the Sius to meet in Oslo and tour Norway before joining the conference in Stockholm, Sweden. The first evening in Oslo, Stanley announced he was retiring as Executive Director of the Hawaii pension fund. I asked the owner of the fine restaurant where we were dining to recommend a good bottle of red wine to celebrate Stanley's retirement. Better than making a recommendation, he led us into his stone-walled wine cellar that contained several hundred cases of wine. The owner selected a properly aged vintage, which we enjoyed with our superb dinner. On the trip we traveled by bus, auto, and train and saw some of the most spectacular scenery in the world. We spent one day on a ship sailing deep into a fjord on one of the coldest days I can remember. On a Sunday, we were scheduled to catch a small commuter ship to Bergen. From there we were to fly to Stockholm. To our surprise, we found the ship did not operate on Sunday, so we took a van, ferry, and two small taxis to the airport arriving only one minute before our 1:00 P.M. flight. That evening, when we arrived at the conference, we especially enjoyed the cocktail hour.

As one would expect, Stockholm was a clean, tranquil city on the Baltic Sea. What surprised me were the cobblestone streets and a thirteenth century cathedral. In my mind I pictured everything being a stereotype "Swedish modern." As with all Pension 2000 conferences, the speakers were interesting and the dinner and entertainment were outstanding.

From Stockholm, it was a short flight to St. Petersburg. It was founded by Tsar Peter the Great but was named after the Apostle Peter. The city was unclean, buildings were dirty, and the people were noticeably unenthusiastic. The economy was a disaster. When there was a run on the bank, they closed their doors, and people were unable to access their savings. We saw elderly women selling their family heirloom table linens and handkerchiefs on the street corners. It was heartbreaking to see these proud people losing their dignity. Worse was observing they had little hope for a better tomorrow. The city was a cultural and architectural mecca. The Hermitage Museum had an invaluable art collection; however, it had not been well preserved and was unprotected from tourists touching the treasures on display. The condition of the art reminded me of the Seventeenth Century work, painted on wood, of

"Madonna and Child" we had seen in an East Germany church. The wood had split and had been patched with a strip of tape.

The most spectacular reception and banquet of any conference was at Peterhof Palace, the residence of Peter I. We sailed across a lake where we disembarked and walked a quarter mile to the palace. It was a magnificent edifice with bright yellow walls and contrasting white stucco decorations. The terraces were dominated by sixty-four water fountains. A uniformed band played. We ascended the marble stairs and were led to a reception room with several bottles of Russian vodka chilling on ice sculptures. The room was impressive with mirrored walls, gold sconces, and crystal chandeliers. Dinner was served in another, equally beautiful room. The ambience exceeded the dinner, but the female soloist, men's choir in black tie, and dancers were outstanding.

Hermitage

Peterhof

Judy   Stanley & Edwina Siu

Mike and Dani Rueff, Mari's parents, owned a condo at Princeville on the North Shore of Kauai. When Mike's parents passed away, he wished to sell their fifty percent interest in the property. Judy and I were elated when we decided to purchase the fifty percent that was for sale. The condo had an unparalleled view of Hanalei Bay and Bali Ha'i. Kauai is known as the "Garden Island," because of its prolific and beautiful flora due to an abundance of rain. The island has less tourism than Oahu and

Maui, because construction has been discouraged. My Navy pal, Woody Clum and wife, Lulu, had a lovely home on Hanalei Bay with a gorgeous view of the ocean and the North Shore of the island. Their home was near our condo. We planned vacations together on Kauai whenever possible. My associate, Jason Pilalas, and wife Rena took their family to Kauai annually and rented a large home on the beach at Hanalei. We looked forward to the evenings when all the families would meet at Tahiti Nui's for dinner. The food was mediocre, but the Hawaiian music and poi in a large community bowl were excellent.

Lulu & Woody   Jason & Rena

Early in 1999, I notified Capital of my intent to retire at year-end. Because I knew most of my potential replacement candidates and the market to be served, the decision regarding a new hire was primarily my responsibility. Midyear, I recommended Gene Waldron for the position. He had been a competitor, but I believed him to be the consummate relationship manager. Gene was highly ethical, knowledgeable, and had strong relationships with plan sponsors nationally. Gene went through the normal Capital interview process and was hired. He came on board several months before year-end with time to learn about the Capital organization and its investment style and process. This allowed me the opportunity to introduce him to our clients, most of whom he knew. In retrospect, he was a brilliant selection.

With retirement looming, Judy and I participated in our final Pension 2000 conference, a trip to Rome and Istanbul. Having been to Rome twice, we had seen most of the many attractions. The business meetings were informative, and the food and entertainment, especially the singers, were excellent. We never had a bad meal in Italy.

The food in Istanbul was not as good, but the historic mosques, churches, palaces, and market places were spectacular. Istanbul straddles Asia and Europe and is located on the shore of the Bosphorus Strait. The most impressive site was the Blue Mosque. We were privileged to tour inside with its opulent décor. Ground breaking was in 1609 when Sultan Ahmed, carrying soil in his lap, prayed, "O Lord, Ahmed is your most loyal servant, please accept his offering." After the serenity of the mosque, we ventured into the hectic, thriving Grand Bazaar, a covered area housing 4,000 shops where 300,000 shoppers visit on a normal day.

The finest palace was Topkapi with extraordinary jewels, artifacts, books, and manuscripts from the 17th and 18th centuries. The palace had been the home of sultans and was renowned for the Imperial Harem with four hundred rooms occupied by the sultan, his concubines, wives, and the rest of his family-very cozy. We visited a fine rug merchant where we were herded into a room, served refreshments, and then viewed dozens of rugs of every size and color. Judy didn't like the high-pressure of the salesmen, so we left without a purchase. Later, we did buy a lovely silk rug at a reputable store. Today, it welcomes friends inside our front door.

While in Istanbul, September 28, 1999, Steve called to announce that Mari had given birth to our second granddaughter, Alexandra. Having complications during the delivery, Mari had bled profusely. She recovered after a few days in the hospital, but there had been some tense moments. Judy informed me we would never be out of the country when another grandchild was born.

In the Fall of 1999, we received an invitation to the wedding of my sister, Susan, to Jack Caple. It was to be held in San Diego. Susan had been single for about twenty-five years. I was excited and happy she had found a nice guy, as well as a successful businessman. At that time Jack owned several boats which were available for rent in the San Diego Harbor for harbor cruises, parties, and weddings. The thirty guests witnessed the wedding vows under the Coronado Bridge onboard the "Playtime."

In December 1999 Capital honored me with a retirement dinner at Annandale Golf Club in Pasadena. I was overwhelmed and a bit embarrassed when over two hundred business associates, family, and friends arrived for cocktails and a sit-down dinner. My great friend and partner, Mike Nyeholt, was the master-of-ceremonies. He did a superb job of keeping the program light and fun. I did not receive a gold watch. Of more value were the warm and gracious comments from David, Steven, and Judy. Cody Ferguson, Steve Brennan, David Fisher, Robert Ronus, John McIlwraith, Phil Swan, and Gene Waldron did a mild roast.

People brought many gag gifts. The classic was 50 one-pound bags of peppercorns. I have always been known to use excessive amounts of pepper on food.

Not only was year-end approaching, but also the beginning of a new millennium, January 1, 2000. People were uneasy, because many technical gurus predicted all computers would crash and be unable to transition from midnight to the New Year. Undaunted, I took the family to Princeville to celebrate my retirement and the new millennium. David, Rosemary, and three-year-old Sophie; Steve, Mari and three-month-old Ali; P.J. and Aunt Marge; Mike and Dani Rueff; and Mari's brother, Cameron, and wife, Pam, comprised our family celebration in Hawaii. It was hectic but full of infinite laughter and fun. We attended a luau on New Year's Eve at the Princeville Hotel. When a Hawaiian band didn't show up to

play, the ambiance was disrupted by a musical substitute, a hard-rock band. Consequently, it was not like a normal luau. And, to top things off, the food ran out before everyone was able to get through the buffet line. The good news was that all the computers and clocks continued to operate after midnight.

"ALOHA"

David   Sophie   Rosemary   Mari   Steven   Ali   Judy   Bob

Chapter Eight

Politics and Public Service

"We make a living by what we get, we make a life by what we give."
Ronald Reagan, August 8, 1992

I have put on paper a few beliefs. They pretty much summarize my political ideology.

The Constitution is the supreme law of the land and should be interpreted from an "originalist" perspective, not as a "living" document subject to political interpretation.

We are endowed by our Creator with certain unalienable rights, which cannot be compromised.

The Executive, Judicial, and Legislative branches of government have defined authority and no one branch should infringe upon the role of another.

We are a sovereign nation with sovereign borders.

U.S. foreign policy should be predicated on what is in the best interest of our country.

A strong military is essential to the safety and security of our country and its people.

A "free market economy" is responsible for the strength and stability of the U.S. economy.

Limited government and "states' rights" are best.

A free and independent press must be intellectually honest.

Freedom of religion and the free expression of one's faith are essential.

Some call me "conservative," to which I readily admit, but I prefer to be called an "American." My political activities have been dictated by my belief in our founding documents and the principles and values found therein. Liberty and freedom are fragile. I have prayed my efforts may help in some small way to preserve American values for my grandchildren and generations to come.

Judy and I were honored to attend Ronald Reagan's First Inaugural speech as Governor of California, January 5, 1967. He spoke words I believe to be true. "Freedom is a fragile thing and is never more than one generation away from extinction. It is not ours by inheritance; it must be fought for and defended constantly by each generation, for it comes only once to a people. Those who have known freedom, and then lost it, have never known it again."

Except to vote Republican, my parents were not politically active. Yet, during my teenage years, our family would sit around the dinner table and discuss current events. My earliest memory of being involved in a serious political discussion was in a debate class in high school. One debate focused on President Franklin Roosevelt's "New Deal." Was it evolution or revolution? The debate was spirited and probably helped initiate my interest in politics.

A few years later, I was accepted for admission to Stanford University. I declared Political Science as my major intending to pursue a law degree. I enjoyed the classes, although I suspect the professors were predominately left leaning politically. Constitutional Law, Administrative Law, and International Law were elective classes I enjoyed. Gratefully, Tax Law was not an offered course, because accounting was my least favorite subject.

We had a Political Science Club which hosted political officials and other relevant speakers on campus. The first "name" speaker we invited was Pat Brown, Attorney General of California. He was later elected Governor of the state. Pat was a plump, reddish-faced man who, in his speech, told jokes, related uninteresting trivia, and laughed too much. He did not discuss his job or the critical issues facing the state. I remember thinking, "How can a person this inept be elected Attorney General?" In ensuing years, I learned the answer to that rhetorical question.

Our club did have a memorable experience with Aleksandr Kerensky who was writing his memoirs at the Hoover Institution. When Czar Nicholas II, the last of the Russian Czars, was overthrown and murdered in 1917, Mr. Kerensky headed the first interim government. He instituted freedom of speech, assembly, religion, and the press. Unfortunately, he was overthrown by the Bolsheviks in the Revolution of 1917.

During my active duty with the Navy, there were few political discussions. In fact, the Navy had a rule that no one was to discuss politics, sex, or religion in the mess (dining) room. I completed my active duty requirement in December 1959 and returned to California from Guam. Richard Nixon was the Republican candidate for President in 1960. Shortly after returning, I was invited to a rally where Mr. Nixon spoke. That was the beginning of a lifetime of political activism. Having been out of the country for a few years, I was caught up in the moment and felt the excitement of the crowd and their enthusiasm for the speaker. It was good to be part of the political process.

My great friend, Berkeley Johnston, invited me to attend a South Pasadena Young Republican (YR) meeting. In this group I developed many lifelong friendships. We were active in supporting local candidates for the Legislature, Congress, School Board, and City Council, as well as President every four years. After a few years in the group, I was elected president. As such, I represented our group at the Los Angeles County Young Republicans.

In 1964 I was elected Vice Chairman of the County Young Republicans. We were deeply involved in the presidential campaign for Barry Goldwater. Tim Holabird and I helped provide special effects at a rally for Goldwater. The rally was held at Dodger Stadium. Goldwater drew a crowd of 50,000 supporters for his speech. Security was very tight, and the Secret Service agents were concerned for Goldwater's safety, especially after arresting a man with a telescoped rifle on a hill outside the stadium.

I spent some time working with the California State Young Republicans and served as Legislative Chairman at the annual conference. When we adopted provocative proposals, people would excuse us because of our "youth." My friend, Al Williams, still laughs at my proposed resolution to "nuc" the Chinese Communist nuclear facilities. This was in the mid-1960's. Perhaps we should have!

In October 1965, five of us from the County Young Republicans were invited to Ronald Reagan's home in Pacific Palisades. Mr. Reagan had never held public office but was exploring the possibility of running for Governor of California against Pat Brown. Governor Brown was running for re-election on the Democratic ticket. Our group had been searching for a conservative candidate; however, we did not know much about Mr. Reagan's political views. We did learn a few things from his speeches, but we had to determine if he was for "real" or just an actor.

Upon arrival at the Reagan home, we were welcomed by Mrs. Reagan and introduced to young Ronnie and daughter, Patti Davis. We were led into a warm, beautiful library with dark wood shelves filled with hundreds of books.; most had political and historical themes. Mr. Reagan entered the library casually dressed and was extremely cordial and friendly in his greeting to us. His broad smile and pleasant demeanor made us feel comfortable even before we began a serious discussion.

Ron was not loud or bombastic. Instead, he spoke softly with conviction and authority. During our three-hour discussion, we covered issues ranging from those important to California and the United States, as well as international concerns. We were amazed and pleasantly surprised at his grasp of critical issues. We were even more impressed at his formulated, practical common sense, and conservative solutions. His solutions were refreshing, because they were not dependent on government which, we all agreed, was the problem and not the solution. I had the temerity to ask Ron how many books on the shelves he had read, to which he replied, "Most." His knowledge certainly validated his short answer.

After the meeting, the five of us stood in Ron's driveway, looked at each other, and said, "He's the man!" Within a few days, we contacted Ron's exploratory team to inform them the L.A. County Young Republicans were prepared to put ten thousand members in the precincts should he decide to run for Governor. We strongly encouraged his candidacy and were confident the Young Republican organizations in California would share our enthusiasm.

Not long after Ron declared his candidacy, I was asked to be Co-Chairman of his campaign in Region 1 of the Citizen's Committee to Elect Ronald Reagan Governor. Los Angeles County was divided into seven regions. Region 1 encompassed the 43rd, 47th, 48th, and 54th Assembly Districts. Geographically, these included the cities across the foothills from Monrovia in the east to Silver Lake and La Crescenta in the west, as well as El Sereno and Temple City to the south. Those of us running the campaign on the local level were "worker bees;" however, the State campaign executive committee included many of the titans of industry and society, such as Henry Salvatori, Leonard Firestone, Asa Call, Justin Dart, Charles Ducommon, and William French Smith.

Being a full-time stockbroker meant most of my campaign work was done in the evenings and on weekends. Fortunately, we recruited a dedicated staff of volunteers who headed the functional committees for fund-raising, advertising, precincts, etc.

Ron and/or Nancy visited the region several times for fund raising events or to speak to various organizations. Ron always spoke from 3x5 notecards to share the comments he had composed. When making appearances in our region, I was given the opportunity to travel with Ron in his car. He was always upbeat, positive, and friendly, as well as focused on the election. Nancy was more reticent to communicate in private. When Judy and I traveled with her to meetings, Nancy was pleasant but not as outgoing as Ron. We did have one unpleasant experience when Ron came to our region for a full day of appearances. He was accompanied by John Tower, the Texas Senator, and a large entourage in several limos. Upon leaving one meeting, I rode in the car with Ron to the next appointment. Judy rode in the limo with the Senator. Upon arrival for the next meeting, Judy told me Tower had made several sexual advancements while in route. She told me she would not ride in the car with him during the remainder of the day. Judy was justifiably irate. I arranged for her to ride with me. I didn't tell Ron why Judy was joining us in his car. In retrospect, I should not have been surprised, as the Senator had a known reputation as a philanderer.

The Hollywood actors and actresses with whom Ron had headlined for many years were an important support group for the campaign. Having been the head of the Screen Actors Guild, Ron was popular with those "stars." An interesting aspect of my position was the opportunity to attend fund raising events and commercial filming where many celebrities were present. Being from Southern California, I was not impressed with the "stars." In contrast, Judy, being from Michigan, was excited when we had an opportunity to dine with Robert Stack or Rock Hudson. She was equally thrilled to sip French champagne while chatting with Cesar Romero. After filming a commercial at the Pantages Theatre in Hollywood, Judy asked if I knew who the person was seated next to me on stage. Not knowing, she told me it was Ray Bolger. He was best known for his part as the Scarecrow in "The Wizard of Oz." The only actor I would liked to have met was John Wayne who famously said, "Now why in the hell do I have to press 1 for English."

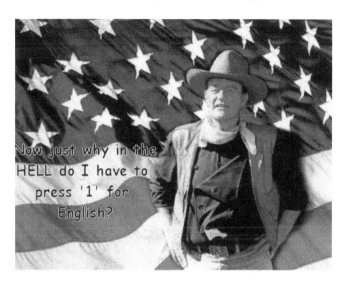

After a year of strenuous campaigning, it was time for the voters to decide who would lead California for the next four years. Ron had run an outstanding campaign. We were hopeful of a victory; however, Pat Brown held a comfortable lead in the polls. As we waited for the results at a "victory" party, the crowd was subdued and feared the worst. You can imagine the joy and relief as we witnessed the vote tallies. There was a thunderous applause when Ronnie took the stage and declared victory. He always had a big smile, but that evening it was as wide as the Grand Canyon. The "dumb cowboy actor," as he was described by the press, had defeated the most "elite"of the Democratic Party. With victory, a year of pro-bono volunteer work all seemed worthwhile. Now, it was time to spend time with family and business.

Even though the campaign was over, there was much to be done during the transition. Governor-elect Reagan had 1,350 appointments to make to state boards, commissions, and departments. Bob Finch was elected Lieutenant Governor. As such, Ron gave him half of the appointments to make. Finch lived in the region. I knew him to be a moderate Republican but not philosophically aligned with Ron. I spent much time documenting the reasons why several of Finch's appointees should not be confirmed. To Ron's credit, they were not approved. Ron gave each of the campaign chairmen a business card with the private telephone number to the phone on his desk in the State Capitol. We were to call if problems with the staff could not be resolved. I never had to use the card.

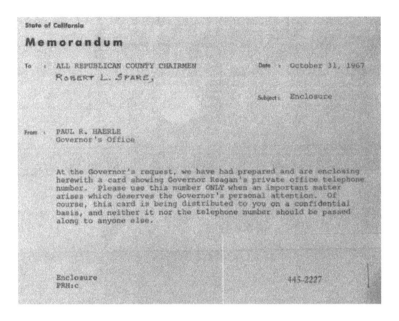

Many of those involved in the campaign accepted positions in Sacramento with the new administration. This opportunity did not appeal to me as a career path, especially with a family and job in Southern California. My final official duty was to attend the Inauguration and Ball in Sacramento. Judy and I invited my college friend, Chet Bjerke, and his wife, Tonya, to join us for the festivities. The highlight of the evening was when Judy and I were invited to join Ron and Nancy for a commemorative photograph. Ron was gracious and took time to thank us for our efforts on his behalf. This campaign was over. Four years later

Ron   Nancy   Judy   Bob

when Ron ran for re-election, I was asked why I didn't work on his campaign. I replied, "He doesn't need help."

Citizens Committee To Elect

RONALD REAGAN GOVERNOR

State Chairman
  Philip Battaglia
Southern Calif. Co-Chairmen
  Dick Eldersoon
  Thomas Pike
Northern Calif. Chairman
  Thomas Reed

August 31, 1966

Mr. Bob Spare
Eastman Dillon
2374 Huntington Drive
San Marino, California

Dear Mr. Spare: Bob

You will recall that during the primary we outregistered the democrats for the first time in 24 years. This was due inlarge measure to an operation called "Round Up". It was a real slam-bang success. "Round Up" was repeated during the current registration drive on Saturday, August 20, and for some reason it was not as successful as it could have been.

I am writing you this letter for the purpose of urging you as strongly as I can to call a meeting immediately and lay detailed plans to insure the most efficient participation of our organization in the second "Round Up" which is scheduled for Saturday, September 10. Let me repeat that we are going to have a second "Round Up" on Saturday, September 10. The purpose is to make absolutely sure that the entire state is blanketed to find unregistered Republicans and register them.

I just can not over-emphasize the importance of this project. Please cancel whatever needs to be cancelled and alter whatever plans need to be altered to insure maximum participation in this critical operation. I know I can count on your unstinting cooperation in this project. As a means of measuring the success of our participation, I would appreciate hearing from you by letter on September 11 as to the number of Republicans that were registered in Region I.

I look forward to hearing from you on the 11th with a report of continued outstanding success in Region I.

Sincerely,

Ronald Reagan

Ronald Reagan

NORTHERN CALIFORNIA HEADQUARTERS: 48 KEARNY ST., SUITE 620, SAN FRANCISCO, CALIFORNIA 94108 PHONE (415) 392-8295
SOUTHERN CALIFORNIA HEADQUARTERS: 3757 WILSHIRE BOULEVARD, LOS ANGELES, CALIFORNIA 90004 PHONE (213) 381-6731

RONALD REAGAN
PACIFIC PALISADES

October 11, 1966

Mr. Bob Spare
Eastman Dillon
2374 Huntington Drive
San Marino, California

Dear Bob:

You are probably reading this note as you dash from one campaign function to another while trying to catch just a few minutes at home. I wish you'd sit down for just a moment and try to absorb just a small part of the gratitude this note represents.

The outlook at this point is very optimistic. The indications are that victory is within our grasp if we can sustain our efforts for the next thirty days. Dirk and Tom have told me of your untiring efforts in Region I.

My purposes in writing you today are two. First to tell you of my deep personal gratitude for your outstanding efforts so far in the campaign. The second is to ask that during the thirty-day "stretch drive" we are about to enter that you continue to give the campaign all the drive and leadership you possibly can.

Thank you again for all you have done, Bob.

Sincerely,

Ronald Reagan

Ronald Reagan

RR:dg

RONALD REAGAN
GOVERNOR-ELECT
STATE OF CALIFORNIA

November 21, 1966

Mr. Bob Spare
Eastman Dillon
2374 Huntington Drive
San Marino, California

Dear Bob:

I have thought many times that even if we had lost the Election, I would have won in a very important way. I refer to the wonderful friends like you that I have made during the last year.

Thank you for the great amount of help and support you have given me during the campaign. Your efforts have had a great effect on the outcome of the Election. That fact is a real tribute to your leadership and organizational ability.

Bob, I appreciate all the work you did on fund raising. I realize this is a difficult task and Region I was most successful. Nancy told me that she had a wonderful day in your Region and was pleased to meet with so many people.

Again, my heartfelt thanks for your friendship and help. I hope to see you at the Inauguration.

Sincerely,

Ronald Reagan

Ronald Reagan

RR:dg

Proposition 1 was on the California ballot and adopted by the voters in 1966. The bill would allow public pension funds to invest 10% of the assets in equity securities beginning in 1967 and up to 25% in five years. The bill authorized the purchase of stocks, but it was left to the Legislature to determine guidelines for asset management, stock eligibility, and the trading of the securities for the pension funds.

Senate Bill 601 and Assembly Bill 913 enabled the legislation to implement Prop. 1. I had met Senator John Harmer during the Goldwater campaign. I asked his office for copies of the pending legislative bills. John responded quickly and asked me to comment on the bills. Evidently, John appreciated my input, because he asked me to join him in testifying before a Senate sub-committee in Sacramento. Feeling a bit inadequate, I invited Jim Fullerton to testify with us. Jim was a senior executive with Capital Research and Management Company and was able to provide expert testimony. The legislation passed with our recommendations.

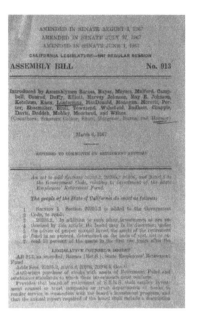

While I was working with Senator Harmer on the legislation, Bob Evans, managing partner of my employer, Eastman Dillon Union Securities, told me not to get involved. The reason for his request was that Eastman Dillon Union Securities and other California stockbrokers were lobbying to allow only California firms to execute trades for the pension funds. If that provision had been adopted, it would have been a gross violation of fiduciary responsibility, as most of the firms who provided "best execution" were headquartered in New York City. At this point, I assumed my future at Eastman Dillon had dimmed significantly. I began to make plans for a change, but with no regrets.

During the next few years, I was active in the Republican Party and campaigned for local candidates for Congress and the State Legislature. In the early 1970's State Senator Bill Richardson came to our house in Pasadena late one afternoon. As we sipped a glass of wine, we chatted about local politics. Judy did not join us, as she had the flu and was in bed. Soon, Bill disclosed the reason for his visit. He and the Republican leadership wanted me to run for the soon to be vacated 54th Assembly District seat. Seventy thousand dollars had been raised to kick off the campaign. I was honored and flattered to be asked to run for public office. I was confidant I could win, but my reply was an emphatic, "Thank you, but no." Bill was surprised with my response and attempted to change my mind. He even asked if he could talk to Judy hoping to convince her of my candidacy. Judy said it was up to me and would support my decision. It was difficult saying "no" to Bill; however, I had contemplated running for public office and concluded it was not the job for me. Indelicately, I expressed that for a legislator to be successful, one must occasionally compromise values and principles. I was not prepared to do so. Also, it would have been lousy to work in Sacramento five days a week and return home only on weekends. Even though Bill was clearly agitated at that moment, we remained friends and had other opportunities to work together.

In 1974, Judy worked for our dear friend Kathy Crow. Kathy was Chair of the California Conservative Union. One evening, Kathy and a few influential Republican ladies in town came to visit. They asked if I would run for a seat on the Pasadena Area Community College Board of Trustees (Pasadena City College). Judy was a teacher, and I had more than a passing interest in education. I also believed the Board could use another conservative voice. The area was divided into five districts. Each trustee was elected by voters in their district. Kathy and the ladies were persuasive, and I consented to run for the Board. My Young Republican friends, Berkeley Johnston and Bruce Davis, organized a campaign committee comprised mostly of personal friends. Because I was working, campaigning was limited to evenings and weekends. The key to winning an election at the time was getting out the vote. This meant working in the precincts and meeting the voters face-to-face. Our young sons, ages 9 and 7, walked the precincts, too. Their efforts may have made the difference in my margin of victory, 52 votes. I was pleased to have won the election, especially since my opponent was a PhD professor. I believed it was a conflict of interests for educators to be on a school board.

1. KATHY CROW   2. JUDY

Why BOB SPARE'S

FINANCIAL EXPERIENCE
IS IMPORTANT TO **YOU**

and to the

Pasadena Community College District

Board of Trustees

AREA 4

(Map on Reverse Side)

1975

BOB SPARE'S
ENDORSEMENTS

PARTIAL LIST

Mr. and Mrs. Robert Edmonston
Mr. and Mrs. Thomas Thiel
Mrs. George Wright
Mr. Richard C. Fildew
Mr. and Mrs. William W. Clary
Mr. and Mrs. Robert Early
Mr. and Mrs. Clifton P. Wolfe
Mr. and Mrs. Dareld Shaver
Mr. and Mrs. James Knight
Dr. and Mrs. Edward Oberc
Mr. and Mrs. James D. Ryan
Mr. and Mrs. Jack C. Flynn
Mr. and Mrs. Edward Hodgkin
Mr. Stuart Snyder
Mr. and Mrs. Robert F. Hayes
Mr. and Mrs. Michael McGee
Mr. Jens Christie
Mr. and Mrs. William Miller
Mr. and Mrs. Robert Martin
Mr. and Mrs. Berkeley W.
  Johnston
Mrs. Sue J. Garrison
Mr. and Mrs. Bee R. Waples Jr.
Dr. and Mrs. D. Clinton
  Bennett
Mr. and Mrs. Douglas Porteous
Mr. and Mrs. Frank J. Noble
Mr. and Mrs. Willard Chilcott
Mr. and Mrs. Melvin Burt
Mr. and Mrs. Bruce Reagan
Mr. Francis Eppes Shine III
Mr. Thomas E. Smith
Mr. and Mrs. William Hahn
Mr. and Mrs. Henry Braun
Dr. and Mrs. Ulric Bray
Mr. and Mrs. Durward
  Howes III
Mr. and Mrs. William T. Huston
Mr. and Mrs. Gleason Payne
Dr. and Mrs. Russell Decker
Mr. and Mrs. Sam T. Hayward
Mrs. Emma S. Nolting
Mr. and Mrs. Clayton M.
  Hurley
Mr. and Mrs. J. Bradford Crow
Mr. and Mrs. Thomas J. Sherritt
Mrs. John Schulz
Mr. and Mrs. R. W. Brand
Dr. and Mrs. C. M. Woodward
Mrs. Neil Ross
Mrs. Lawrence A. Odlin
Mrs. Dixie McIntee
Mr. and Mrs. Joseph M. Crosby

Mr. C. Anthony Phillips
Miss Janet Codding
Mr. Bryson Kratz
Mr. and Mrs. Elliot N. Sax
Mr. and Mrs. Jon N. Dawn
Mr. and Mrs. Gerald L.
  Whitehead
Mr. and Mrs. L. B. Harbour
Mr. and Mrs. Richard Snyder
Mr. and Mrs. Horace H.
  Mickley
Mr. and Mrs. Edgar F.
  Whitmore Jr.
Mr. and Mrs. John W. Harris Jr.
Mr. and Mrs. Clyde E. Holley
Mr. and Mrs. John G.
  Armstrong
Mr. and Mrs. Hugh J. McDonald
Mr. and Mrs. Peter Kaplanis
Mr. and Mrs. Franklin
  Thornton
Dr. and Mrs. D. Lloyd Nelson
Mrs. Joan T. Day
Mr. and Mrs. David Cashion
Mr. and Mrs. Andrew
  Vollero Jr.
Mr. and Mrs. John Fox
Dr. Tjaart Nanninga
Mr. C. Milton Henshilwood
Mr. and Mrs. Bruce Davis
Mr. and Mrs. Charles Hale
Mr. Clifford R. Anderson Jr.
Mr. Charles L. Rogers
Mr. Richard Shooshan
Mr. and Mrs. Austin H.
  Hathaway, Jr.
Betty Snedeker
Mrs. Fred E. Rhodes
Dr. and Mrs. Henry Myers
Mr. and Mrs. Arthur C.
  Withrow
Mr. William P. Barry
Mr. and Mrs. Roland DeWees
Mr. and Mrs. George Wenger
Mr. and Mrs. Gary Hayward
Mr. and Mrs. William Chelf
Mr. and Mrs. Ronald Childs
Mr. and Mrs. Marshall Barnes
Mrs. Ray Untereimer
Mr. and Mrs. John Loucks
Mr. and Mrs. James Gilloon
Mr. and Mrs. Ronald Martin
Mr. and Mrs. Harold T.
  Angerhofer

The five years on the Board was an education. I am quite sure I learned more than I contributed. The position of Trustee was a non-political position; however, it was not long before I learned where the philosophical lines were drawn. I arrived early for my first Board meeting. While sitting in my assigned seat, a beautiful leather chair, Walter Shatford, patriarch of the Board, made a grand entrance. He was a twenty-year member of the board, as well as a radical, left-wing attorney who had been cited by a government committee for his ties to Communist organizations. Much to my chagrin, he sat in the chair next to me. Pleasantly, I said, "Good evening, Walter," to which he made no response. Walter did not recognize my bi-monthly greeting for the first six months of my tenure. During meetings, Walter used the strategy of waiting until each trustee had commented on an issue, both pros and cons, before summarizing and then declaring how the Board should vote. Fellow Trustee Roger Gertmanian was a Stanford friend and a staunch conservative. After one meeting when Walter swayed the board with his brilliant "summary," Roger and I decided he would no longer have "the last word." Henceforth, either Roger or I would wait until Walter finished his comments and recommendations to make our closing comments. Needless to say, Walter was furious.

Some of today's events remind me of an incident that happened forty years ago. The board received a proposal from the black students requesting a dedicated space for meetings on campus. The administration recommended approval of their request. I argued that such an action would be polarizing and divisive. If approved, we would be obligated to provide separate meeting spaces for Hispanics, Asians, and Whites, as well. The proposal was defeated; however, I believe it was more because of cost than philosophy.

During my tenure as President, the school sponsored a series of travel films that were open to the public. The showing of a film on South Africa drew protests. Fifteen minutes prior to the showing, the school received a phone call stating that a bomb had been placed in the auditorium and was due to explode before the film was to begin. I consulted with the Chief of Police. We cleared the auditorium, found no explosives, and ran the film 45 minutes late.

In 1979, while President of the Board, it was evident that Proposition 13, limiting property tax escalation, was going to be adopted by the voters of California. I requested the administration present a pro-forma budget reflecting a 15% cut in the prior year's budget. After three months of stonewalling, the board received a hypothetical budget. Because 87% of the school's budget was for salaries and benefits, cuts were going to have to come from personnel. The teacher's union recommended that the budget cuts come from terminating the youngest teachers to protect the older, tenured employees. The end of my term on the Board happened coincidently at the same time Judy, the boys, and I planned to move from Pasadena to San Marino. No longer being a resident of Pasadena would make me ineligible to run for re-election in District Four. This was also a time for re-drawing geographic lines for congressional, legislative, and local governmental districts, something done every ten years. It was clear those responsible for drawing the new district lines were intent on eliminating either my friend, Roger, or me from the Board. We reached an agreement that I would voluntarily be gerrymandered out of my region. The good news was that Roger's district was protected, so he won re-election. Was this a conspiracy? Being on the board was a rewarding experience for me. I hope my conservative voice added something to the dialogue and direction of the college.

The year 2000 was a watershed year. Not only was it the millennium but the year I retired from Capital Guardian Trust Company. At the time, Congressman Jim Rogan, who represented us in the 27th District, was the lead prosecutor in the impeachment of President Bill Clinton in the House and in the Senate. Jim was also running for re-election. The Democrats targeted his seat and raised huge campaign funds from the Hollywood elite. Because of the continuing impeachment trial, Jim was unable or unwilling to return to the District to campaign. I believe this led to his defeat. Adam Schiff beat him by three percentage points. I had the honor of serving on Jim's Finance Committee. I admired Jim as much as I admired Ronald Reagan. Jim had all the attributes one would want in an elected official. He was intelligent and humble, intellectually honest with integrity, courageous, and an unapologetic patriot. He loved our Country. For you historians, I recommend Jim's book, <u>Catching The Flag</u>. It is a compilation of his private diaries written during the Clinton impeachment trial.

Mike Antonovich represented the Fifth Supervisorial District in Los Angeles County. We became political friends during our days in the L.A. County Young Republicans and Goldwater campaign. Judy and I visited Mike in his office after my retirement. I offered to serve pro bono on any board or commission where I could be of value. Not long after our meeting, Mike called

John McCain   Mike Antonovich

to ask if I would be interested in serving on the Quality and Productive Commission for the County. After some due diligence, I accepted the appointment. The mission of the Commission was to introduce best practices from private industry into the seventeen County departments. The work was interesting and the commissioners, who came from very diverse backgrounds, were dedicated and enthusiastic about making the County operations more efficient. My favorite project was to encourage departments to rewrite documents in plain, easy to understand English for the public to read. The attorneys were not happy, but the public was elated.

Two years later, Antonovich called to inform me that he had an appointment to the L.A. County Employees Retirement Fund (LACERA) Investment Board. This was exactly the Board I wished to join. I was very familiar with LACERA, for it had been a client when I was at Capital Guardian. LACERA had a defined benefit plan that was funded by the public with county taxes and county employee contributions. This group included the sheriffs and firemen. Although the pension fund had assets of $40 billion, it was underfunded. The trustees would not set an actuarial assumption level low enough to meet anticipated benefit payments. This is a systemic problem in the public fund world, because the boards are controlled by the unions. They do not adopt the actuary's recommended assumed rate of return for the fund. To do so, employee contributions would have to be increased. One of the frustrations on the Board was that some of the trustees promoted their personal agenda rather than fulfilling their fiduciary responsibility. Two of the Hispanic trustees were more interested in an investment manager's Hispanic head count rather than their investment returns. Another frustration was with trustees who had no investment experience, which was a requirement to be on the Board. During the economic disaster and stock market crash in 2008, a trustee who was an attorney from Beverly Hills suggested we sell all of the equity securities in the fund! Lisa Mazzocco, our highly competent and experienced Chief Investment Officer, and I explained the risk in TRYING to sell a huge portfolio in a stock market that was already down 35%. One good question was, "Sell to whom?" We then asked him, "If we sold all our stocks, when should we repurchase the securities?" Needless to say, the Board did not sell the stocks. On the contrary, we purchased stocks as part of our strategic rebalancing program. In the following year, the fund assets rebounded significantly.

Robert L. Spare Joins the Board of Investments

L ACERA is proud to welcome Mr. Robert L. Spare to the Board of Investments. He attended his inaugural board meeting on February 13, 2002. Mr. Spare was nominated for this position by Supervisor Antonovich and appointed by the Board of Supervisors.

Mr. Spare brings more than 40 years of investment experience to the Board of Investments. His educational background includes graduating from Stanford University and the Naval War College. He served his country in the U.S. Navy and retired with the rank of Captain from the Naval Reserve Intelligence Program.

Before his retirement in 2000 from his second career, Mr. Spare was Senior Vice President of Capital Guardian Trust Co., one of the largest investment management firms in the world, specializing in providing portfolio management services to large retirement plans. Prior to his position there, Mr. Spare was deputy manager of the First Boston Corporation, a major investment banking firm, providing economic and securities research to institutional clients. Additionally, as a Trustee of the Pasadena Community College Board, he shared responsibility for approving and overseeing a $30 million budget.

Mr. Spare held the position of 2nd Vice Chair on the Los Angeles County Quality and Productivity Commission, and is looking forward to serving in his new position on the LACERA Board of Investments.

Mr. Spare was born in Alhambra, California and has spent most of his lifetime in the Pasadena area where he and his wife, Judy, raised their two sons.

Again, we wish to extend a very warm welcome to the newest member of the Board of Investments, and we are anticipating an exciting and productive term of service.

At the end of my term on the Investment Board, Antonovich asked if I was interested in serving another term. I told him I was interested for only one more term. I was surprised when Mike appointed his Deputy's brother, John Barger. There is an old expression, "Politics make strange bedfellows." I was disappointed, because I believed I knew the investment process and the capital markets which was not the case with most of the members. But, the Lord works in mysterious ways. It was not long after I left the Board that Judy had physical problems. If I had continued on the Board, I would have had to resign my position.

For many years, Judy and I focused our charitable contributions for organizations supporting children, medical research, special schools, church, and our local hospital. However, after retirement we started supporting politically conservative "think tanks." We could see there were people dedicated to changing our form of government and economic system, as well as others who were brain washing our children in school. Students were being taught they were responsible for the sins of their ancestors and that those transgressions had to be rectified. They were being taught our economic system caused minorities to be disadvantaged and that social justice could only be accomplished through the redistribution of wealth. Understanding the greatness of our Country, as well as the advancement of civil rights and personal liberty, was not being taught. Most children do not understand the immense sacrifices Americans have made in terms of blood and treasure in order to free other nations of the despotism of Nazism and Communism. As I write today, we are witnessing the result of the radical left's control of the minds of young people for an entire generation. Nothing is more important to the future of our Country than to provide students with a BALANCE of economic and political thought. Teaching history in a fair and balanced way must be renewed. Children need to learn to think critically, understand free and open debate, and hear views from those with whom they may disagree.

Today, one of the most egregious, ideological positions of the left is climate change. Thirty years ago, Al Gore popularized the "THEORY" that the earth was WARMING due to man-made emissions of carbon dioxide (CO_2) from fossil fuel burning. At the time, Al predicted New York City would be under water in ten years if the CO_2 emitting did not stop. Every few years the alarmists predict the end of the world in "the next ten years." Since there are inconvenient periods of global cooling, the predictors of doom have changed the terminology from global warming to "climate change." Unfortunately, this unproven science is being taught in schools, and it is scaring the diapers off of our children.

Judy and I joined the Claremont Institute. We had a close relationship with the Director Brian Kennedy, primarily because of our mutual interest in missile defense. The Institute sponsored an annual Winston Churchill black-tie dinner to honor prominent conservatives. We sponsored a table at several events and took friends who were politically active. We were able meet and be photographed with honored speakers including Vice President Dick Cheney, Secretary of Defense Don Rumsfeld, Senator Ted Cruz, former Ambassador to the United Nations John Bolton, and our favorite honoree, Rush Limbaugh.

Cheney

Rumsfeld

Limbaugh   Sue Williams

Bolton

Cruz

Oli North

Next, we joined the Heritage Foundation. I believe they publish the most thorough research on major current issues, often presenting their "white papers" to members of Congress, governors, and other interested stakeholders. My friends Berkeley Johnston, Tom Meehan, and I hosted a luncheon for Heritage at Annandale Golf Club. After a delicious lunch, which included glasses of fine California wine, seven guests joined the Foundation. This was a new but pleasant way to be involved politically.

Jim Talt

In 2019 I joined the Hoover Institution, a conservative, political think tank domiciled on the Stanford campus. The Institution was founded by Herbert Hoover in 1919. Forty years later, he reaffirmed the mission of the organization with these words: "This Institution supports the Constitution of the United States, its Bill of Rights, and its method of representative government. Both our social and economic systems are based on private enterprise from which springs initiative and ingenuity. Ours is a system where the Federal Government should undertake no governmental, social, or economic action, except where local government, or the people, cannot undertake it for themselves. The overall mission of this Institution is, from its records, to recall the voice of experience against the making of war, and by the study of these records and their publication, to recall man's endeavors to make and preserve peace, and to sustain for America the safeguards of the American way of life. This Institution is not, and must not be, a mere library. But with these purposes as its goal, the Institution itself must constantly and dynamically point the road to peace, to personal freedom, and to the safeguards of the American System."

The Hoover Institute sponsored Aleksandr Kerensky when writing his memoirs. I was a student at Stanford University at the time.

I joined the Institution not only because of their published research, but because of the vast conference program they sponsor. I have been able to attend seminars at Stanford, San Diego, Palm Springs, Pasadena, Santa Barbara, Carmel, and Napa Valley. The agendas have been topical and important with speakers acknowledged as experts in their field. A side benefit of attending such events has been the opportunity to see and visit with many friends.

Cashions   Sister Barb   Spares   Melinda Gordon

Boards   Newtons

I urge everyone, especially students, to read and assimilate the wisdom found in the Declaration of Independence and the Constitution of the United States of America in order to understand and appreciate the freedoms and rights which we are guaranteed and, equally important, the limits which are imposed upon government.

The Declaration of Independence was adopted by the action of the Second Continental Congress on July 4, 1776, the unanimous Declaration of the thirteen United States of America. It declares, "We hold these Truths to be self-evident, that all Men are created equal, that they are endowed by their Creator with certain unalienable rights, that are among these are Life, Liberty and the Pursuit of Happiness..."

The Constitution of the United States of America was signed on September 17,1787 and begins, "We the People, of the United States, in Order to form a more perfect Union, establish Justice, insure domestic Tranquility, provide for the common defence, promote the general Welfare, and secure the Blessings of Liberty to ourselves and our

Posterity, do ordain and establish this Constitution for the United States of America."

The final founding document is the Bill of Rights, adopted on December 15, 1791. Congress established a process to add Amendments to the Constitution. It required that two-thirds of both Houses concur in proposing an Article (Amendment) to the state legislatures, then requiring ratification by three-fourths of the said legislatures. Among the twenty-seven (XXVII) articles is the right to free speech, the right bear arms, and states' rights.

Well, I only rented this soapbox, and it is time to get off.

God bless America! I pray that all of us will dedicate ourselves to preserving the fundamental values and freedoms of America. These have been bought at the great expense of others.

Chapter Nine

The Golden Years, 2000-2009

Upon returning from Hawaii, life felt less meaningful, like a half empty vessel. David and Steven were married with children, and I was unemployed for the first time in forty-five years. Fortunately, boredom did not have time to intrude. We planned to travel extensively, and Judy and I agreed it was time to sell our home in San Marino and purchase a condo in Southwest Pasadena. Judy's friend, Kim Atkinson, found an interesting tri-level condo on South Orange Grove where the Rose Parade formed every January 1st. We loved our new home but quickly tired of the traffic noise. We remained there for two years and then moved to the perfect condo at 345 W. Bellevue Drive in Pasadena.

New Year's Eve and New Year's morning became a tradition. Our children and grandchildren would arrive to welcome in the New Year, sleep overnight, and go to the parade route early in the morning. Prior to the start of the parade, we walked in the street, up and down Orange Grove, and watched bands tune-up for their eight mile march; we talked with the caballeros preparing their festively adorned horses for the parade, and we marveled at the workers putting the final orchids and roses on the floats. The biggest attraction may have been when the queen and her court climbed into their regal seats on the Queen's Float.

Believing it was a cost-effective way to reach hundreds of millions of people globally, David convinced Dole Pineapple to enter a float in the parade. He approached Raul Rodriguez, the preeminent float builder at Fiesta Floats, with a proposition: "I don't care what it costs, but I want to win the sweepstakes." Fiesta delivered, and Dole won the first of many major awards in the world renowned Pasadena Rose Parade.

After retirement, one of our first "short" driving trips was to Arizona to see Judy's mom and aunt. On the return trip we stayed overnight in La Quinta near Palm Springs. Judy had often commented on how much she enjoyed the desert and how nice it would be to have a little hideaway there. We talked with a realtor, just to "get a feel for the market." Soon thereafter, we purchased a modest three bedroom condo overlooking the 14th green on the Arnold Palmer golf course at PGA West. Of course, we had to remodel the bathrooms and kitchen and build a spa in the backyard. Suddenly, our little retreat was not so "modest." The view from the backyard looked across the golf course to the majestic mountains rising sharply from just beyond the fairway. It was spectacular, especially when it was illuminated by floodlights at night.

Edwina Siu

Judy and I had traveled extensively for business but had not been on a pleasure cruise. When Fred Betts, my Capital Guardian pal, called to say that he and Bettye were booked on a Silver Seas cruise to the Greek Islands, we immediately made a reservation. The extent of my cruising had been aboard the U.S.S. Ranger and several other aircraft carriers.

We met the Betts in Athens, Greece where we spent a day touring local attractions, such as the Olympic Stadium and the Acropolis which had been a fifty-year building project initiated by Pericles. As we ascended the rocky hill, we were in awe of the Parthenon ruins and how majestic it must have been when dedicated to the goddess Athena in 438 B.C. On May 6, 2000 we boarded the Silver Wind, an upscale ship with a manageable nine hundred passengers. The accommodations, food, service, entertainment, and land excursions were superb.

Our first stop was in Mykonos, a mostly desolate island with a quaint resort known for its summer party atmosphere. The only architecture of significance was a row of 16th century windmills, not an auspicious start to our cruise.

Our stop in Rhodes was much more interesting. It is famous for the Seven Wonders of the Ancient World. Our tour guide took us to Lindos, one of the most beautiful villages in Greece. We hiked up several hundred steps to a hilltop acropolis with temple ruins and a castle. This was a picturesque island where you could enjoy visiting the delightful seaside resorts and fine sandy beaches.

Our first stop in Turkey was in Kas, where we boarded a small tour boat to motor up a river to a most unusual site. On the sheer, rock mountainside were Daris style graves formed by carvings of women's figures in the walls to the entrance to the tombs. They were truly remarkable works of art.

To us, the highlight of the cruise was docking in Kusadasi, Turkey and taking a day trip to Ephesus where the Apostle Paul established a Christian church; his letters to this congregation are recorded in the Book of Ephesians in the Bible. We walked through the town on a marble road with tracks carved into the marble from chariot wheels. As we walked, archeologists were excavating in the dirt with spoons and small tools. Our guide was very knowledgeable and kept us mesmerized with stories of what life was like for the Ephesians in the first century A.D. Our tour culminated with an opportunity to sit in the arena where Paul had preached.

Bettye & Fred

Visiting Istanbul was exciting; however, Judy and I had been there and much of the tour was repetitive. From Istanbul we sailed to the marvelous island of Corfu. It was the greenest of the islands with dense vegetation and lovely beaches. Of the islands we visited, Corfu was the one we all agreed would be on our return list. The culture was unique, because it had been under Venetian, French, and English rule at various times before being united with Greece in 1864.

We sailed up the Adriatic Sea to the Croatian city of Dubrovnik, which had suffered significant damage during the Serbian bombardment in 1991. Ten years later the city was rebuilt. The buildings had stunning red tile roofs. The view from the stone wall, which surrounded the city, provided a magnificent view of the Adriatic coastline. The people were friendly, especially the women who made embroidered handkerchiefs, which we purchased for Christmas gifts. Judy could not leave this enchanted city without acquiring a set of delicately painted wine glasses. They are now in the bar at our lake home.

After two weeks aboard the Silver Wind on our first, but not last, cruise, we arrived in Venice early in the morning. I vividly remember standing on the forward deck shortly after sunrise as we approached the city. There we had a splendid view of Ponte di Rialto, St. Mark's Basilica, and the Campanile Bell Tower on Piazza San Marcos. We have many warm memories of our few days in Venice: riding the romantic gondola through a myriad of canals, dining at our favorite restaurant, Ristorante Antica Martina, and exploring the sights and shops of this fascinating city. No one can leave Venice without taking a speedboat to Murano to visit the glass-blowing facilities. Venetian glass is exceptional in detail and color, and it has been an art form for fifteen hundred years. No one is obligated to buy a piece of glass art, but, if you don't, you may not get a ride back to your hotel. That was not a problem for Bettye and Judy. For Judy, it was love at first sight. She selected a large piece consisting of three Tatori birds perched on tree limbs. The hand-blown glass birds were in vibrant colors: red, blue, yellow, and green. Not to be outdone, Bettye found an equally spectacular piece-three geese flying in formation. I can still see the look of disbelief on Fred's face when the salesman presented him with the bill.

Buying Tatori Birds

Our first cruise was a wonderful experience: the food, entertainment, tours, and even the black tie dinners. Sharing the time with great friends, made it extra special.

Bettye and Fred   Judy and Bob

I have always appreciated beautiful woods. With more free time, I joined a woodworking club, which utilized the vacated shops at McKinley Junior High School in Pasadena. Besides having every piece of equipment known to man, we had expert woodworking advice and instruction. What little artistic talent I possessed was exhibited in the pieces I created: toy boxes for the grandchildren, a classic rocking chair, inlaid boxes, turned bowls, tables, and book shelves. The only really creative piece I designed and carved was of a wooden seagull with a three and one-half foot wingspan, flying low over ocean waves. The process involved cutting and gluing one-inch walnut wood strips, drawing an outline of the bird, sawing around the outline, and finally doing the fine cutting and sanding. It was a work of love and patience. The piece proudly sits in my living room in Arcadia. The woodworking shop has since closed; however, I accumulated enough equipment to complete some projects on my own at home, like the Tiki Bar, which we use for our annual Polynesian party.

Judy and I enjoyed our first cruise so much that we quickly booked an ocean cruise to Spain and Portugal along with the Betts, my sister, Barbara, and her husband, Al Martindale. We boarded the Silver Cloud on April 11, 2002 in Monte Carlo. Prior to boarding, the six of us took a long walk around the town to stretch our legs before meeting the ship. When we attempted to enter the renowned casino, we were asked to pay an entrance fee. This was the first time I had to pay to lose my money. The city was small, clean, and overlooked a spectacular marina occupied with large, meticulously maintained yachts. The boats, cars, and people were all a bit pretentious.

Betts   Spares   Martindales

After departing Monte Carlo, the captain informed us that we would not stop in St. Tropez because of inclimate weather. Our substitute port was Villa France, a small, cliffside town. Then, we were unable to visit Corsica because of weather, opting to dock at Toulon where we spent a pleasant day enjoying "country French" food and people.

Our stop in Marseille was memorable for the rain and a delightful lunch at a country farm. The ride through the hills, filled with farms and vineyards, was enjoyable and gave us a feel for rural France. The city of Marseille was home to the largest group of Muslims in France. We were warned not to venture alone into the city.

Our first port of call in Spain was Tarragona, a dirty industrial city and port. It was a change from the picturesque harbors and marinas in France. As disappointing as Tarragona was, Palma de Mallorca was remarkably delightful. It is a resort destination for rich  Spaniards and Europeans with attractive beach resorts. Our drive into the interior of the island culminated in a fabulous five or six course luncheon at a hillside restaurant. On reflection, that may have been the best meal of the trip.

Our next destination was Granada, which was the primary reason I was excited about visiting Spain. On a hilltop overlooking the city was the

Alhambra with the most spectacular buildings and architectural creations I have seen. Originally built as a fortress in the 9th century, the current Alhambra structures were developed by the Moors (thus the Moorish design) and then enhanced and completed by the Muslims in the 14th century. The beauty and intricate designs of the walls, ceilings, and doors cannot be described any more than I can describe a gorgeous sunset.

There was not enough time to fully appreciate the magnificence of the Alhambra, but it was time to move on to the historic and strategic Gibraltar, an important, British naval base. The fortress at Gibraltar has a commanding presence over the Straits of Gibraltar, which controlled the western access to the Mediterranean Sea. We had a brief tour of the city, punctuated with an exciting cable car ride to the top of "the rock."

It was a short trip around the southern tip of Spain and up the west coast of Portugal to Lisbon. Sadly, our one day in the city was spent at an endodontist's office where Judy endured a partial root canal procedure.

We stopped at the Madeira Islands where we visited Porto Santo whose claimed of fame was that Christopher Columbus lived here when not discovering new continents. The most interesting island was Funchal, which had tropical vegetation reminiscent of the Hawaiian Islands. Here, we had perhaps the most "fun" event of the cruise, a sled ride like none other. Judy and I sat in a sled and were launched down a steep cobblestone street covered with straw. The sled had no steering or brakes, but the descent was controlled by two men, running alongside, with ropes connected to the sled.

En-route to the fabled port of Casablanca, we spent a day in Tenerife, Canary Islands. The topography and vegetation varied significantly between the tropical beaches and 12,000 foot mountains. After a day tour, we appreciated why this alluring island was a resort destination for Europeans.

As in Istanbul, we felt a bit uneasy in Casablanca, a Moroccan city in North Africa. The most spectacular site was the Hasan II Mosque, which was modern and magnificent. However, we most enjoyed visiting the open-air market with hundreds of stalls exhibiting beautiful fresh flowers, every fruit and vegetable imaginable, and wicker baskets full of colorful, aromatic spices. George Miller would dissent, but the produce and products were more bountiful and attractively displayed than the marketplace in Bali.

Sagrada Família Church

Our final port visit was in Barcelona. It was a beautiful, delightful city to enjoy as our final destination on what had been a fabulous cruise. The city is known for its art and architecture and, specifically, the fantastic Sagrada Família church designed by Antoni Gaudí. The church construction began with ground breaking in 1882 and, as of our visit, was still "in progress." Clearly, Barcelona was the center of the "modernist" movement when you consider that Picasso and Dali resided in the city. Barcelona has wide, tree-lined streets with vibrant, friendly people. It is definitely a city where we would like to have spent more time.

After returning from a delightful cruise, we moved into our new condo on Bellevue Drive; the size and location of the unit was ideal for us at that time. We upgraded the bathrooms and kitchen and knocked out part of a wall to install French doors between the dining room and a private, tree shaded patio. A high priority for me was to build a Viking BBQ with utility drawers and refrigerator. There were only three units in our complex, and we were blessed with lovely, considerate neighbors. Our unit was split-level with two bedrooms, two-and-one-half-baths, and an attached garage with access from it into the kitchen/breakfast room area. We loved our new home and were happy to be away from the noise of Orange Grove, but still close to the parade route.

Judy and I continued our friendship with Steve and Diane Andrews from the days when Steve was on the San Diego County Retirement Board, a client of Capital Guardian. Steve and I played as a team in at least a dozen golf tournaments, and he was the most enthusiastic player and golf fan I had ever met (Judy's brother John Jay runs a close second). The Andrews were a young, black couple, he a banker, and she a children's advocacy attorney. For several years, we invited them to our condo at PGA West for the Bob Hope charity golf tournament. We had a wonderful, fun-filled time with them, along with our neighbors Woody and Lulu Clum. I remember walking out on the patio early one morning before the girls were up, and there was Steve, completely relaxed, drinking a cup of coffee, smoking a cigarette, and reading the Bible in preparation for his young folks Bible study class.

Several years later Diane asked me to give a eulogy at Steve's memorial service before a mostly black audience. Upon making a comment relating Steve's life to a verse in the Bible, I was interrupted with a loud "Amen brother," and later several "Hallelujah, Amens." It was not surprising that Steve died on the golf course. The memorial was held there. God bless my golfing buddy and friend.

On July 14, 2002, we met Stanley and Edwina Siu and Woody and Lulu Clum in Fairbanks, Alaska. I had spent significant time in the state on business, but never had much time to explore outside the main cities. Our four-day land tour took us by train and bus to Danali National Park. The park is home to grizzly bears, wolves, moose, caribou, and Dall sheep. It is dominated by Mount McKinley, at 20,000 feet, the tallest mountain in North America. We were not able to see the top of the mountain, because, as is normal, it was shrouded in clouds.

Our land venture ended in Anchorage where we made a short flight to Juneau to meet the Wilderness Explorer, our ninety-four passenger ship. Accommodations were Spartan, but so was the dress code. We spent a day with Bob Storer and his wife as our tour guides. Bob was Chief Investment Officer of the Alaska Permanent Fund and a client of CGTC. They took us to see the Juneau glaciers and then visited their more than one-hundred-year-old house; we then dined on fresh, wild caught halibut at their favorite, small, intimate restaurant.

To ease the Spartan pain, we took bottles of excellent wine on board the ship. White wine was for the women and red for the men. We saw no reason to ruin a beautiful meal with a cheap house wine. Our seven-day cruise explored only the Inland Passage with our first destination being the Tracy Arm Fjord. It is a classic fjord with several elevated glaciers on breathtaking sheer rock mountains, and waterfalls cascading down from the mile-high mountaintops.

The ship was small enough that we could approach close to the glaciers, but not too close, because of glacier calving, which is the sudden breaking away of a mass of ice from the glacier. Glaciers start to look alike, except for some exceptional in size like Mendenhall (a thirteen mile glacier) and Glacier Bay. We had pleasant weather with sunshine that glistened off the crystal blue ice. On a few occasions we anchored in a quiet bay and launched canoes, so we could explore the shoreline and hopefully sight a bear or moose.

Near Glacier Bay we boarded Avon inflatable rafts with outboard motors and visited Elfin Cove, a small fishing village with a population of twenty. We had just finished buying smoked salmon and halibut for our evening "happy hour" when another boat from our ship arrived to announce that the whales were running. Hurriedly, we departed and found the area where several Orcas playfully sounded and surfaced near our small, fragile rubber boats. For nature's final act, a magnificent bald eagle circled above us as we returned to mother ship. Our final stop was Sitka where we disembarked and caught a flight to the "lower 48," grateful to have been with close friends while enjoying the beauty and majesty of Alaska.

The final "event" of 2002 (December 10th) was the birth of Matt and Charlie, identical DNA twins. Gratefully, Mari did not have the problems she suffered with the birth of Ali. However, Matt, the oldest by a minute, had a problem with the "soft spot" on his head. It was closing prematurely and required surgery before he was four-months-old. The family spent a tense six hours while two teams of doctors performed the surgery. There was much relief and a few tears when the lead doctor came out and announced that the operation was successful. Matt required minor cosmetic surgery when he was four years old, but otherwise he is healthy physically and mentally-many prayers answered.

Steven   Matt   Ali   Mari   Charlie

P.J., Judy's mom, was nearing the time when it was no longer safe for her to live alone, so Judy and her brother and sister agreed to move her to California where family could ensure she would be well cared for. Gratefully, P.J. was agreeable to relocating, which made it easier when we all met in Arizona to determine what limited pieces of furniture, furnishings, and art she could take with her. The remainder was divided among her children or given to charity.

Judy and I arranged for P.J. to move into an assisted living room at Villa Gardens, one of Pasadena's best facilities. Her dementia/Alzheimer's was progressing slowly; however, she knew all her family members, as well as most of the staff and caregivers at her new home. The person she could not locate in her mind was her husband, Elden. On several occasions she would say, "Where is he? If he doesn't show up pretty soon, I'm going to get rid of him." As was her demeanor, she said it with a smile.

P.J. was happy at Villa Gardens where she helped the staff in the office. She assisted other residents, pushing a little lady in a wheelchair and helping to feed a blind man. We lived close-by and would visit her often, including lunch most Sundays after church. She was mobile and joined our family for birthdays and holidays. On August 18, 2007, P.J. was called home by her Lord. Her ashes were placed next to Elden's in Sun City, Arizona. Her sister Marge probably said it best, "I don't know anyone who didn't love Priscilla. She was always so kind, loving, generous, and never complained." Amen, and God bless her.

P.J.   Judy   Marge

On our fortieth wedding anniversary, Judy and I took our sons and their families to Hawaii, our favorite vacation destination. Matt and Charlie were under two years of age and apparently unhappy with our outbound flight. They vocally expressed their displeasure, but, fortunately, nearby passengers were surprisingly understanding. As we left the plane in Lihue, Steven was overheard saying, "They're not flying again until they can shave."

Although we owned a condo on the north shore of Kauai, we selected three condos in Poipu Beach on the south shore for our vacation where the grandchildren would have more activities. There could not have been a better way to celebrate our anniversary than being with family in exotic Hawaii, enjoying the water, tropical flowers and trees, refreshing trade winds, and delicious Pupus and Mai Tais. We did take a day trip to cruise up the Wailua River to the Fern Grotto where we were serenaded by a lovely Hawaiian wahine who sang the romantic, "Hawaiian Wedding Song." It was the perfect song for the perfect trip-more warm memories of our visit to paradise. Aloha 'till next time.

Wailua River Boat

Berkeley and Maria Johnston were some of our closest, long-time friends, and we were excited when they agreed to join us on a tour of the Canadian Rockies. Berk was a fraternity brother at Stanford and a conservative political ally for decades. We both lived in San Marino where our sons were in the Boy Scouts. Berk and I were in the troop's "Old Goat Patrol."

We met in Vancouver a day prior to the start of the tour. We had a wonderful day walking around the city and visiting Queen Elizabeth Park, which although not as manicured as Butchart Gardens, was as enjoyable to see. The Tauck Tour began with a short ferry ride to Victoria Island. Upon arrival we walked to the island's main attraction, Butchart Gardens, which had acres of spectacular, colorful flowers and plants. Judy and Maria had a surprise; they had made reservations at the Empress Hotel, a charming Victorian hotel, for high tea. The tea wasn't anything special; however, the finger sandwiches, especially the cucumber, were exceptional. We were flown back to Vancouver on a seaplane, which gave us a marvelous view of the Gulf Islands. The "Rocky Mountaineer" train was late departing that evening, but, once underway, we slept well to the "singing" of the rails.

Our first stop was at Jasper Park where Judy and I played golf. We saw our first of many pristine, deep blue mountain lakes surrounded by majestic mountains. The golf course was unique, because each "tee box" faced a different mountain peak. En-route to the spectacular Fairmont Chateau Hotel at Lake Louise, we stopped to hike on Athabasca Glacier where we had a photo taken of the four of us holding the San Marino Tribune newspaper, a tradition in our hometown.

On the way to Banff, we stopped at Moraine Lake, and I took a photo which I believe was the best of the trip. I have thought about commissioning an artist to paint the scene: pine trees in the foreground, the glittering lake with gradations of color from navy to emerald blue, and snow capped mountains in the distance.

The Fairmont Banff Hotel was our last stop on the tour. The hotel was as outstanding as the Fairmont at Lake Louise. We had a day of leisure, but with one planned event, a short, but not short enough, rafting trip on the Bow River. Having done a fair amount of white water rafting, this excursion was like paddling in a swimming pool.

Our tour ended in Calgary where we rented a car and drove into the United States, through Montana, to Jackson Hole. Here, the Johnstons had asked us to be guests in their magnificent log house, which they had built.

Flying back to California, Judy and I talked about the quality of the Tauck Tour with great accommodations, food, scenery, and wonderful friends. It had been truly outstanding.

Judy and I loved our adventures to foreign lands, but Hawaii would beckon often. We would spend a week or two at our Princeville condo. When we, or the Rueffs, did not use the condo, it was in a rental pool for vacationers from the mainland. We coordinated many of our trips with the Clums, who owned a home on nearby Hanalei Bay. Our friends the Sius would fly over from Oahu and join us for golf at the challenging Prince course. Prior to returning home, we would fly to Honolulu and stay at the splendid Halekulani Hotel on Waikiki, play golf with Stanley and Edwina, and have dinner at the exquisite Orchids Restaurant at our hotel.

During one visit to Princeville, we were introduced to Harry Wishard. We commissioned him to paint the scene from the balcony of our condo. Judy appreciated his use of color and composition of subject. We had a high degree of confidence he would capture the look and feel of the magnificent view. He did a wonderful job of portraying the  intermediate sandy beaches, bays and jungle, and the iconic Bali Ha'i on the horizon. The original hangs in our breakfast room. Dave and Steve each have a giclée print of the painting.

For several years our former neighbors and wonderful friends, Bill and Sally Farwell, invited us to stay with them at their new home in Grass

Valley, California. Bill is an architect who designed and built their house on a beautiful mountain golf course. Both had lost spouses and had only been married for a few years. They were happy and fun to be with, and we enjoyed golfing with them and dining on the patio of their country club on a gorgeous summer evening.

We took advantage of the trip to visit Mother Ellen in Auburn, where we went to her favorite steak house for dinner. The conversation was pleasant, but it was frustrating, because Ellen would not talk much about our life before the family was separated.

After retirement I found I had time to get involved in new and interesting activities. Steve's friend, Chris Atkinson, wanted to organize a small syndicate in thoroughbred horse racing at Santa Anita race track in Arcadia. We reached an agreement with John Sadler, a reputable trainer, to stable and train our horses, as well as to assist us in acquiring horses. Our early purchases were of low-priced "claimers" (a horse that can be "claimed" for a pre-determined price prior to a race). Over time, friends joined the syndicate. We grew the size of the stable, and we began to focus on horses with better breeding, resulting in higher acquisition prices. As the number of investors grew in "Joy Ride Racing,"our stable grew to ten horses at one time. We raced our horses at Hollywood Park, Del Mar in San Diego, and Santa Anita, which may be the most beautiful race track in the United States with its impressive view of the San Gabriel Mountains beyond the track. These are the same stunning mountains which are enjoyed by millions on T.V. during the Rose Bowl game on New Year's Day. We had some "good" horses-Lord Albion, Count Orange, Cadillac, Pat The Cool Cat, Kool Suggestion, Kaffeinator (never liked that name!), Domonation, Afleet Ruler, Pure Class, and Curvey Star, all of which won races. However, it was not until we acquired Noble Court that we had a great horse.

Mike Smith, the Hall of Fame jockey, rode Noble on his first big win at Santa Anita. This race was followed by his victory in the San Vicente, Grade II race and then his win in the Ack Ack Handicap, Grade II, 7 1/2 furlong, $100,000 feature race at Hollywood Park. In addition to the Kentucky Derby, the other event which every horse owner and trainer covets is to have a horse qualify for the Breeders Cup.

Noble Court qualified for the Breeder's Cup $1,000,000 Turf Sprint race (6 1/2 furlongs) to be run at Santa Anita. We were excited about Noble's entry and confident that he could compete against the strong field. We were confident until they drew for the horses' post positions. Noble was not a

"speed" horse and preferred to lie back before closing from the outside in the stretch run. He drew the # 1 post-position, which, in a field of twenty horses, was a disaster. On November 7, 2009, the horses broke from the gate, and Noble was quickly swallowed-up by the "speed" horses. He fell back on the rail and was unable to work his way through so many horses to get to the outside and have a chance to run in the stretch. We were disappointed but proud of the fact that Noble had earned a start in the prestigious race. After nine years we terminated the syndicate with regrets, but with fond memories of many of our horses closing in the stretch and winning by a head; few things are as exhilarating.

Our four grandchildren lived within an hour drive from our condo; however, we never saw them as much as we would have preferred. This was partly because we spent lots of time at Lake Arrowhead and the desert condo when we were not off on a cruise or a tour. On one very special occasion, Ali invited us to attend her first grade class presentation of the classic musical play, "The Wizard of Oz." The play was performed in a large gym-like building where we sat on wooden folding chairs. We were near the stage in what must have been the "orchestra seats." Ali had the leading role, portraying Dorothy, and we were amazed at how professionally she sang and recited her lines. She danced around the stage in the mandatory red patent leather shoes with the Tinman,

Scarecrow, and Lion. Four years later, Matt was a guard and Charlie was #2 Tinman in the same play. These were not auspicious roles, but important to the storyline.

About the same time, Sophie invited Judy and me to "show and tell" time at her school. It was a pleasure to share our experiences at Mala Mala, a game reserve in South Africa, with well-behaved and inquisitive students. They enjoyed the photos of the lions, leopards, rhinos, hippos, and elephants, as well as the spear and hide covered shield and native wooden masks. What better way is there to spend a day than with your granddaughter?

Ali

For many years I told Judy of my desire to attend a cooking school. We found a one-day class in the Napa Valley and enticed our friends, the Sius and Clums, with the opportunity to stay and play golf at Silverado Resort and Spa. The class was much too brief; however, we did learn how to make several Mexican dishes, which we enjoyed while consuming cerveza and local wine. My contribution was searing and peeling the poblano chiles for chile rellenos. After golfing the following day, John Coleman and Cathy O'Callaghan, arranged for a dinner at a charming, intimate restaurant which served marvelous food. We were joined at dinner by George and Janet Miller, the Siu's son, David, and his fiancée, Lara, who were students at Stanford University. It was a brief outing but a world of fun with great friends.

Judy   Lulu   Edwina

Every golfer's dream is to visit Ireland and Scotland. We booked a Tauck Tour for twelve days in Ireland and eight days in Scotland. Stanley and Edwina Siu joined us from Hawaii, as well as Bill and Pat Hibschman from Pennsylvania. Bill is a long-time friend and competitor in the investment business and a close friend of the Sius.

We all arrived a day prior to the start of the tour and had an enjoyable free day in Ennis before boarding the bus and heading to our first stop, a walk along the Cliffs of Moher. The sheer cliffs, which rose sharply from the Atlantic Ocean, were reminiscent of the White Cliffs of Dover. We drove through the sparsely populated countryside, which was as green as advertised but with little vegetation and few trees. What was not lacking were the stone ruins of former castles, homes, and walls.

Our first accommodations were perhaps the most spectacular of the tour. Ashford Castle is located on the shores of Loch Corrib and was advertised as the "quintessence of Old World elegance." That description does not do justice to one of the finest hotels in the world. We spent two days hiking, eating, relaxing, and "falconing." We went into the woods with trained falcons that would launch off our forearm and return when we offered a piece of meat to the bird. We took a brief side trip to the remarkable Kylemore Abby and Gardens overlooking a striking royal blue lake.

Ashford Castle

Kylemore Abby

We departed Ashford with Dublin as our destination. En-route, we made several stops including Killybegs, one of Ireland's major fishing ports. The landscape changed, and we began to see working farms and ranches with grazing cattle and sheep. However, the sheep were not always in the pasture. Several times our bus had to wait patiently while a shepherd cleared them from the road. Dublin was a lovely city. With smiles and cheerfulness, the Irish were happy people. We had time to explore the city and visit the exquisite Powerscourt Gardens in a small valley which was beautifully landscaped with brightly colored seasonal flowers and well-manicured, delicate trees and shrubs.

On our ninth day in Ireland, we stopped at the Mount Juliet Conrad Hotel in County Kilkenny, where we had our only opportunity to play golf. It was not one of the better courses in Ireland, but we were able to say we had played golf in this golfing mecca. We visited the Waterford Crystal factory and observed the artisans cutting crystal bowls, vases, and glasses. The glassware was beautiful, but there were no bargains in the gift shop. One of the most historic visits was to the scenic port town of Cobh. Here, we visited the Heritage Center which commemorates the mass emigration of the Irish to the United States.

Bill lifting the Blarney Stone

No tour of Ireland would be complete without climbing the steep winding stairs to kiss the fabled Blarney Stone. There was a line of visitors waiting to perform the ritual, so Bill volunteered to represent our group. After crossing that off our "bucket list," we spent a day following the world-renowned "Ring of Kerry," a one hundred-ten mile drive along the coastline of the Iveragh Peninsula. We saw some of the most dramatic scenery in Ireland: picturesque villages, coves, and sandy beaches. Our last night and farewell reception was at the Dromoland Castle, a magnificent baronial estate built in the fifteenth century.

Ireland had been everything we envisioned, and more. We had enjoyed the pastoral countryside, gregarious people, excellent food, and great friends with whom to share the experience. We were transferred to Shannon Airport to fly to Glasgow for the second leg of our sojourn. The Hibschmans had been to Scotland, so they did not join us there. However, we were happy that our old friends, Woody and Lulu Clum, would be meeting us for our tour of Scotland.

We remained in Glasgow for two days with time to roam around the city and enjoy the Victorian and Gothic architecture. We stayed at the De Vere Cameron House Hotel, which was surrounded by acres of green lawn and trees on the shores of famed Loch Lomond. We were invited for lunch and a tour of Glenturret Distillery, by reputation one of Scotland's fine distillers. At lunch, they served a small bottle of their finest scotch to each of us. It was Woody's lucky day, because Lulu, Judy, and I did not drink scotch. He had our portions which provided him with more than his minimum daily requirement.

Clums & Sius

We traveled into the Scottish Highlands to Glen Coe where we saw the remains of Urquhart Castle, one of Scotland's most visited sites. The castle has a storied history dating to the thirteen hundreds when it was prominent in the Scot's struggle for independence. Even in ruin, the fortress is still magnificent to view. That evening we enjoyed Scottish bagpipes and highland dancers at the hotel. A well-clad Scotsman attempted to describe haggis to us, but I could not understand a word he said. For the record, haggis is the chopped liver and heart of the sheep mixed with oatmeal and spices, packed in a casing, and then baked. No, I did not appreciate their delicacy.

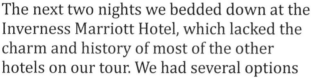
Urquhart Ruins

The next two nights we bedded down at the Inverness Marriott Hotel, which lacked the charm and history of most of the other hotels on our tour. We had several options for activities. The Clums and Sius elected to play golf. Judy and I spent a day leisurely exploring the city and taking a long walk. I asked our guide if we could visit Ullapool where our friend Jack MacLeod's ancestors had lived, but he explained that it was too far from Inverness.

During our tour of the Scottish Highlands, we made the mandatory drive to see where the Monster, or Nessie, is said to inhabit the Loch Ness. We did not see her, but we saw many signs stating this was where she lived.

En-route to our final destination, Edinburgh, we visited the Blair Castle. It is a magnificent, whitewashed baronial structure that would look at home in Disneyland. The castle was built in 1269 for the Clan Murray and is currently owned by the current Duke, Bruce Murray, who lives in South Africa (he can't be too bright).

Our final two nights were spent in the lovely Balmoral Hotel in Edinburgh. As avid golfers, we were excited about our visit to St Andrews, one of the most prestigious golf courses in the world. We walked across the Swilken Bridge where all of the world's greatest golfers have traversed on their way to the eighteenth green. What a thrill! We watched a few foursomes tee off from the first tee, including two young men with Stanford University golf bags. I am certain they had dreams of following in the footsteps of Tiger Woods who had preceded them at Stanford.

Balmoral Castle

Edinburgh reminded me of London, a modern city with remarkable, medieval palaces and military fortresses. We visited the awesome Edinburgh Castle, atop Castle Rock, overlooking the city. The massive stone buildings inside the fortress are built on a hillside and are connected by wide, winding streets and walkways. The most impressive exhibit in the castle contained the scepter, sword, and crown of the Scottish crown jewels. The final visit of our eight day tour was to the Palace of Holyroodhouse, the Queen's Edinburgh residence. After the tour, Judy and I took the train to London to visit Charlie and Kaaren Hale for a few days prior to returning to California.

Edinburgh Castle

Palace of Holyroodhouse

This was our second tour with Tauck. They again delivered a first class experience. As I reflect on the trip, Ireland had the best food and happiest people, while Scotland had the most beautiful scenery, especially the trees, plants, flowers, exquisite ponds, and small lakes. The tour was especially memorable for the time we spent with our beautiful friends, the Sius, Clums, and Hibschmans.

Steven maintained a close relationship with several of his high school football buddies. Many of their fathers were my friends. We arranged a father/son weekend at our lake house where Larry Stone, John Wagner, Monte Ross, and I enjoyed a memorable time with our sons.

Rosemary Sophie Ali Mari

Charlie Steven Matt David

The Citrus Choir is a group of students at Citrus College who audition to become members of the singing group. They train year-round with a full-time conductor and have performed around the world. Each Christmas holiday they appear at Annandale Golf Club, and we have not missed this special evening in nearly twenty years. Typically, our group consists of Steve and Mari, Dave and Rosemary, Mari's parents, and Don and Judy Fickas. The eighty or so singers are dressed in formal attire, the women in full-length, deep-red velvet dresses. All of the Christmas songs are professionally and beautifully performed, but the favorite of the evening is "Little Drummer Boy." When Sophie and Ali were old enough (in their parent's opinion), they were included in the festivities. They were so cute in their holiday dresses and black, patent leather shoes. They bubbled over with excitement in anticipation of seeing and hearing the group. A few years later, Matt and Charlie were included, and we were proud to show-off our grandchildren to our friends.

The one destination which was always at the top of my travel list was Normandy Beach, France. In 2008, the stars were finally aligned and I organized a trip with Berk and Maria Johnston, Woody and Lulu Clum, and Stanley and Edwina Siu. We arrived two days prior to the start of the Viking river cruise, and arranged for a full–day private tour. Long before arriving in Normandy, I communicated with our guide and told him what we would be seeing on the Viking one-day tour of Normandy. After reading several books on the invasion, I suggested eight other sites to visit. I asked him to take us to places he considered important, as well. We were fortunate to have hired a guide who was born and raised in Normandy and was a fount of knowledge. He arrived at our hotel in Honfleur at 8:00 a.m. We were gone all day and did not return until 8:00 that evening. We saw points of interest that were not in any of the literature I had read.

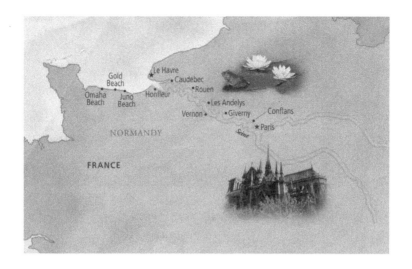

General Dwight D. Eisenhower was Supreme Allied Commander of "Operation Overlord" which commenced at dawn on June 6, 1944. Three airborne divisions landed by parachute; others were delivered by wooden gliders which crash–landed in the fields above the beaches. Naval forces shelled German gun emplacements for hours prior to 0630 hours when American, British, and Canadian troops landed on Utah, Omaha, Gold, Juno, and Sword beaches in history's greatest amphibious invasion. The heroism of those who died, and those who survived, cannot be told in words. It was a miracle the allied soldiers survived the rain of gunfire on their landing craft and on the beaches before scaling the cliffs to drive the Germans into retreat. Within a week the allies had secured the beaches, and within three months had defeated the Germans in the area. The troops were now ready to advance to Paris and then to Germany. The victory at Normandy was as important to the victory in Europe as was the Battle of Midway in defeating the Japanese in the Pacific war. First, we toured the invasion landing beaches and then the American Museum and Memorial. With reverence and in silence, we walked among the 9,238 white marble crosses and 149 Stars of David. I felt as if I were in church and that God was there watching over the brave men who had died to preserve freedom. I teared up and prayed as I read the names on grave after grave. It was a deeply emotional and humbling experience for each of us. Judy and I walked alone on Omaha Beach and picked up a few seashells for the grandchildren before continuing the tour.

Our guide took us to a little known bunker where German long guns shelled our troops seven kilometers away on Omaha Beach. In Sainte-Mère-Église, we saw the church where a paratrooper landed. His parachute was caught on the side of the building, and he hung suspended in his harness.

Incidentally, the Americans are still revered by the French people in Normandy. Each stop during our tour was emotionally charged as we envisioned the soldiers involved in that particular engagement. Closing our eyes we could envision the soldiers in the 2nd Ranger Battalion scaling the cliffs on rope ladders at Pointe de Hoc. A highlight for all of us was visiting the monument at Omaha Beach where President Reagan spoke on the fortieth anniversary of the Normandy invasion. We returned to our hotel exhausted emotionally but grateful for the opportunity to share this awesome experience with dear friends.

Omaha Beach   Pointe du Hoc

The next day we joined the Viking tour and visited a few sites bypassed the prior day, but the tour was anti-climatic after our awesome adventure. That evening we boarded the ship in Le Havre. The next morning we did a walking tour of Honfleur, a delightfully restored port town founded in the eleventh century. The attractive houses and shops on both sides of the harbor were colorful and well kept.

We began our four-day cruise down the Seine River to Paris with an overnight stop in Rouen, which was full of history. It was the capital of Normandy and infamous for the imprisonment of Joan of Arc who was tried for heresy and burned at the stake in 1431. We had a delightful walk through the shopping area. The streets were clean and the shops carried quality merchandise, especially in the inviting candy store. The shopping area ended at a beautiful and ornate Great Clock Tower, which told the time, weather, and season.

We cruised down to Les Andelys where we hiked up a mountain and toured the ruins of Chateau Gaillard, which were built by Richard the Lion Hearted in the twelfth century. It was quite windy and cold, but the view down the Seine and beyond was spectacular.

The most delightful day of the cruise was when we docked at Vernon and had an excursion to Giverny, where the impressionist Claude Monet lived until he died in 1926. His home furnishings had not changed, and his exquisite collection of Japanese engravings was still exhibited. As we strolled through the gardens with weeping willows, water lily filled pond, and Japanese bridge, we felt as if we were in the middle of one of his paintings. After a brief stop in Conflans, we arrived in Paris where we docked close to the Eiffel Tower. We boarded a river boat that evening and had an enjoyable tour of the city from the river. The next day we strolled around the city and did some "modest" shopping. That evening we attended the Captain's farewell dinner.

We slept on board the ship that night. The next morning we were bused through the countryside to Chalon-sur-Saone and boarded our ship for the second leg of the Viking tour. We stopped for lunch in Dijon. We dined in a small, quaint restaurant on a delicious boeuf bourguignon, which is a beef stew braised in a good French Burgundy wine.

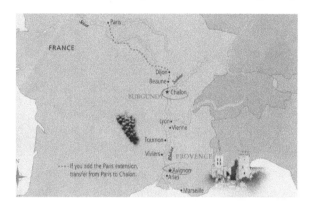

From Chalon we boarded a bus for an excursion to Beaune, the wine capital of Burgundy. We spent a delightful few hours tasting the regions finest wines in a charming, old, rock wine cellar; the ambiance seemingly improved the aroma and taste of the wines. The next morning the weather was clear and cool as we cruised past lush vineyards, farms, and quaint villages.

We docked in Lyon for a brief tour and then continued on to Vienne which was a Roman Colony in 47 B.C. under Julies Caesar. Roman ruins were prominent in the city, and a section of a Roman stone highway still exists. It was interesting to learn that Roman road-markers were placed every thousand steps by Roman soldiers. This equated to about one mile; however, we did not step it off to determine the accuracy of the markers. A splendid remnant of that era was the first century Temple of Emperor Augustus and Livia.

We cruised into the Rhone River and docked in Tournon at midnight. This area is famous for its red wines and its fine chocolates which are supplied to chefs in more than thirty countries. I am not a big chocolate fan, but it was as delectable as advertised. After a brief stop in Viviers, we cruised to Arles, the town much loved by Vincent Van Gogh. In 1888 he wrote to his brother Theo, "Nature here is extraordinarily beautiful--- I can't match its beauty in my paintings, but I take so much in that I can let myself go without restraint." His friend Paul Gauguin also painted in Arles for a brief time. We were excited to visit Espace Van Gogh, the cultural center dedicated to him.

Arles was a Phoenician trading port prior to the Roman conquest in 123 B.C. Today, there are many impressive ruins of buildings and bridges, especially the ancient Arles Amphitheatre, which now hosts plays, concerts, and bullfights (in France?).

Our final destination was Avignon, a magnificent walled city on the Rhone River. It is known as the "City of the Popes." For most of the fourteenth century all the popes resided in the Papal Palaces, which we visited. As you can imagine, the Italians were not happy with the pope being in France. Today, the pope and Vatican are located in Rome. During our land tours, we visited many churches and castles. In Avignon, we had an opportunity to enjoy two outstanding museums. First was the musée Calvert with a collection of ancient silver housed in an eighteenth century neoclassical mansion. The second was the musée Louis Vouland with an exhibit of marvelous seventeenth and eighteenth century porcelain, chandeliers, tapestries, and other extraordinary antiques.

As we flew home, we reminisced about our unforgettable experience in Normandy, as well as the beauty and history of the cities we visited and the scenery we enjoyed. The only negatives about the trip were the shipboard accommodations and the food. We were on an old Viking ship with beds that should have been updated. The food was far below average. Perhaps this was due to the fact that the chef was Russian, cooking on a tour of France! Despite a few annoyances, it had been one of the greatest trips in our lifetime. In a significant way, this was due to sharing it with the Johnstons, Sius, and Clums.

Sadly, a little rain must fall in every family. We returned home to learn that David and Rosemary were separating, which was a shock to Judy and me. After sixteen years of marriage their interests had become very diverse. Rosemary enjoyed staying home, baking, decorating for the holidays, and attending swap meets at the Rose Bowl. David preferred going to parties, meeting with friends, and attending sporting events, especially at the Rose Bowl or the Coliseum. As Vice-President for marketing at Dole Packaged Foods, Dave worked long hours and traveled extensively. After marriage counseling was ineffective, they negotiated the terms of a divorce without attorneys. If a separation can be amicable, this one was. They have remained friendly, and both attend birthday parties and holiday gatherings with our family.

Sophie lived primarily with her mother, but also spent significant time with her dad. She was accepted as a student at Oaks Christian High School and both parents were supportive of her academic and social activities. All of us were delighted and proud when she made the girl's golf team. David faithfully took Sophie to church on Sunday mornings where he taught her Bible school class. The three of them made the best of an unfortunate situation.

On another sad day, but less traumatic, Dani and Mike Rueff told us they wanted to sell our jointly-owned condo at Pali Ke Kua on the island of Kauai. It would have been difficult to sell half a condo, so we agreed to sell, also. We have wonderful memories of our many visits to our little corner of paradise and especially miss the gorgeous sunsets. Although our condo is gone, we have continued to vacation on the North Shore of Kauai, which we believe to be the most beautiful part of the "Garden Island."

In June of 2009, Judy and I received an offer we could not refuse. Our friends, Jason and Rena Pilalas, invited us to join them at their home in North Palm Beach, Florida and cruise on their 146-foot yacht to Noack, Connecticut. The trip was billed as "A Culinary Journey," It was that and more.

A
Culinary
Journey

From North Palm Beach, Florida
To Noank, Connecticut

The ship had four staterooms for invited guests: Jerry and Judy McGrath from Hawaii, Charles and Alla Campbell from the east coast, Bob and Barbara Brockmair from Orange County, and Judy and me. Our suite was spacious with every necessity provided. We stayed at the Pilalas' gorgeous home while the ship was being provisioned and fueled. After we boarded the next morning, we waved goodbye to Palm Beach and headed out to sea. Soon it was time for our "Welcome Aboard Lunch" as we cruised up the Florida coastline heading north. The menu for lunch listed "Green Salad, Prosciutto Wrapped Shrimp Salsa, Lobster Salad and Teriyaki Beef Satay Salad." This was all prepared by Chef Pete. It was a glorious day, and we enjoyed our culinary feast on the canopied aft deck. Our lunch was a foretaste of what we would experience at every meal. The ship was skippered by Ken Bracewell and had a crew of seven, including a young lady who drove the Pilalas' Suburban up the coast to meet us at each port.

The first stop was in Charleston, a charming and beautiful Southern city. The ladies met a friend of Rena's for lunch and a tour of the city. Jason, being a military historian and collector of Navy memorabilia, opted out of tea and finger sandwiches for a tour of the aircraft carrier Yorktown at Patriot's Point. The USS Yorktown (CV-10) was built in sixteen and one-half months during W.W. II to replace Yorktown (CV-5), which was sunk in the Battle of Midway in June 1944. Known as the "Fighting Lady," she was a significant factor in the defeat of the Japanese in the Pacific offensive. We made a short visit to the Citadel, one of the six U.S. military colleges. Our final military objective was to see the H.L. Hunley, which became the first successful combat submarine with the sinking of the USS Housatonic in 1864. She vanished shortly thereafter, was not found until 1971, and not recovered until 2000. As of our visit, the sub was being preserved, and we were able to get a close-up view of the process to conserve the submarine.

The ladies seduced us away from the military attractions to visit historic Fort Sumter. It is a sea fort which was occupied by Union troops in 1861 when South Carolina Militia artillery fired on the garrison from shore. The bombardment lasted all day, and the next day the fort surrendered. These were the first shots that started the disastrous Civil War, which tore our country apart.

Dinner aboard the "Rena" at the Charleston City Marina was another gourmet's delight: "Caprese Salad, Artisan Bread Basket, Alaskan King Crab Legs, Potato Crusted Chilean Sea Bass, Slow Roasted Barbeque Baby Back Ribs, Grilled Green Spice Lamb Chops, Herbed Goat Cheese Infused Purple Smashed Potatoes, Vegetable Melange, Pecan Pie with Vanilla Bean Ice Cream, and Warm Brownie Sundae with French Vanilla Kahlúa Fudge." Mercifully, the portions were not King Henry VIII size.

Our next destination was Norfolk, Virginia. The guys visited the Mariner's Museum where the turret and other artifacts from the Monitor were being restored. She was an "ironclad," and the first one built by the Union during the Civil War. At the same time, the Confederacy built the "ironclad" Virginia (or Merrimac). The two Revolutionary War ships met in battle in 1862. Although neither claimed a clear victory, the ships had shown the superiority of "iron and steam" over "wood and sail" warship construction. In 1862 the Monitor sank in a storm off of North Carolina's Outer Bank. The wreckage was not discovered until 1973.

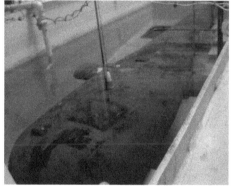

I looked forward to our next destination, Annapolis, and a visit to the U.S. Naval Academy. As we approached the harbor in late afternoon, the clouds were ominous, dark, and low-hanging. The wind blew briskly, and it began to rain heavily. The next morning the weather cleared. We explored the town and met John Gallaudet, an old Navy buddy who was a recruiter for the Academy, for coffee. We had a great tour of the Academy, visiting the Chapel where Judy and I had attended the wedding of our friend, Susan Booth. We were fortunate to visit the Academy Museum, because it had just reopened after a complete renovation. The Museum dates back to 1845. The exhibits include flags, uniforms, weapons, photographs, and twelve hundred paintings. The Roger's ship model collection is remarkable and includes ancient wooden sail-powered ships, as well as modern-day warships, all built with intricate detail.

The end of a wonderful day was followed by a delightful birthday party for my Judy. Rena and the crew decorated the dining room and provided leis for everyone. We enjoyed hor d'oeuvres and cocktails before sitting down for another wonderful meal created by Chef Pete. For this special occasion he prepared a "Raw Bar with Maine Lobster Tails and Claws, Wild Caught Shrimp, Alaskan King Crab Legs, Steamed Aromatic Clams and Mussels, Bread Basket, Chesapeake Chicken, Annapolis Blue Crab Back Fin Meat, Zesty Hollandaise, Garlic Spinach, and Strawberry, Apricot, Raspberry Trifle." I don't know how we slept after such an extravagant feast, but the gentle motion of the boat and the fine wine did the trick.

Because of weather, we made a brief unscheduled stop at St. Michaels, Maryland where we had a delicious dinner at "208 Talbot." The weather cleared overnight, and we departed for New York City. We docked on the East Side of Manhattan after cruising close to the majestic Statue of Liberty rising regally against a grayish-blue sky. The statue was a gift from the French government in 1886 and a symbol of freedom and democracy to the world.

Jason and Rena hosted an all-day open house for their daughter, Debbie, and her husband, Ian O'Malley, as well as a dozen other young folks. It was nice to have a day to relax and sunbath on-board the "Rena." The next day Judy and I walked to the 9/11 Memorial and Museum which was under construction. A temporary museum was open. It provided a stark reminder of the day 2,977 people died in the Muslim terrorist attack on the Twin Towers in 2001.

On the last leg of our voyage, we cruised along the beautiful Atlantic coastline, nearing our final port much too quickly. Noack is a community of historic houses on a peninsula at the mouth of the Mystic River and known for its fishing and boat building. We remained overnight at the Pilalas' updated Cape Cod home. It is connected to a restored lighthouse, which serves as the depository for Jason's extensive Naval memorabilia. Silver Seas cruises are elegant. However, this cruise was more delightful and memorable, because it was small and intimate and provided by Jason and Rena, the consummate host and hostess. We were grateful to have been included in this "cruise of a lifetime."

Rena and Jason Pilalas

Pilalas Lighthouse

Judy and I returned to California and our comfortable condo in Pasadena. We were happy and full of thanksgiving for the good life God had provided us. We had no idea that "in the twinkling of an eye," our lives were about to change dramatically.

Chapter Ten

Tragedy and Triumph

We returned to California to enjoy the rest of the summer with family and friends. Our entire family gathered at the lake to celebrate July 4th and host our traditional BBQ. Judy made macaroni salad (Steven's favorite), Sheila Ross brought her famous five-bean casserole, Karen Pinter prepared delicious hot appetizers, and I barbequed bratwurst and hotdogs. As nightfall approached, all of us went out on our ski boats to watch the fireworks, which were launched from a barge in the middle of Lake Arrowhead. The show was spectacular with the bright bursts lighting up the ponderosa pines and glistening on the water. After the forty-five minute extravaganza, we returned to the house for dessert, coffee, and adult refreshments.

A few weeks later, Judy and I went to the lake for a couple of days to get out of the August heat of Pasadena. On August 8, 2009, we drove back to Pasadena, arriving about 11:30 in the morning. We had been home about ten minutes when Judy complained of a pounding in her head. She sat down at the kitchen table but after a minute went to lie down on the coach in the living room. I was mindful of an aneurism in the brain which Judy had coiled two years prior, so I gave her a quick neurological test, checking her grip, her speech, and eyes. Everything appeared normal. About five minutes later her eyes started to glaze over, and her speech began to slur. I called the paramedics at 911. Paramedics from the nearby Fair Oaks Fire Station arrived in approximately five minutes, just after Judy suffered a hemorrhage in the brain. She was unconscious, so they gave her oxygen and injections. They rushed her to the Huntington Hospital emergency room, which was only a few blocks from our condo. I gave one of the paramedics our "gold" donor card and followed the ambulance to the hospital.

I was allowed in the emergency room where I met Dr. Lance Gravely, a neurosurgeon. He explained that Judy had a serious bleed in the brain, and he asked permission to perform a procedure which required inserting a tube in her head to relieve the pressure caused by the hemorrhage. After they shaved off a large patch of her beautiful hair, the doctor inserted the tube. He bluntly explained the seriousness of a sub-arachnoid hemorrhage and said, "Few people walk out of here after a bleed like this." Dr. Gravely, I was to learn, is a renowned neurosurgeon and just happened to be in the emergency room when Judy arrived. I don't believe it was just "luck" he was there at that moment in time; I prefer to believe God put him there for a purpose.

Judy was moved to intensive care that afternoon. Dr. Teitelbaum, who had coiled the aneurism in her brain two years prior, was contacted at St. Joseph's Hospital in Burbank and asked to go to the Huntington to perform an exploratory angiogram. Upon finding the previously coiled aneurism secure, he searched for the source of the bleeding and found a second aneurism, which he coiled to secure the bleeding.

Dr. Rich Spitzer had been Judy's neurologist for several years. The two of them had a special relationship, as one of Dr. Spitzer's children had been in Judy's kindergarten class. He visited Judy every day in the intensive care unit and performed all the neurological tests- - -flashlight in the eyes, squeeze of the fingers, stick pins in the toes, but always with no response. Dr. Gravely, realistic as he was, continually reminded me that the first fourteen days were the most critical due to the risk of pneumonia, infection, stroke, or additional bleeding. The stress was made more tolerable with the support of family, friends, and constant prayers.

Dr. Spitzer   Judy

Dr. Gravely is a Board Certified
Neurological Surgeon.
College: Harvard University
Medical School: University of Southern

After nearly two weeks in intensive care, Dr. Spitzer made his usual morning visit to check on Judy. He checked her eyes, no response. He squeezed her fingers, no response. He poked her big toe with a pin, and her toe moved. This was her first response and an indication that there was hope. The emotion was overwhelming. I quietly cried with joy, and I believe Dr. Spitzer had a tear in his eye. It was not long before Judy opened her eyes, which were clear and, to me, sparkling. Then, she talked with a clear but weak voice. Fourteen days had passed and Judy was on the road to recovery. It was time to give thanks and praise to our Lord.

I will always be indebted to the many doctors, nurses, and staff personnel who cared for Judy and were significant support to me. My daily routine was to arrive at the hospital at 6:30 in the morning to talk to the night nurse who was going off duty. I spent the day with Judy before leaving at 7:30 in the evening, after the night nurse came on duty. Early on, I learned every patient needs an advocate. Judy did not have diabetes, but one morning a nurse was ready to give her a shot of insulin for diabetes, to which I objected. Judy had never had diabetes, and I don't know why that malady appeared on her chart. Dr. Spitzer called me at home at 11:30 one evening to say he had visited Judy and she was "doing well." This was dedication above and beyond the call of duty. Joe Pachorek, our primary care doctor, had no responsibility for Judy's care in the hospital; however, he visited her often just to say "hello" and to encourage her.

When Judy was moved from intensive care to D.O.U. (a lower level of care), our family and friends were allowed limited visitation. Judy was quarantined the first few days, and I remember walking into her room and seeing Judy Fickas sitting in her yellow quarantine gown and cap. Judy had a "shunt" permanently implanted in her head to control the pressure on the brain. At one point Dr. Gravely was concerned that Judy was not as responsive to commands as she had been, so he adjusted the shunt with a magic, metal "o-ring." She became noticeably more alert.

After two weeks in the D.O.U., Judy was moved to a neurological unit which was a bit unnerving, because she did not have as much personal attention in this unit. However, it was recognition of the great progress Judy had made and an affirmation she could make further recovery.

I believe a major contribution to Judy's recovery was the many loving get-well cards she received, as well as the personal visits by our extended family and friends. David and Steven visited almost daily, and every one of Judy's friends visited more than once. John Bitzer, who was best man in our wedding, flew from Pittsburgh to see the two of us. George Miller drove down from San Francisco and coined the phrase "Bobby time," meaning that I should spend some time away from the hospital for my own emotional and physical well-being.

Judy's brother and sister visited, as did her cousin, Jan Meyerott. Literally, every one of Judy's friends visited with flowers in hand and with words of encouragement. Her room could have been mistaken for a flower shop. Dick Babb, my Stanford roommate and a doctor at the Stanford Hospital, called weekly for progress reports; Edwina Siu called every two days for updates. Judy's wonderful, faithful friends, Sheila Ross, Judy Fickas, and Coyla Grumm, were at the hospital so often they received "lifetime" visitor's passes.

John   Josh   Mary   Larry

When Judy was significantly improved, it was determined she could begin therapy. Dr. Hegde told me it would be best for Judy to be transferred to an outside facility. The Huntington had an excellent therapy program, and I pleaded with the doctor to allow Judy to stay at the hospital for her therapy. He was concerned Judy would not be able to perform three-and-one-half-hours of therapy each day, which was a requirement. I argued that she needed to be where she had access to her neurosurgeon and neurologist. On decision day, Dr. Hegde, nonchalantly, said that he was moving Judy to rehab in the hospital. I was relieved and grateful to God for answering my prayer one more time.

After five weeks in recovery, Judy was moved to rehab on September 14th. One small procedure remained. The feeding tube needed to be removed from her stomach. This was the last of the many tubes she had endured. I have not presented many of the details of this traumatic experience and of Judy's recovery, but through it all she was courageous, positive, and grateful for her caregivers, doctors, family, and friends. She made remarkable progress physically, but she still had short-term memory lapses. Judy had no problem recognizing family and friends, and she looked forward to each visit with a beautiful smile for all.

Little did we know what challenges lay ahead. Judy went from the beauty spa to boot camp. Starting on day one, she had seven, 30-minute sessions per day: three with the physical therapist, two with the occupational therapist, and two with the speech therapist. She had to re-learn how to dress, brush her teeth, walk, and use utensils to eat. She regained strength slowly, but her balance was a continual problem.

When Judy completed the rehab program at the hospital, she was prepared to perform most of the every day functions at home. Dr. Hegde recommended transferring Judy to another rehab facility where she could continue her regimen. I had arranged for home care and believed she would be happier in her home. Her doctor consented, and Judy came home on October 13th, the answer to nine weeks of prayer.

I arranged for Carlota Brizuela, a registered nurse, and Josie Mendoza, a certified nursing assistant, to care for Judy. Fortunately, Carlota wanted to work the night shift and Josie preferred daytime work, so everyone was happy. Judy worked diligently to improve her memory, playing word games, doing puzzles, and anything to stimulate the brain. Dr. Wortheim recommended that Judy create a list of "affirmations" to enhance her self-esteem and confidence. Judy comprised the following points, which I wrote down, so she could recite them each day:

1. I have a good singing voice. I love to sing, and it gives me, and others, much pleasure.

2. I have many friends. I am a good listener and express my love and compassion for others. I am a good communicator with all family members and friends.

3. I have made remarkable progress in improving my physical strength, mobility, and memory. Dr. Spitzer and Dr. Wortheim tell me so!

Carlota

Josie

The first two years after coming home was a period of exultation but also of despair at times. We had always enjoyed walking. We started again, first with Judy in a wheelchair, then with her walker, and finally without assistance except for holding her hand. The terrifying moments were the two or three occasions when Judy had a seizure (but not a hemorrhage), and the paramedics had to take her to the Huntington Hospital where she underwent extensive tests for a few days before returning home.

We began to have a limited social life. We invited a few friends at a time for a BBQ dinner, and we would go to Lacy Park in San Marino to walk for an hour in the beautiful, quiet, peaceful setting. On special days we would take

a picnic lunch and enjoy our lunch with friends while sitting under large shade trees.

Soon we returned to worshipping at the Church of Christ in Sierra Madre. Yordana, a nursing school student, worked for us on Sunday to give Josie a day off. She was good company for Judy and would attend Church with us. After the service, we enjoyed going out to lunch with our family or a few friends from the congregation. On special occasions, such as Valentine's Day, Easter, and Mother's Day, Judy and I would invite our sons, their families, and Mari's parents to a fabulous brunch at Annandale Golf Club. Grandsons Matt and Charlie were "kings" of the buffet, never quitting before devouring three substantial plates of food, followed by several decadent desserts.

There was a period of several months when Judy had hallucinations, which seemed to intensify when a doctor added Keppra to her drug regimen. The unwanted side effects of the drug were irritability, low energy, and dizziness. She told Josie that her Lord told her to "go to California where you will meet Bob." More disturbing was when she locked herself in the bathroom and told us, "The devil locked me in the bathroom, but God freed me." With the consent of the doctor, she ceased using Keppra.

Judy had dramatic mood swings between depression and elation. After dinner one evening Judy insisted on talking to her best friend, Sheila Ross, in person. Judy was feeling unwanted and unloved, so I called Sheila. She came to our condo and talked with Judy for nearly an hour. When Sheila departed, Judy's attitude was changed 180 degrees. She was happy and positive about her life. Judy had firm religious faith and trust in God, but I became concerned when, on a few occasions, she said God wasn't listening to her. I called Maurice Hall, a retired minister and elder in our Church, and asked him to visit Judy and to discuss her concerns. Their conversation ended with a prayer. After Maurice left, Judy expressed faith in her Lord and acknowledged He loved her and would care for her. With the help of friends like Sheila and Maurice, as well as a change in her medication, Judy's mood changed dramatically and the hallucinations disappeared. She was back to being her sweet, happy self.

My life was made easier with Carlota and Josie caring for Judy. She became ambulatory but needed assistance in showering and dressing. Importantly, they administered her medications, which consisted of fifteen prescription drugs and vitamins each day. The day started with a probiotic at 5 a.m. and ended with two drugs, as well as eye and nose drops at bedtime. Incidentally, Judy interfaced with eighteen doctors during her illness.

My responsibilities were simple. I marketed and prepared the meals. Breakfast was easy to prepare with orange juice, hot tea, and hot or cold cereal. Occasionally, I would treat Judy and Josie to hotcakes or French toast. Lunch was a cup of soup and a tuna or other sandwich. I often barbequed chicken or fish for dinner. Occasionally, we had beef, lamb, or pork. We always had a starch and vegetable. Well-balanced and healthy meals were important. I was retired, healthy, and had the time and interest to help Judy in her recovery. I was fortunate to have outstanding insurance coverage with Medicare, Anthem Blue Cross PPO Plus, Tricare for Life (military insurance), and Unum Long-term Care to provide for a significant part of Judy's medical, drug, and homecare expenses.

Over time, I needed to find additional caregivers who could relieve Carlota and Josie. Ruby Mercado, RN, was a godsend and helped when I was desperate to find additional help. Mary, Yordana, Beatrix, and Nereyda, were invaluable on a limited basis. When Josie announced she had to leave us because of medical problems, God was there with the solution. Sylvie Castenada came into our life and was wonderful with Judy. In addition to caregiving, she cleaned the house, ironed clothes, and, once a week, relieved my dinner cooking duties. Sylvie asked Judy what she wanted for her Wednesday night dinner. It was always, "Chicken and dumplings."

Sylvie

Vicki Lonzarata was Judy's hairdresser at The Gates in San Marino for twenty-five years. Not long before Judy had the hemorrhage, the two of them decided that Judy would let her hair grow out to its natural color. Judy's hair turned a beautiful silver-gray. When she entered the hospital, half of her hair was shaved off in the emergency room. When she came home from the hospital, one of the first things Judy desired was to visit the hairdresser. As a welcome home present, Vicki offered to come to our condo to do Judy's hair. It had been nearly three months since Judy had had a manicure and pedicure. Tran, her friend of twenty years, came to our condo and put Judy's favorite French tips on her finger nails. This lifted her spirits. It's remarkable how friends react in a time of need.

I have written about Judy's love of music and how much she enjoyed singing and playing the piano. However, during her rehab, music became more than just a "pleasure." It became therapeutic and invaluable to her recovery. When Judy was well enough to go out to dinner, we went to our favorite restaurant, Stoney Point. Amadeo and Antoinetta, the owners, prepared the finest Tuscan dishes for us: fresh homemade pasta and Judy's favorite, petrale sole. My favorite entrée was their incredible osso buco, served with angel hair pasta and a light tomato-basil sauce. They always had the perfect wine from Tuscany to enhance any entrée.

The restaurant was small and intimate. Over time, we got to know many of the regular customers, especially those who came Saturday evenings to hear Lou McMullin entertain on the piano. Lou was a voice teacher. Prior to Judy's hemorrhage, he came to our condo weekly to give Judy voice lessons with his accompaniment. After a few months of training, Lou invited Judy to sing a song for the small group of Saturday night patrons at the restaurant.

Judy and Lou McMullin

At a singing lesson during Judy's recovery, I suggested that Lou and Judy do a musical recital at our condo. They prepared for several months and on October 15, 2012 they performed before a full house of twenty-three friends. Judy sang seven songs including "Some Enchanted Evening" and "Bali Ha'i" from her favorite movie "South Pacific." Song selections also included a religious hymn, "How Great Thou Art." After an intermission where we served coffee, tea, and cookies, Judy sang our favorite song, "Love Is A Many Splendored Thing." For the finale, I played a CD recording of "The Hawaiian Wedding Song," circa 1962, performed by our dear friend, Edwina Siu, and Ke Kali Au. This was the first of four recitals Judy would sing over a six-year period.

We were getting back into a period of normalcy and engaging in previously enjoyed activities. We again attended the Citrus Choir Christmas performance at Annandale Golf Club; it was wonderful to have all the family there, plus Don and Judy Fickas, as well as a new guest, Judy's caregiver, Carlota. Once again, we were able to walk to Orange Grove Boulevard and view the floats prior to the start of the Rose Parade. Because David headed the float project for Dole Foods, Sophie was allowed to ride on the float, which was a thrill for her and us.

Once again we were able to celebrate birthdays and special occasions as a family. God truly blessed us. One of the occasions we missed was getting together with the family at Lake Arrowhead for holiday weekends, especially July 4th. Judy and I treasured the opportunity to be with our children and grandchildren; we enjoyed our many friends who joined us for a barbeque and fireworks. And, we had a special treat when sister Sue

and her friend, John, visited us at the house. It was a treasured time, because we had not been together for several years.

Sophie graduated from high school in 2013 and was accepted at Boston University, which meant that she would be spending most of the next four years in Boston. I received permission from Judy's doctor to take her and the family to Hawaii. On July 11th, we celebrated our forty-ninth wedding anniversary in Princeville, Kauai.

We stayed in three condos at Pu'u Po'a with a view of Hanalei Bay and Bali Ha'i, similar to that from our condo at Pali Ke Kua. We picnicked and swam at Anini, our favorite beach, located near the Kilauea lighthouse and bird refuge. We drove through Hanalei and up the picturesque North Shore to Bali Ha'i, stopping at Lumaha'i Beach for a swim. It is a beautiful, romantic setting and, not surprising, scenes in the movie "South Pacific" were filmed there.

Dave and Steve played golf with their daughters at the Makai course, which is owned by the Princeville Hotel. We had many great meals, but two were memorable: dinner at the Dolphin in Hanalei Bay where Steve and Mari became engaged, and a spectacular gourmet meal on our last night in Hawaii. When I was on the Investment Board of the L.A. County Employees Retirement Association, we bought the Princeville Hotel for the pension fund. When we arrived on Kauai, I visited the manager. He gave us a tour of the hotel and offered to make a reservation for us at their five-star restaurant. To give you a "flavor" for the menu, Steve had "chipotle infused salmon sushi" as an appetizer. When the waiter presented the bill, I questioned the amount because it was considerably less than I had expected. The waiter informed me the manager had discounted the bill by fifty percent.

Everyone had a marvelous time on the trip, especially Josie who had never been to the islands. As always, we were sad to leave Hawaii, but we were already planning our return to paradise.

Back on the mainland, it was time for me to pay for my past "sins." After wear and tear on my right shoulder from rugby, volleyball, body surfing, and golf, I had a tear in the rotator cuff and right bicep. These were repaired by Dr. Greg Adamson. A few months later, I had my right knee replaced. After two previous knee surgeries and countless cortisone injections, Dr. Todd Dietrich informed me it was time for a total knee replacement. Those surgeries, as well Judy's medical condition, convinced us to move to a single-story residence.

2015 was a tranquil, happy year of contentment. Ali, Matt, and Charlie were soccer players. Judy and I spent many enjoyable afternoons watching them play. It was especially fun for me, because I had played the game in college. We spent several holiday weekends with the kids at the lake, swimming, water-skiing and barbequing their favorite meals.

We celebrated Judy's birthday on June 10th at the Annandale Golf Club with a dinner for forty family members and friends. She had made amazing progress physically, mentally, and emotionally. We were excited to share that blessing with those we loved.

A month later, on July 11th, we hosted a magnificent event at the Valley Hunt Club in Pasadena, a reception and dinner to honor our 50th wedding anniversary. We sent out engraved invitations and received nearly one hundred positive responses. The club was beautifully decorated. We ordered lovely floral centerpieces, which we offered to our guests. The filet and Chilean sea bass were outstanding, the service superb, the entertainment delightful, and the speeches mostly flattering. Our friends Ann Louise and Geno Escarrega played the piano and sang Judy's and my favorite songs, including, "Love Is A Many Splendored Thing." The outflow of love and friendship was overwhelming. It was an unforgettable evening. I thanked God Judy and I were able to celebrate it together.

We searched for a three bedroom, single story condo or house for eight months before purchasing a home in Arcadia. We bought our first house nearly fifty years earlier. This new house had been owned by a Chinese family (families). It was well built but needed lots of cosmetic work, at least that is what I believed after reading the inspection report. In fact, the electric panel needed replacing and a new, second panel installed. The sewer pipes were cracked. There were rats in the attic and animals living under the house. A few exterior doors needed replacing. The house required painting inside and out. The pool had cracks in the plaster, which caused the pool to lose water.

Before   After

I questioned my sanity in purchasing a home needing so many repairs, but we were anxious for a place with no stairs and more room for caregivers and guests. After much work and expense, the house was beautiful, and more importantly, Judy loved it. She especially enjoyed sitting on the newly built patio overlooking the tropical landscaping we had professionally designed and planted. It reminded us of Kauai. My favorite addition was a new, built-in Lynx barbeque with a small refrigerator and storage drawers. Kevork Babian was a one-man construction crew who singly did the remodeling and construction, including the patio and BBQ. Kevork could perform any task. He was professional, pleasant, and considerate of Judy's condition. Equally professional were Akef Faqouri, who brought the plumbing up to standard, and Robert Mercado, who replaced the old and potentially dangerous electrical system.

Before   After

Judy continued to receive "well–wishes" from friends, notably at Christmas time. Bill Russ, a rugby pal from Stanford days, said he was praying for Judy. At Christmas he sent a postcard with a photo of the men's Bible study group at Menlo Park Presbyterian Church with a message saying they were all praying for Judy. Judy was moved by their gesture of Christian love. It further confirmed her belief in the goodness of people and was a reminder of how important friends are in our lives.

In the mid-1960's, Don and Judy Fickas had been our neighbors in Arcadia. They had remained in Arcadia, and when we moved back, they invited us to a picnic and summer concert in Arcadia Park. We enjoyed the patriotic music and gourmet picnic dinner so much that we made it an annual event with the Fickases, Cashions, Newtons, Rosses, and Rueffs.

Don and Judy Fickas

With great remorse we decided to sell our condo and golf membership at PGA West, because we were no longer playing golf. We were spending more time at the lake. We sold it to a young couple who appreciated the care that had gone into making it a lovely home. Our biggest concern was where to move the art objects and paintings. Between the lake house and our Arcadia home, we were able to place our notable pieces. We donated the remaining items to the Huntington Hospital.

At the urging of Lyman Newton, I joined The Valley Club. A group of men met monthly, listened to interesting speakers, and shared cocktails and a meal. This gave me an opportunity to visit with many old friends, and once a year we invited our wives to a black-tie dinner and dance. There were several of us in the group who discussed politics, the economy, and capital markets. From this group we organized a small investment club, not to co-invest, but to discuss our individual investments. Jack MacLeod, Dean Stephan, and Bob Twist were engineer/businessmen

who had significant knowledge in the world of finance. Bill Richards and I had worked in the investment industry and brought a different perspective to investing. My belief was that asset allocation was the most important factor in determining investment returns. The engineers were interested in individual stock selection from a business point of view, which was driven by virtue of them having owned a business enterprise. It was a great group of friends. I always learned something at each meeting from my erudite buddies.

It became a tradition for us to celebrate our wedding anniversary with a luncheon at Annandale. For our 51st the club prepared a fabulous buffet: several choices of salad, a variety of finger sandwiches, whole chilled salmon, and trays of sinful desserts. Our musical friends, Ann Louise and Geno, were in attendance. After lunch, she conducted a piano bar sing along which everyone enjoyed, especially the two Judy's, Spare and Fickas.

When our friend and Judy's accompanist, Lou McMullin, passed away, we were blessed to find another pianist, Ann Louise. She came to our house weekly to give singing lessons to Judy. In addition to being a fine teacher, she made the lessons enjoyable. She taught Judy breathing, projection, and the importance of stage presence. They worked diligently and performed two recitals to a full house in our home. Again, the music came from Broadway shows, such as "The King and I," "Finian's Rainbow," "The Sound of Music," "Camelot," "My Fair Lady" and, of course, "South Pacific." We finished the program with everyone singing "You Are My Sunshine," by the Pine Ridge Boys, 1939. Ann Louise was another of our godsends.

Music is in the Air
So, Join Us
for

"A Spring Sing"
featuring

Judy Spare - soloist
Ann Louise Christensen - pianist

Enjoy
Delightful Refreshments
April 20th
at
2:00 P.M.
1311 Oakwood Drive, Arcadia
R.S.V.P. by April 14th   Dress: Casual
(626) 538-4755

Bob   Ann Louise   Judy

On several occasions, including Christmas, Lyman and Gloria Newton invited us to be their dinner guests at the Valley Hunt Club. It is a private social club and best known for starting the Tournament of Roses Parade in 1890. Professor Charles F. Holder announced at a Club meeting, "In New York people are buried in snow. Here our flowers are blooming and our oranges are about to bear. Let's hold a festival to tell the world about our paradise." Little did the professor know the Rose Parade would incentivize throngs of people to migrate to California from the Midwest and East Coast.

In 1965 I built a Tiki bar at our first house in Arcadia. I have written about our love of Hawaii and the South Pacific. I had lots of free time in 2017 and needed to be at home with Judy, so I decided to build Tiki II. It turned out to be a "work of art" with split bamboo sides, a thatched roof of palm fronds, and three authentic tapa cloth panels on the front. Two interior shelves to store the Mai Tai ingredients, and it is on wheels, so I can roll it out for pool parties. That year we hosted over fifty guests for a luau which featured lovely Hawaiian music, tropical drinks, and exotic Hawaiian cuisine. Our friends, Stanley and Edwina Siu, brought gorgeous fresh orchid leis from Hawaii for each of the wahines (ladies). I had a wooden sign carved for the patio that welcomes guests. It reads, "Pu'uhonua," or "A place of refuge."

Stanley & Edwina

Ali graduated from West Ranch High School in 2017 with an excellent academic record. She chose to attend Pepperdine University at their spectacular campus in Malibu overlooking the vast Pacific Ocean. She had played soccer since her 6th birthday and was an outstanding player for her club teams and high school. After twelve years of soccer competition, she decided not to pursue the sport at Pepperdine.

Ali

Because she sustained several injuries requiring rehabilitation, she became interested in sports medicine.

At that time, Sophie was a senior at Boston University and working part-time for a small company that promoted entertainers, musical bands, and singers. As graduation neared, she was offered a full-time position; however, she wanted to move to New York or Los Angeles. Evidently, her mentor recognized her talent and allowed her to represent his company in New York City, where she moved after graduation. Early on she realized it was important to learn to defend herself, so she took boxing lessons.

Sophie

Judy was a student of the Bible most of her adult life. With unfailing faith and absolute belief that Jesus had died for our sins, she believed Jesus had "gone to prepare a place for us" in His Father's kingdom. One day she asked me to select Bible passages that discussed life after death and God's promise of salvation. I marked the verses in my Bible. One of them resonated with her. "Though you have not seen him, you love him; and even though you do not see him now, you believe in him and are filled with an inexpressible and glorious joy, for you are receiving the goal of your faith, the salvation of your souls." 1 Peter 1:8-9

After the readings, Judy said to me in a soft voice, one a mother might use in speaking to a child, "The body dies but the soul lives forever." She had a radiant smile as she spoke. As our conversation continued, Judy said her wish was to rise into Heaven on the Wings of Angels and to see "the shining face of Jesus." Specifically, she was looking forward to reuniting with her parents and three of her closest friends: Mimi Bitzer, Kate Martin, and Janice Board.

In 2017, Aunt Allene, P.J.'s youngest sister, passed away in San Diego. She was always the life of every party, happy and vociferous. Allene was a fine artist, and her paintings of animals were stunningly realistic. I made a large toy chest for Matt and Charlie on which she painted wild African animals: an elephant, giraffe, lion, zebra, and gazelle. Her daughter, Jan, and husband, Bob Meyerott, hosted a small "celebration of life" ceremony at the La Jolla Beach and Tennis Club. We had much in her life to recount. Her husband, Wayne Sanders, attended but was not in good health. He passed away not long thereafter.

Judy and I enjoyed celebrating our wedding anniversary with family and friends. As had become a tradition, we hosted a luncheon to commemorate our 54th anniversary in June, 2018 at Annandale Golf Club. Judy had suffered two hairline fractures in her lower back, both of which were "cemented" by Dr. Bill Costigan. Her physical condition had deteriorated, but she wanted to enjoy the special day with her favorite people. She looked beautiful. We had a happy, joy-filled day. Later, she talked about each of our guests and how much she loved and cherished them. We did not know then that we had celebrated our final anniversary together.

Sheila Ross   Judy   Sylvie

Judy developed respiratory problems and the doctor ordered an oxygen machine to assist her in breathing. The oxygen provided some benefit; however, other medical problems developed which caused her lungs to malfunction. Judy was admitted to the Methodist Hospital where they tried for a few weeks to restore her failing organs. Finally, the attending physician informed me that Judy could not breath on her own. The only recourse was to put her on a respirator, which would require an induced coma. The other option was to bring her home with hospice care. I called our sons, as well as Judy's brother and sister, to seek their advice. We all agreed that Judy would want to be at home. Over the ensuing seven days, many of her friends visited her. Although she could not talk, she gave each a beautiful, warm smile. Dave and Steve were with Judy every day. Carlota and Sylvie helped make Judy comfortable. The people from hospice were loving and caring and of immeasurable assistance in helping us through the last few days. Most importantly, they kept Judy comfortable and free of pain. Judy was ready to meet her Lord. Early in the morning of October 6, 2018, as I was holding my beautiful Sweetheart's hand, she peacefully left this world and rose into Heaven on the Wings of Angels.

"Let not your heart be troubled; you believe in God, believe also in Me. In my Father's house are many mansions; if it were not so, I would have told you. I go to prepare a place for you. And, if I go and prepare a place for you, I will come again and receive you to myself; that where I am, there you may be also." John 14:1-3

For nine years my prayers had been that God would keep me healthy physically, mentally, and financially for as long as Judy needed me. He answered my prayers for which I am eternally grateful.

Our friend, Coyla Grumm, asked if I planned to hold a Church service for Judy, to which I responded in the affirmative. She and several other ladies at the Church of Christ in Sierra Madre organized the service, which I was probably incapable of doing at the time. Prior to the church memorial, the family held a private burial service at the Mountain View Cemetery Chapel on October 11th. Chris Collins, one of our young preachers at church, officiated. It was followed with a solemn luncheon at Annandale. Just three months prior we had celebrated the joyful occasion of our wedding anniversary at the club. I believe Judy approved of the headstone David, Steven, and I designed.

Judy was an amazing person, uncompromising in her faith, as well as her love of family, friends, and country.

The memorial service at church was magnificent because of the planning and the participants. The "Celebration of Life" of Judith Jay Spare was conducted at the Sierra Madre Church of Christ on October 20, 2018. At my insistence, the service started at 11:00 a.m. and concluded at 12:00 noon, exactly. Dr. Jack Scott officiated and eulogies were presented by David and Steven Spare, Judy Fickas, Coyla Grumm, Ray Tripp, and Judy's faithful caregiver, Carlota Brizuela. Judy's piano accompanist, Ann Louise, sang "Amazing Grace," which she and Judy had sung together many times. Gary Baker led the attendees in singing "How Great Thou Art," one of Judy's favorite hymns. Our friend, Geno Escarrega, sang Judy's and my favorite song, "Love is a Many Splendored Thing." The service was followed by a reception at Annandale Golf Club where Judy and I had hosted so many memorable parties. Somehow, I could feel Judy's presence there with me enjoying her family and friends, one last time, until we meet again!

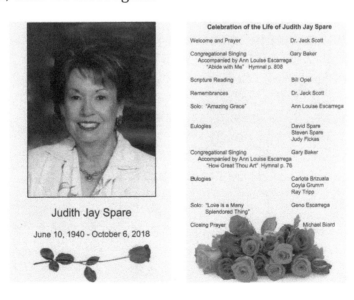

Chapter Eleven

The Rest Of The Story

Paul Harvey may be the greatest radio commentator of all time. He would tell part of an intriguing story, go to a commercial, and then in a low, melodious voice say, "And now for the rest of the story." It has been more than two years since my beautiful Judy passed away, and I have been conflicted on where to end my memoirs. Chapter ten would have been a logical ending point; however, much has transpired in my life and in the world since then. I didn't want to risk having my memoirs referred to as the "Unfinished Memoirs," as was the fate of Franz Schubert's famous "Unfinished Symphony in B minor," because it had no fourth movement.

I haven't mentioned it previously, but friends say I am hyperactive and have a type-A personality. (Sometimes they mean it as a compliment!) However, after Judy's "Celebration of Life," I was content to stay home alone, cook a meal, and read or watch a sporting event on T.V. My family and friends were of great comfort and support, but I felt I had no sense of purpose. After a pleasant Thanksgiving dinner at Steve and Mari's, I drove north to visit friends, many of whom I had not seen in a decade.

My first stop was in San Luis Obispo. I had a pleasant visit with Jim and Ann Farmer, old Pasadena High School friends. Jim and I played football together, and we double-dated to the senior prom, he with his then girlfriend, now wife, Ann. Next, was a traumatic visit with my close friends Berkeley and Maria Johnston. Berkeley was suffering from Alzheimer's disease and was in a mental facility. When I told Berk I was on my way to attend a Stanford football game, there was a slight hint of recognition. In reality, he did not know me. It was heartbreaking, because Berk had been a double type-A, energetic and a leader in every aspect of his life.

Jim and Ann Farmer

Berk and Maria Johnston

I know no Christian couple more dedicated than those two. Berk passed away recently. Mercifully, Maria was allowed to spend the final few days with him. God bless them both.

During a sobering drive to Paso Robles, I had time to reflect on the fragility of life, the importance of enjoying the beauty of each day, and loving and cherishing family and every friend. In Paso Robles, I had dinner with Cody and Donna Ferguson. Cody was a client and a fellow investment board member for Los Angeles County. Cody was my tour guide as we visited several fine wineries where I was able to purchase a nice variety of local wines. This area has become a second Napa Valley with miles of fertile land in the beautiful rolling hills of Central California. All of the vineyards were planted subsequent to my trips through what was desolate land in the 1950's.

My next destination was Los Altos Hills where I stayed with Bob Meyerott and his son, Greg, who was a senior at Menlo College. The Los Altos home is a second residence for Bob and Jan, Judy's cousin. During my visit, I made the short drive to the Stanford campus and visited the Hoover Institution and had a much too brief meeting with Dick Babb, my former Stanford roommate.

I planned the trip so I could attend the Stanford-Cal football game in Strawberry Canyon on the University of California, Berkeley campus. George Miller was my host, and we attended

Bob and Greg

226

the game with Cal fans John Coleman and Cathy O'Callaghan. I enjoyed the "Big Game" more than they, since the Indians beat "the dirty Golden Bears." I stayed with George in San Francisco for a few days where we dined at Sam's Grill, the oldest restaurant in the city. George and a few of his pals bought this renowned establishment a few years earlier.

My last stop was in Monterey where I was welcomed by Woody and Lu Clum in their new home at Pasadera, an impressive, new development with a limited number of Tuscan styled homes scattered in the rolling hills overlooking the golf course. It was good to end my driving trip with close friends who had loved Judy as a sister, as well as reminiscence about the many happy ventures we had experienced together.

Back in Arcadia, the holidays were approaching. I looked forward to spending time with family, especially my grandchildren. The Citrus Choir made its annual appearance at Annandale Golf Club. The Newtons, Fickases, and Rueffs joined our family for an extraordinary performance and gourmet dinner. It was the first time in fifty-five years Judy and I had not been together to celebrate Christmas; although pensive, it was comforting to be with family and close, special friends.

Steve and Mari hosted Christmas for our extended family. In the midst of joy and thanksgiving, we had the painful reminder of who was missing at the dinner table. But, I had to remember that Judy was in God's care in His Kingdom. I visited her gravesite often, and we had quiet chats in the peaceful surroundings near the San Gabriel Mountains. I told Judy how much I loved her and missed her, but, also, how happy I was that she was where she wanted to be, singing with the Angels.

Early in the new year, I departed for San Diego on another driving trip. I stayed with Bob and Jan Meyerott and their sons, Johnny and Jimmie, at their charming home in La Jolla. They were gracious to allow me to use their residence as a "home base," so I could visit other longtime friends in the area.

Bob Sandroni was a competitor and friend in the investment business; Judy and I spent many pleasurable times with Bob and Lora at Lake Arrowhead before their house was destroyed by fire. Subsequently, they bought a magnificent Tuscan home in the hills east of Del Mar. Our visit was delightful. We lunched at their golf club and spent the afternoon drinking iced tea and talking.

I had not seen my great friend and Theta Xi brother, Chuck Arledge, and his wife, Barbara, since our fiftieth wedding anniversary. Together, we spent a wonderful afternoon at the La Jolla Beach and Tennis Club. It doesn't get much better than savoring a delicious lunch with friends and watching the seagulls circling above the waves crashing on the sandy beach. We talked about our

sixty years of friendship and recalled our annual picnics and attendance at Stanford football games when they played USC or UCLA in Los Angeles. Our tailgate group always included other Stanford friends, Fred and Phyllis Crosby and Jack and Lynn Laack.

My final rendezvous was with old Navy buddies. Bob Olivari is a master builder of model military aircraft and aircraft carriers. Six of us, including Tom Hart and Terry Kaltenback, had lunch on Coronado Island. We were then invited to view Bob's collection of planes and ships at Commander Naval Air Forces, Pacific headquarters. Bob's collection is museum quality and will hopefully reside in the Smithsonian Institute one day.

Being a collector of American Indian pottery and rugs for fifty years, Al Williams wanted to offer three of his finest "pinch" vases on consignment to a reputable dealer in Scottsdale, Arizona. So, together we drove there in the early spring to meet with the vendor. In Scottsdale, we hiked in the spectacular red rocks which dominate the landscape, and after a short tour of the town, we headed north to visit my sister, Susan, and her companion, John Fielding, in Cottonwood. It was Sue's birthday, so we went to her favorite restaurant in Cottonwood for dinner. Would you believe we had Thai food in Arizona?

In 2019, Ali spent her sophomore year at the Pepperdine campus in Florence, Italy. I was excited when Steve and Mari invited me to go with them to meet Ali at the completion of the school year. My only regret was that Matt and Charlie could not join us because of school and soccer conflicts.

After an on-time, pleasant flight in first class, we arrived late-morning on a lovely Spring day in Florence. We were tired but anxious to see Ali, so we walked two miles to the campus, which was set in a classic Italian mansion. It was great fun meeting the other students and seeing how excited they were about their nine months in one of the greatest cultural centers in Europe. All sixty students were melancholy about leaving Florence, but they were looking forward to reuniting in the Fall back on the Malibu campus.

Ali had a "goodbye" dinner and evening with her classmates and then joined us the next day to conduct a twelve mile walking tour of Florence in all its grandeur. We visited the dramatic Duomo Cathedral, Michelangelo's "David" in the Galleria dell'Accademia, and the Uffizi Gallery where Botticelli's, "The Birth of Venus," is exhibited. After ravishing pizza at Ali's favorite parlor, we walked across the Plaza de la Republica and saw the Palazzo Medici. From there it was a short one-mile walk across the Ponte Vecchio Bridge to Ali's favorite sorbet shop. It was a well-deserved and appreciated respite.

Judy and I had been to Florence twice and never tired of seeing the magnificent Renaissance art and architecture in that cultural mecca. Judy loved art and had been a docent at the Huntington Library and Gallery in San Marino. On one of our visits to Florence, I fondly remembered the joy   Judy had in describing a masterpiece and the difference in style and technique of artists, such as Rembrandt and Reynolds.

Ali said "goodbye" to Florence and her friends, and we drove to Lerici in the far northwest corner of Italy. There we stayed at the Doria Hotel, high on the hillside overlooking a quiet, peaceful coastal town. From the seaport we planned to board a boat and stop at the five villages of Cinque Terra. Poor Ali was incapacitated with food poisoning, so she and Mari did not join Steve and me for the day-trip to the villages, which are built on steep, rugged terraces overlooking the Ligurian Sea.

We were disappointed the ladies had missed the trip to Cinque Terra. But, Ali felt better after a day of rest, and we were able to fly to Madrid as scheduled. Sophie flew to Madrid from New York and surprised Ali when we checked into our hotel. It was wonderful the cousins could be together for the remainder of the trip. From Madrid, we booked a guided day-trip to Toledo, an imposing ancient walled city with a history of Arab, Jewish, and Christian influences.

Being soccer fans, we were delighted to tour Santiago Bernstein Stadium, the magnificent home of the Real Madrid soccer club. However, we were disappointed the team did not have a game scheduled during our time in Madrid.

The Museo Nacional del Prado is as impressive as any of the better-known museums housing the works of renowned artists circa 15th-18th century, including Rembrandt, El Greco, Velasquez, Vermeer, Goya, Rubens, and Titian. Of less interest to me were the works of Salvador Dalí and Picasso at Museo Nacional Centro de Arte Reina Sophía.

Steven's dinner reservations in Madrid took us to an amazing restaurant, "Bodega de los Secretos," which was in the converted caves of a former wine cellar. The ambiance, food, and wine were spectacular.

Sophie continued on with us to London for the final stop in our travels. Steve and Mari made reservations at an Airbnb in Covent Gardens. It was spacious, well located, and kept us in shape with the climbing of three flights of stairs to our "view" rooms. One evening we enjoyed a glass or two of wine at Charlie and Kaaren Hale's lovely home and then dined at Lucia's, their favorite Italian Restaurant in London.

The next day, we arranged a full day of sightseeing and were blessed to have a tour guide who was exceptionally knowledgeable and pleasant. We visited the Tower of London (home of the Queen's jewels), White House Armory, and Westminster Abbey. We had a delightful pub lunch and then traveled to our final destination, a tour of the Churchill War

Room where Winston and his military staff met underground during W.W. II. We dined that evening at "Ivy," one of London's finest restaurants; it was a bit formal but charming, and the food was exceptional.

The girls spent our final day in London shopping and walking around the city. For dinner, Steve selected his all time favorite dining experience in the city at "Sale e Pepe" (salt and pepper). It is a "happening" place where the owner and waiters have as much fun as their patrons, and the food is memorable.

What a great experience it had been spending quality time and sharing experiences with Steve and Mari and my two, beautiful granddaughters.

I returned home to a bevy of activities with family and friends. Sister Sue and John Fielding drove from Arizona to Lake Arrowhead where we spent a few restful days hiking, boating, and barbecuing. I then spent a few days with Al Williams at his timeshare condo on the beach in Ventura. That was followed by several days in Newport Beach with Steve, Mari, and Mari's family. It was organized confusion, but we had a wonderful time and lots of laughs.

In those first two years after Judy was gone, I spent time with my two bachelor buddies, Mike Nyeholt and Greg Board. Mike and I had worked together as a team at Capital. Greg was a longtime friend whose wife, Janice, had taught kindergarten with Judy before passing away. We spent many pleasant evenings on my backyard patio enjoying adult beverages and perfectly barbecued, Taylor steaks. Great friends!

One hot, July evening, I received a strange phone call from our long-time friend Judy Fickas. In a serious tone of voice she said, "Bob, I want to ask you something," to which I responded, "O.K. what do you wish to ask." Still serious, she repeated her hesitancy to ask. Finally, she said, "Bob, I know you have social functions where you may wish to have an escort, and I have someone in mind whose company I think you would enjoy."

I wasn't sure that I would be good company for a young lady; however, there were dinners and other functions where an escort would be desirable. I was surprised when Judy mentioned the mystery woman's name, Barbara Kirmsse. Judy and I had met Barbara and her husband, Ken, when we all attended Judy and Don Fickas' Christmas parties more than fifty years ago. Ken passed away in 1988 and Barbara never remarried. She raised two children, Ken and Mindy, in a lovely home perched high on the hillside in Alta Loma with a spectacular view of the valley below. Mindy and her husband, Paul, live nearby, and Ken and his wife, Cindy, recently moved to Henderson, Nevada. Barbara's ninety-eight-year-old mother, Mrs. Wilma

Steeve, lives nearby and does not drive, so Barbara spends a significant amount of time helping her.

On July 23rd the Fickases, Barb, and I went to lunch at Spaggi, a charming Italian restaurant that served food which rivaled the finest in Rome or Venice. We enjoyed a delightful afternoon. I learned that Barb is a private pilot, an accomplished artist, and insists on a prayer before a meal.

I was concerned about Dave and Steve and how they would feel about me having a date just ten months after Judy's passing. They were encouraging and suggested that at my age I should "go for it." There was more discussion needed. I visited Judy at the Mountain View Cemetery and asked her permission to go out with Barbara. I knew that she would approve. Judy and I had discussed dating if and when one of us predeceased the other. The Fickases then hosted a picnic at one of the summer concerts in Arcadia Park; it was the kind of event where it was nice to have an escort. Barb and I enjoyed Judy's gourmet picnic and sitting out under the canopy of trees and stars listening to many favorite songs. Judy Fickas smiled like a Cheshire cat, proud of having gotten Barb and me together for at least a first date.

John Bitzer invited me for a visit at his very old farmhouse on Martha's Vineyard. Although his health was deteriorating, John and MaryElla were great hosts. In typical fashion, they had a houseful of guests: son Charlie and wife Shelly, Lance and Marilyn Spiegel, and Dan and Mara

Redden. During the day, guests were on their own for food and entertainment. At night each couple was responsible for preparing dinner for the group. Each meal was a lavish feast, preceded with cocktails around the "rock" which overlooked the ocean. On my assigned night to cook, Dan took mercy and assisted me in purchasing and then grilling three-inch thick wild-caught swordfish. Served with grilled vegetables and several salads, the meal was appreciated by a hungry crew. Although John was on oxygen some of the day, one evening he took the group to dinner at his golf club where he enjoyed "holding court' with his friends.

Shelly   Liz   Mara

Charlie John   Dan Bob

After having my full quota of fun, I caught the ferry to Nantucket to visit Charlie and Kaaren Hale. Their primary home is in London; however, they have a magnificent home and guesthouse beside a beautiful lake on the island. Kaaren is an artist of some note, and the rooms are filled with her colorful watercolor paintings. The island is renowned for its plethora of artists who create art in several media. They are probably best known for their fine scrimshaw

237

engravings and the Nantucket handwoven baskets, both of which are works of art. The Hales are the consummate hosts whether in London or Nantucket. I always enjoy the time we spend together.

Every October, I enjoy hosting the Tiki Party in our backyard. Sylvie and Misael prepare food which rivals any lūʻau in the islands. We had the usual forty plus guests, and, for the first time, my Navy pal, Bill Poteet, and wife, Becky, visited from Lubbock, Texas. Sadly, my dear friends Stanley and Edwina Siu could not join us from Hawaii. Always generous and thoughtful, the Sius sent fresh orchid leis for all the wahines. Oh, and Barb was my "escort" and beautiful co-host that evening.

Larry Stone, my political and social buddy, was a significant financial donor to the Young America's Foundation, which owns the Reagan Ranch in Santa Ynez. Larry arranged a private tour of the Reagan Museum in Santa Barbara followed by a visit to the ranch. I did not need an escort for the tour; however, I knew Barb and I would enjoy the time together. Since Barb was a big fan of President Reagan's and I had worked for Ronald Reagan in the 1960's, we were thrilled to see Rancho Cielo, the small, modest Spanish styled hacienda secluded on a 688-acre ranch in the rolling, oak covered hills on the central coast of California. Ronnie and Nancy loved their refuge, which was as humble as he. This was their destination when they wanted to escape the hectic pace and pressure of the presidency. President Mikhail Gorbachev of the Soviet Union and Prime Minister Margaret Thatcher of Great Britain were a few of the notable    guests they hosted at their ranch. Once, when the President was presented with a receipt for a case of wine he ordered for a reception for Mrs. Thatcher, he signed his name. When asked to fill in his occupation, he wrote, "Public servant." Today, most publicly elected politicians could learn something from the humility of President Reagan.

Woody Clum telephoned me with the tragic news that Tom Hart, our close friend and Navy buddy, had been informed by his doctor that his yearlong treatment with his battle against bone cancer was unsuccessful. I called Tom and told him that Woody and I would like to visit him and his "very significant other" Sydene Kober at her exquisite

home in Los Gatos. She and Tom had agreed he would spend his final time at her home, with hospice if needed.

Woody, Lulu, and I spent three days in Sydene's home reliving fifty years of the special camaraderie Tom, Woody, and I had been blessed to experience. Tom looked well and was in good spirits belying the doctor's prognosis. He insisted on taking us to lunch and then dinner where we shared two bottles of excellent wine (the only kind Tom would drink) interspersed with many heartfelt toasts. Three weeks later Tom was gone.

My friend, Barbara, and I drove north to attend the "celebration of life," which was presented by Sydene and Tom's two daughters. Sydene's eulogy said everything about their relationship, "Tom was not perfect, but he was perfect for me." Our hearts went out to her, because she had lost her husband a few years prior after caring for him during a lengthy illness. It is those left behind who hurt the

most. We referred to Tom as "Mr. Navy," so it was fitting that he have a military burial. Terry Kaltenback, Tom's Navy buddy in San Diego, arranged for a ceremony and burial at the Miramar Marine Corp Air Station Cemetery. It was an opportunity for many of us who had served with him to hand salute Captain Tom Hart one more time. Rest in peace, Tom.

Terry is a volunteer tour guide for the U.S.S. Midway CVA-41, which is now a museum anchored in San Diego Harbor. He invited Barbara and me to an early morning private tour before the ship was open to the public. Our squadron had operated with the Midway in the Western Pacific in the 1950's; however, I had not been on board previously.

The Christmas holidays in 2019 were filled with family events and other social activities. The Valley Club held their annual black-tie dinner at the Valley Hunt Club and provided an opportunity for many of my friends and wives to meet Barb. The Club decorations were extraordinary and enhanced by the Christmas carolers, smell of wood burning in the fireplace, and laughter of friends enjoying a magical evening together.

I love the Christmas holidays, because I can spend more time with my grandchildren. Sophie flew from New York City where she was gainfully employed. It was fascinating hearing how an attractive young woman survived in the big city. Believing it important to defend herself in an emergency, she had become a proficient boxer (not competitively) and hit with power.

To say "farewell" to 2019, Barb and I invited Ann Louise and Gene Escarrega, Gloria and Lyman Newton, and Judy and Don Fickas to Annandale Golf Club to celebrate New Year's Eve. We had a marvelous evening, but little did we know or suspect what was ahead for us in 2020.

Ali was back at Pepperdine University after a memorable year of study in Florence. Being a kinesiology major, she was proud to have been hired by the athletic department to work with the training staff and student athletes with sports injuries. Ali's #1 wish and goal is to return to Florence.

Matt and Charlie were juniors at West Ranch High School. They were good students and key members of their club and high school soccer teams. Steven encouraged the boys to lift weights to build their leg and upper body strength. The boys have started playing golf, which is a sport that they can play forever in business or just for pleasure. The college application process has been problematic for them because of COVID. Standardized tests have been suspended, and needless to say, they have had an unusual senior year.

After returning from a visit in February 2020 with John Bitzer and MaryElla in Fort Worth, Dan Redden called to tell me John's health had deteriorated since our time together on the Vineyard. Dan suggested it would be an appropriate time to visit John. I called to say I was making reservations to fly to Fort Worth. John insisted I bring Barb, explaining, "I want to meet the young lady you think is so special." John was in a rest home and spent most of the day on oxygen; he was able to use his wheelchair to go to the dining area where we enjoyed lunch together. In the evening, Barb and I shared dinner with MaryElla and Shelly Bitzer, John's daughter-in-law. Shelly had been John's greatest patient advocate in dealing with the facility staff. She ensured he received proper care. Our dinner at the Fort Worth Club was marvelous. It is an exquisite club, quiet and reserved with beautiful hardwood paneling and soft lighting. Over a bottle of superb wine, we had a difficult but important discussion about John's health. During our time together at lunch, John got to know Barb while the three of us chatted for several hours. Before I departed for home, John and I had a private conversation. He confided in me saying, "Bobby, she's a keeper!"

Late at night a few weeks later, John told a pastor he was "ready to meet Jesus" and died peacefully. Because of exogenous events occurring in our country, the family was not allowed to have a memorial service or celebration of life at that time. The family planned to have a memorial service on Martha's Vineyard at a later date.

In March 2020, we began to hear increasing reports of a new, potentially deadly virus, Covid-19, which many believe originated in Wuhan, China. As I write this chapter, a year has passed, and the virus appears to be subsiding. The virus has been devastating with the deaths of 500,000 in the United States and 2,700,000 worldwide. It has been a difficult year for people on all continents. Early on, when the virus was spreading rapidly, President Trump took bold action and launched "Operation Warp Speed" to develop a vaccine to protect against the virus. Naysayers opined that it would take at least five years to develop an effective vaccine. They had not learned the truth of American spirit and ingenuity. Private industry, with the encouragement of our federal government, went to work. Former President Trump may have been the only person who was not surprised when Moderna, Pfizer, and Johnson and Johnson received FDA approval to begin administering shots in less than twelve months.

Sadly, this success was too late to preclude the closing of a great number of small businesses, restaurants, beauty shops, and gyms, as well as amusement parks, churches, and sporting events. Despite the fact that children are less susceptible to contracting the virus, they have had to attend school classes remotely using the computer. This has done immeasurable damage to their mental and emotional health.

Perhaps the cruelest result of the pandemic has been the separation of older couples in retirement communities or rest homes. Because of different medical needs, for more than a year two of my friends have not been allowed to visit their wives who have memory problems even though they live in the same complex.

Barb and I have been fortunate to live in our own homes and have escaped being "locked down." We have not been able to go to any "events." Even the hiking trails in the local San Gabriel Mountains were closed for a time. However, we have been able to get together, BBQ, read books, watch movies, and join Church on Zoom on Sunday morning. The quarantine has allowed me time to write my memoirs which I have completed in just over a year.

The house at Lake Arrowhead has provided everyone in the family a wonderful opportunity to get out of their homes and into a lovely environment. Even though the Covid restrictions at Lake Arrowhead were similar to those in Los Angeles County, being in the mountains has offered a welcomed change of scenery. Spending a few days overlooking the lake and sitting under

the majestic ponderosa pines has helped restore the psyche and the soul. Barbara and I have enjoyed walking/hiking in the mountains and have been grateful for mini-vacations at Lake Arrowhead.

Barbara and Chita Johnson

With the virus especially dangerous for older folks, I did not see my family for many months. Barb and I were not overly concerned about being together, as we were careful about our exposure with other people. It was a blessing we could get together every week or two and deepen our relationship in a relaxed atmosphere. Barb is comfortable to be with, considerate of others, generous, and loves animals, as well as people. Most importantly, we share the same religious values and political principles.

Barbara grew up on a farm in Iowa. Consequently, she experienced living off the land as the farm was self-sufficient. She was driving a tractor, cooking, sewing, and ironing at an early age. Today, she enjoys flying airplanes, book club, golf, and tinkering with mechanical gadgets. She can repair just about anything that needs to be fixed. It's embarrassing how much more she knows about mechanical things than I. This is not all bad. When I need to purchase a gift for her, I know what to buy...tools!

As Covid restrictions lift, Barb is anxious to take additional flight lessons and get back into the cockpit. For my birthday, she gave me one of her oil paintings, a landscape of snow-capped mountains and a stream in the Swiss Alps. I have encouraged her to take additional painting lessons when they are available to add to her significant skills.

Barb has been a blessing in my life, and we have enjoyed our time together; however, we are anxious to see friends and go places, little of which has been possible for the last year.

Barb and I are used to doing things the way we have done them for years. Often, we "discuss" if food should be cooled before placing it in the refrigerator or the best way to bake a potato. Google has become our "go to" arbitrator.

In October 2020, Arizona lifted some restrictions, so we planned a family reunion in Scottsdale. Brother Ray flew in from North Carolina. Sister Sue and John drove down from Cottonwood. Sister Barbara was out of lockdown at her retirement community. Barb and I drove from California. Brother Jim had reservations to fly from Idaho, but cancelled when he was given incorrect information regarding Covid testing. All of us were disappointed Jim did not make the reunion, but we carried on in family tradition. Sister Barbara's son, Ken, and wife Sharon, opened the beautiful, artistic front doors of their fabulous home to all of us and allowed us to use it as a base for the reunion activities. Our hosts were gracious, generous, and hospitable. Although younger than their guests, I believe they had as much fun, maybe more.

Ken   Sharon

Barb Bob Sue Ray   Barb Bob

The first of three evenings I prepared cowboy beans and BBQ baby back spareribs which everyone seemed to enjoy. The next evening Ken and Sharon brought in a gourmet caterer who prepared and served a magnificent feast. Our dessert was served under the stars which was preceded by an incredible sunset with a broad stream of clouds in gold, red, blue, gray, and yellow. It was a magical evening during which we relived the miracle of our initial reunion nearly thirty years prior.

I opened the memoirs with a recounting of us five siblings being reunited after forty-nine years of separation, and now conclude with this most recent reunion.

The sky is blue, the sun is shining, the outlook is for "fair winds and following seas." I look forward with the curiosity of a kid to what God has planned for me in the homestretch.

From the fourth chapter of Philippians, verses 6, 11-13:

"Do not be anxious about anything, but in everything, by prayer and petition, with thanksgiving, present your requests to God."

"...for I have learned to be content whatever the circumstances. I know what it is to be in need, and I know what it is to have plenty. I have learned the secret of being content in any and every situation, whether well fed or hungry, whether living in plenty or want. I can do everything through Him who gives me strength." AMEN!

Postscripts of Siblings

James Kerby Jennings

My memories date back to the summer of 1940 when we five children, our mother, and a man (Uncle Donny), singing, carousing, and having a gay old time, took a joy ride in a crowded car with the top down. Barbara was told she could not take her favorite possession with us and was pouting. Lloyd (Bob) and I were rough housing. Raymond was just looking around at everything whizzing by and transfixed by it all. Mother held Billy.

We arrived at a large house (building) and were met by a tall, stern woman, Mrs. West, who took us to another room filled with toys and books. Barbara took possession of a doll and a book. That was the last we saw of our mother or Uncle Donny, and we began our stay at the Children's Home Society. While at the orphanage, I remember Mrs. West threatening me, especially when I did not want to eat my custard which tasted like glue. Being located near Hollywood, entertainers came to perform. Shirley Temple was one. Another was Edgar Bergen who brought his puppet Charlie McCarthy. I remember talking to Mr. Bergen while sitting on his lap.

Billy (renamed Ben) and I were adopted by Lola and O. J. Jennings in December 1940. Initially, we lived in El Centro, California. O. J. was a vegetable grower. He had significant acreage including a processing plant and a fleet of trucks to haul produce from field to shed. These trucks routed on a perimeter street behind our home which was lined with salt trees. The neighborhood boys and I would climb the trees and spear the lettuce with bamboo spears we made. Ohhh, what fun to tear open the heads to get to the hearts!

In 1941-1942, O. J. (Dad) sold his share of the business to his partner, Chas Freeman. During this time I lived with Lola's cousin, Verda and Pete Peterson in Turlock, while Dad and Mother searched California for another property. We visited a dry land cattle ranch near Gilroy. The most notable feature of the ranch was the classic three-story western ranch house complete with natural gas for light, heating, and cooking. Their search resulted in the purchase of a 1,500 acre Sacramento valley ranch and a 7,500 acre foothill grazing property, which was later sold.

The valley ranch was 10 miles south of Red Bluff, California and was our home from 1942-1968.

We had a very conservative home life and education. Grammar school was from grades 5-8 in a two-room, country school house, Los Robles School, which was some five miles south of town. There were 70 students at the school in total. Graduation and moving to high school was a major life changing event for this shy, farm boy who was lacking in social graces, especially with girls.

My freshman year was noteworthy in that I was initiated into the Future Farmers of America (FFA). I also gained ownership of 2 registered Angus heifers who were destined to be shown, winning grand champion and reserve champion in their class.

Sophomore year I was elected president of Future Farmers of America. It was during this year in high school that I asked O. J. if I could play football. He responded, "Yes, provided you continue to complete your ranch chores." In addition to my heifers, I cared for chickens, two milk cows, and horses. There was no provision for transport to and from football practice. Thus, I learned to hitch-hike five miles and then walk/run two miles on a country road only to sit on the team bench. It was during this year I showed my two FFA heifers in the Tehama County Fair. I enlisted the help of my FFA classmate, Wes Eckels. Ironically, Wes, with my heifer, handled the task of winning the title of grand champion while my other heifer, which I showed, won reserve champion. Otherwise, the school year was nondescript. Ben, five years younger, sat at the living room desk and drew cartoons and listened to something called rock and roll.

It was during junior year I was invited to my first girl/boy party at the home of one of my classmates who lived in town. Being the only person who lived out of town, Mother drove me and stated she would be back to fetch me at 10:30. Refreshments were served. Then, there was time to get acquainted with games such as Spin the Bottle. I experienced my first kiss. The evening evolved into learning (clumsy me) complicated dance steps and CLOSE DANCING!!! I was relieved when Mother arrived to retrieve me from my first exposure to social conduct Red Bluff style.

I remained an aggie (farm boy) with interest in increasing my Angus herd and breeding my two registered heifers who were now two-years-old. As far as football, I was finally able to get some playing time as a line backer. Making the roster encouraged me to tryout for baseball. I bought a baseball mitt for $25, my entire summer earnings on the ranch. Sadly, it was stolen during a round-robin tournament at the high school. This was tough.

Senior year, 1950-1951, was a landmark year at RBUHS. The heifers calved. Both males were sold. This money helped pay off the cost of their mom's to O.J. I showed a carload of O.J.'s Angus feeders at the Cow Palace in San Francisco. Football season ended alright.

My social life began to form with a plea from Linda Lee Ruble asking me if I would take her to the Christmas Formal Dance, as she and her beau had broken up. I reluctantly agreed. The night arrived, and it was very stormy. I wore O.J.'s once used tuxedo with sapphire studs and patent leather pumps that were too small. I departed for the Stover Ranch three miles down the county road for my first real date with Linda Lee Ruble. Driving the family's caddy, I felt like I was living the dream. However, it was too perfect to last. Boom...Boom...the right front tire had a blow out! I was half-way to Linda Lee's and had to make my first real-life decision after changing the tire in a rain storm. Did I wear my patent leather shoes or not and run for home, or face my date soaking wet and totally embarrassed? Choosing the latter, I arrived at Linda Lee's where her startled mother asked me in a threatening tone, "What in the world happened to you, Jimmy?" A brief explanation resulted in her asking me in a heartfelt, concerned tone to strip off my sopping clothing. She departed the room and returned with her husband's bathrobe. Sitting before a roaring fire for an hour allowed me time to warm and my clothing to dry, as well as allowing Linda Lee extra time to finish her grooming. We finally arrived at the Christmas Formal for a dance or two together. Fortunately for me, Linda's dance card was full, because my feet were killing me in the damp, undersized patents.

After the determination and diligence of a half-dozen social, activist senior girls, who thought a cute cowboy was preferred to a townie, hotshot athlete, I was, with reluctance, elected Senior Class President for the Fall term. Christmas vacation ended and 1951 started. The second semester began with another election. The same dynamic election committee set out to continue their success. I was elected Student Body President for the Spring term. Love was everywhere during the last semester. Two under class school mates approached me stating that a friend, Shirley Stillwell, wanted to meet me. We fell in love and were together for more than two years. Our time together was only interrupted by my college schedules at Cal Poly San Luis Obispo. I drove from SLO to Red Bluff every other weekend. Absence does not make the heart grow fonder; it only makes the heart hurt more.

During the summer of 1953, cousin Howard S. Packard and his wife, Carolyn, visited us for a week at the ranch. "Pack" was a World War II United States Navy ace fighter pilot and captured my attention. He asked me if I might be interested in becoming a Naval pilot and officer. Intrigued, I applied, qualified, and began training on the 26th of June 1954 through February 1956. I earned my wings of gold and was commissioned as an ensign of the United States Navy. From March 1956 until March 1959, I was a junior officer jet pilot in Squadron VA 56 aboard the USS Bonhomme Richard CVA 31. We flew F9F8 Cougars; the squadron mission was to deliver nuclear weapons to strategic enemy targets.

After my tour with VA 56, I took a break in service to complete my college degree at Cal Poly San Luis Obispo. Upon graduation I returned to active duty and served as a flight instructor, accumulating 3100 hours at Naval Air Station Meridian, Mississippi from March 1960 to 1963. My next billet was as V1 Flight Deck Officer and Assistant Aircraft Handling Officer on the USS Midway, CVA 41, where I was responsible for 160 enlisted men on the flight deck for both launch and recovery operations from June 1963 until after June 1966, during the Viet Nam conflict.

Sandwiched between my military active duty of fourteen years and my employment as a pilot with Pan Am, I was married for twelve years from 1956 to 1968 and had four beautiful daughters. The eldest, Kim, was born in San Diego on January 2, 1958. Diane was born in San Luis Obispo, November 16, 1959. The two youngest were born in Meridian, Mississippi, Pam on May 5, 1961 and Linda on August 25, 1963. The time in Mississippi was perhaps the most peaceful and stable years of our marriage and parenthood. In my estimation, it was the most important time educationally for my daughters, as it was during the early turbulent years of the racial awakening of the negro citizens' plight. I was invited by a neighbor, who was Southern born and raised, to join him and a half-dozen others in a civil rights incident to stop a so-called Freedom Bus from Philadelphia. I declined the invitation, but the group actually engaged in a standoff which became dangerously hostile on the main east/west highway from Birmingham, Alabama.

After my retirement from the military, I flew for Pan Am from October 1966 until Pan Am went bankrupt in December 1991. I retired after 25 years with the airline and was the last pilot to do so. Sandpoint/Coeur d'Alene Idaho has been my home since retirement.

Pam   Diane   Kim   Linda and son Jimmy

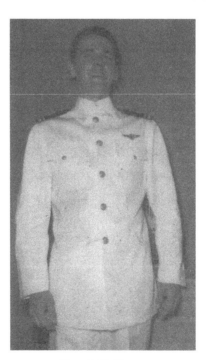

Jim- U.S. Navy

Barbara Tripp Martindale

I grew up in Pasadena, California with my brother Raymond. He is exactly one-year and 12 days younger than I. We were adopted by the Tripp family who changed Ray's middle name from Matt to Leonard and mine from Ellen (my birth mother's name) to Jane. Our mother was overly protective and extremely strict. Our father was a mail carrier, worked long hours, and was almost non-participatory in our upbringing. In this atmosphere I learned compliance, determination, self-preservation, independence, and responsibility for myself, as well as for Raymond.

I also learned NEVER to ask questions, especially after two incidents shortly after we were adopted. When I asked about our brother Bob, then called Lloyd, who had disappeared from our lives a month after our adoption, I was told he wasn't well. Being an insecure four-year-old, I believed he had died. When questioning about our father, I was told he had been killed in an automobile accident. Later, I discovered this was untrue.

I attended Longfellow Elementary School in Pasadena. Because of the positive influence of my 1st grade teacher, Miss Samuelson, I made the decision early to become a 1st grade teacher. She was kind, understanding, and an angel to me, and I wanted to be just like her.

At Eliot Junior High School I was a cheerleader and worked in the school bookstore. I always sought to please others in order to gain acceptance and self-confidence. Many activities, both in school and outside, helped me. One that was especially beneficial was the help and guidance from a high school speech class professor and his critique of my competitive speeches. Another was serving as Honored Queen of Job's Daughters, a fraternal organization sponsored by the Masons. Eliot Junior High School ended in the 10th grade. Regrettably, I missed the graduation festivities due to a severe case of the measles.

Always in a hurry, I took extra classes, so I could graduate early from Pasadena City College. This allowed me to transfer to Occidental College as a junior. I had wanted to attend UCLA, but my mother said, "NO!" At Occidental I graduated Cum Laude with a Bachelor of Science in Education. After I completed my practice teaching in 1st grade at R. D.

White Elementary School in Glendale, California, I was then offered a teaching position there. With my teacher's salary, I was able to rent my own apartment and buy my first car for $300-a grey, stick shift, 1947 Studebaker. I thought I was really living!

My life flipped upside down Friday, April 26, 1958 when I met Al Martindale on a blind date arranged by his cousin's wife, Jane Henry. The Dodgers had recently moved from Brooklyn, New York and were playing baseball at the Los Angeles Coliseum. Our date at the game was great fun. After the game, Al and I continued the evening with conversation in his car until 5 a.m. We were engaged by Monday and married on September 12, 1958. Al and I celebrated 48 1/2 wonderful years together before he passed in March 2007.

Al was my knight in shining armor and the light of my life. Having been raised in a family devoid of closeness, everything I learned about a loving, giving, and sharing relationship I learned from Al. He was an encourager, motivator, challenger, helper, and great listener. He was the most positive influencer I have ever known. We shared a love and life I could have never envisioned.

Al was a UCLA graduate with a degree in business and finance. He proudly served in the United States Army as a First Lieutenant in Korea. His expertise, hard work, and determination in business allowed us opportunities both in the United States and around the world. We eventually visited six of the seven continents and over 90 countries. One of our greatest pleasures was meeting and getting to know many interesting and fascinating people on our journeys, which included thirty cruises. Some remain friends even today.

Our home included three children, a menagerie of stray animals, and always a host of friends. Our son, Ken, was born in January 1960. After three miscarriages, we decided to adopt. We received Jim at 6-weeks-old. He was born October 20, 1963. Deciding we wanted a daughter, Jan came to us at 9- days-old having been born July 14, 1965. With three active kids, there was never a dull moment. Between baseball, basketball, football, hockey, gymnastics, and music lessons, I was the chief carpool driver. As parents, we were active and participating fans and supporters.

Al's business commitments were a big part of our amazing life. One such adventure led us to Salt Lake City for nineteen years. It was here Al agreed to help his friend, Dee Smith, develop a small, local grocery chain with 13 stores into a competitive drug/grocery company with 300 stores in 13 Western states.

As a counter influence to the very dominant Mormon culture, we became very active in our church, Wasatch Presbyterian. Al and I team taught Sunday School. I was chairman of the Christian Education Committee; Al was chairman of the Finance Committee. Aside from church, one of my greatest pleasures was my initiation into the P.E.O. sisterhood in 1976. P.E.O is a philanthropic educational organization which raises funds for women in order for them to continue their education. I am still involved in P.E.O. today.

Other business ventures and consulting opportunities allowed us the fun and experience of living in Las Vegas for fourteen years and New York City for three. While Al worked with Slim Fast in New York City, I struggled in the search for my missing brothers. This journey seriously began after the deaths of my adoptive parents who passed just ten days apart in 1985. While in New York City, I was shocked and surprised to find my youngest brother, Ben (originally named Billy). Finding our oldest brother, Jim, in Idaho was then easy, since he and Ben grew up together in Red Bluff, California.

When I hit roadblocks in my search, I decided to enlist the help of a search assistant. She informed me she could find our birth mother easily. I reluctantly agreed. We found her in Northern California. Al and I flew her down to our home in Laguna Beach for a somewhat awkward meeting. She immediately wanted to be a mother to me and tell me what to do. Soon after, I found Bob, who, I learned later, had grown up not very far from Ray and me. OH HAPPY DAY! ALL WERE FOUND!

We had a grand reunion with all five siblings and spouses in New York City in Ben's apartment. After our reunion, we shared many great times together cultivating wonderful memories. With Al's help, I was able to complete my search and found our papa who was living in Las Vegas. He was an amazing, humble, delightful, and loving man with a fascinating life story of his own. Even though we only had three years with him, we treasured our time together. Both birth parents lived to the age of 93-good genes!

By 2006, Al and I had moved 13 times and were ready to settle down in one place. We chose Newport Beach, California. This was a decision made none too soon. Al passed to his new life with God and the angels in March 2007. After thirteen years back in California, I decided to move to Scottsdale, Arizona in 2019.

I am blessed to have loving, caring, and giving family members. Ken and his wife, Sharon, spend quite a bit of time in Scottsdale. This is fortunate for me, as I get to see them when they are in Arizona. Unfortunately, Jim died in 1998 after a long battle with substance abuse which began after the shooting death of his best childhood buddy. Jan is estranged from the family. Grandson Allen lives in Salt Lake City with his friend, Jessie, and his three children, Mark, Luke, and Ali. Grandson Brandon and his wife, Jess, and their two children, Amelia and Audrey, live in Summit, New Jersey. Granddaughter Lily lives in San Francisco.

As I reflect on my life, I realize I have lived the life I was meant to live according to God's plan for me. I am where I am meant to be, for now. My reflection reaffirms my belief that everything happens for a reason in the way it is meant to unfold in God's perfect time. I AM SO BLESSED! GOD IS GOOD!

Al and Barbara

Ken and Sharon

P.K. and Lily

Jim

Al and P.K.

JANUARY 3, 2005
Marie Allen Ken Barb Papa Al Brandon

Barbara and Lily

Raymond Leonard Tripp

I guess the best place to start my story is the first day of my remembrance at the orphanage, Children's Home Society of California. As a young child, my life was confined to one of many cribs all lined up head to foot in a room that looked like a large football field. Women with starched white uniforms and small white caps scurried around tending to the needs of all the boys and girls who were sitting, standing, or laying down. There were echoes and cries that seemed to reverberate from one crib to the next. I did not know I was there with my three brothers and one sister. All of us were awaiting a thing called adoption.

Eventually, a couple named Tripp came to "replace their daughter," Verna, who had died from asthma at a young age. My brother Bob and I were included in the purchase along with my sister, Barbara. When the Tripps realized that caring for three young ragamuffins was more than they could handle, Bob was returned to the orphanage to await adoption by another family. Even without Bob, Barbara, an obedient daughter, and I proved to be a challenge. Being a hard-headed son, I was told I could test the patience of a saint.

Some childhood memories include our father serving in the United States Navy while our mother attempted to care for us. We traveled on a train to Nebraska with our mother to visit our grandmother. There we attended school. One day after snow had covered the ground, little Raymond got lost. Between tears and crying, a kind teacher was able to get me home safe and sound.

Upon our return to Pasadena, California, I attended Longfellow Elementary and then Eliot Junior High School. Barbara, a good student, was one year ahead of me in school. I remember my Latin teacher, Mrs. Payne, a perfect name for her, saying, "Raymond, why can't you be like your sister?" I had no reply to her question, only self-doubt.

Thinking I may get hurt, my parents did not allow me to participate in any sports. Consequently, I began playing the clarinet in Dr. Palmer's music class. As I became more proficient, he encouraged me to continue. However, I do remember one sports experience. One day after school, there was a track meet against our hated rival, Muir. I was asked by

Coach Reardon to participate in the 100, 220, and high jump. Even though I knew I would get in trouble if my parents found out, I chose to participate. It did not take long for my parents, along with my sister, to appear at the school. In front of all the participants, coaches, and other parents, I was told I had five minutes to pick my clothes up and get to the car. Needless to say, I was TOTALLY embarrassed. This is just one example of the discipline my sister and I faced. No questions asked. Do as I say. Like obedient puppets with strings being pulled and manipulated, we became obedient children.

The next step in my education was at Pasadena High School, which was on the same campus of Pasadena City College. There, I continued playing the clarinet. I was selected to play first chair in the Bulldog Marching Band and marched the 5 1/2 miles in six Tournament of Roses parades. Not to say I was in a hurry to leave home, but I graduated from high school on the 16th of June 1955 and the very next day, June 17th, was enlisted in the United States Army and assigned to the 503rd MP Company. After training at Fort Ord, I was shipped to Fort Knox, Kentucky and eventually loaded onto a troop ship for a leisurely cruise across the Atlantic to Germany. Three years later, I was discharged and moved back to California.

By serendipity, I met the love of my life, Karen Jean King. I robbed the cradle, as Karen was only sixteen-years-old when we married. I was twenty-one. At this time, I divided my life BC/AD-Before Christ and After Christ. Before meeting and marrying Karen, life was all about me. After marrying Karen, which was the first smart decision I ever made, I was forced to think about others. Our first child, Tori, was born. Karen then became pregnant with our son, Mark. During her pregnancy, our friend, Richard Woodall, asked us to attend church with him and his wife. Being really good at making up excuses, we found ways to avoid church. But, God has ways of getting our attention. Richard continued to bug me to go to church. To get him to stop, we went with him to Old Fashioned Southern Baptist Church in Rosemead, California one Sunday.

About a month after we started attending church, Karen gave birth to our son, Mark. Two days later, Mark passed away from double pneumonia. I better not share here the words I expressed with God at that time. For the next five years, we did not darken the doors of any church. The closest we came was driving by them by car. Karen gave birth to our third child, Julie, and then our fourth, Kelly. During those five years, I could not understand why God had taken our son. I said to God, "Look at all we were doing for YOU and this is Your response." Needless to say, I was MAD at God. Truth be told, He did not need us to accomplish His plans for our lives. For five years, we went back to living our lives apart from the interference from God. Weekends were filled with drinking and partying. There was NO time for church. Then, one Saturday afternoon, Karen said to me, "Babe, I was thinking about going to church tomorrow." I stopped what I was doing and responded by asking, "What did you say?" Karen repeated what she had said. My reply to her was, "That is crazy. I have had the same thought." Little did we realize what was about to happen in our lives.

We told our partying friends we were not going to go out with them. We stayed home that Saturday night and the next day attended a Baptist church on Washington Boulevard in Pasadena. The following Sunday we went back to the church in Rosemead. Pastor Starling and the congregation accepted us back with open arms and love. Two weeks later, Karen accepted Jesus Christ as her Lord and Savior. Two weeks after that I did the same. Karen and I started working with the youth group at Hope Union Church in Rosemead. After church we would go with the Hoffman family and their children, Mike and Cindy, to a convalescent facility and sing and speak to the residents about God's love.

A few years passed and I began to feel the Lord directing me to go to Bible school. A couple we knew at Hope Union were attending Grace Bible Institute (GBI) in Omaha, Nebraska. We made the decision to move, so I could attend school. Before leaving Southern California, something special happened. At the time, I was driving for UPS in North Hollywood. One of my stops was at a gas station. One day, while telling the station manager that our family would be moving to Omaha, he asked if I had snow tires for my car. Having lived in Southern California, I did not know anything about winterizing a vehicle. I had not even thought about tires for my Pontiac Le Mans. After learning the make and model of my car, he ran into his shop and appeared two minutes later with four brand new winter tires that were the perfect size for my car. Apparently, a gentleman had bought but never used them. The Lord truly provides!

In December 1971, my wife, three daughters, and I loaded all of our personal belongings into a twelve by eight foot trailer. We hitched the trailer to our two-door, UCLA blue, white vinyl topped Pontiac Le Mans and headed to Salt Lake City where we visited my sister, Barbara, and her family before continuing our trek to Omaha. In the outskirts of St. George, Utah, one of the trailer tires blew out. Once again the Lord showed He was able to meet our needs. We stopped in a gas station where a replacement tire was ordered. Within two hours, we were on our way to Salt Lake City.

Mike and Debbie, friends attending GBI, were able to secure temporary living accommodations in the home of one the GBI professors. It had a first and second story, as well as a basement, and became our home until my graduation in 1974. Big Bertha was the nickname we gave the huge furnace with multiple arms that heated our home. The Lord continued to provide for our needs. I secured a job in the receiving department of Pittsburg Plate Glass in the afternoons and was able to attend GBI classes in the morning. Karen babysat two children plus took care of our three daughters.

When it came time for me to submit my application and enroll, I also needed to pay the tuition to start classes at Grace Bible Institute. I had not received my first pay check. Consequently, I did not have the necessary funds for the first term. When the woman helping me in the admissions office saw my name, she turned around and picked up a business sized envelop with my name handwritten on the front. She commenced to tear it open and onto the counter flowed "manna from heaven." There were one, five, and ten dollar bills, as well as an assortment of change. The money totaled $98. This was enough to pay the school bill in full. Plus, there was enough "manna" left over ($48) to buy food for the family. To this day, I still do not know who sent this money, so that is why I called it "manna from heaven."

After graduation in 1974, our family went to Montgomery, Alabama where I was assigned as an Associate Pastor at McGee Road United Methodist Church. Karen and I worked with the youth. During our ministry there, we saw a dramatic increase in the attendance. Young lives were changed by the power of the Holy Spirit.

From Montgomery we moved to Savanah, Georgia to pastor at Independent Full Gospel Church. Once again, we were blessed to see church growth and people accept Jesus Christ as their Lord and Savior. While pastoring in Montgomery and Savannah, Karen and I did some volunteer work at a local television station for a new Christian program, Praise The Lord Club (PTL Club). After about a year, Jim Moss, Executive Director, and Dale Hill, Executive Producer, for Praise the Lord Club television program asked me if I would consider hosting one of the telethon teams. So, after our moves to Omaha, Montgomery, and Savannah, Karen and I moved to Charlotte, North Carolina where I worked at PTL and hosted one of the telethon teams. I then became Vice President of Trinity Advertising, which was the in-house advertising agency for PTL.

After our parents died, my sister found our adoption papers. Learning our birth names, Barbara spearheaded the search for our birth parents and siblings. Our first sibling reunion was in New York City. We met our mother and were able to have celebrations with her, including her 90th birthday in Lake Tahoe. Eventually, all of the family met our mother and father in Las Vegas where our father lived.

Karen and I have been blessed with three daughters, nine grandchildren, and eleven great-grandchildren. I am reminded of what Ecclesiastes 3:2 declares, "There is a time to live and a time to die." In 2008, the love of my life was diagnosed with Alzheimer's disease which then progressed to Lewy Body Dementia. There were days Karen did not recognize me. After 55 years of a beautiful marriage, her life and memory were fading away. Karen was cared for at White Oak of Waxhaw, a short and long term care facility about a mile from our home. On Thanksgiving in 2014, Kelly and her children went to visit their mama. While Karen sat in her wheelchair, Kelly accessed one of Karen's favorite songs on her cell phone. She played "My Tribute" by Andre Crouch and placed the phone close to her mama's ear. As the words "God be the glory, for the things He has done," Karen slowly raised her left arm heavenward and tears ran down her cheeks. She still knew who her Lord and Savior was. A few days later, on November 30th, Karen took her last breath on this earth. On the natural stone marker located at Forest Lawn East Green Burial Preserve, the words above Karen's remains are inscribed, "The flame of our love never died."

As I close I would like to share a few thoughts. Being placed for adoption has turned out to be a blessing. Sure, I would have loved to have gotten to know my father, who probably would have let me play baseball and taken me fishing, for many more years, but I was blessed by his kindness, thoughtfulness, and appreciation in the years I was able to spend with him. In life there are events that define who we are. The moment that changed the direction of my life was when I was 28-years-old, married for seven years, and the father of three beautiful daughters. I made the decision to accept Jesus Christ into my life when Pastor Starling gave the invitation. Blaise Pascal stated, "There is a God-shaped vacuum in the heart of each man which cannot be satisfied by any created thing but only by God, the Creator, made known through Jesus Christ." I made that personal decision, and as the old gospel song says, "Thanks to Calvary, I'm not the man I used to be. Thanks to Calvary things are different than before." With tears running down my face, I tried to tell my daughters, Tori, Julie, and Kelly, thanks to Calvary they now had a brand new daddy. I invite anyone who can relate to my story to accept Jesus Christ as your personnel Lord and Savior. If you have that God-shaped vacuum in your life, it can be filled with the love of Jesus. And, you will become that new person God created you to be.

Ray-U.S. Army

Ray and Karen

Julie, Tori, and Kelly

Ben (Billy) Wesley Jennings
8/19/1938-2002

Ben passed from this world in 2002. Our family lost its most colorful member at that time. I can give my recollections from the years I knew Ben, following our reunion in the late 1980's, especially during the three years Al and I were in New York City.

My first experience with Ben was our initial phone call when I found him in The Village in New York City. Our conversation lasted almost an hour. It was as if we were old friends and had never been separated. We made arrangements for Al and me to meet at Ben's apartment. At our first glimpse of him, I gasped and said, "He looks JUST LIKE RAY!" They could have been twins; Ben being a heavier version of Ray. Al, commenting about Ben's large, rent-controlled apartment, said, "I thought the earthquakes were in California!" Ben's apartment was a mess, but that was Ben. The kitchen reflected his love of cooking. There was grease everywhere!

At our meeting he explained his circuitous journey from being raised with the Jennings family on a cattle ranch in Red Bluff, California to the Marine Corp Honor Guard in Washington, D. C. for President Eisenhower to Haight Ashbury and finally to New York City. Through later conversations, we learned he had experiences living in New Orleans, Venice, and Paris-all favorite cities of mine. What fun it was to compare the sites we had seen.

Ben was an accomplished artist, writer and musician. Not living on the base when stationed in Washington, D.C. allowed Ben time to pursue his art. After active duty, an art dealer introduced Ben to people in the art community in New York City. He played great blues harmonica and was also a magician. Definitely a free spirit, he marched to his own beat. He was like a magnet drawing an eclectic group of friends wherever he was. Ben's parties introduced Al and me to a segment of New York society we had not known. His gatherings were like being in a movie!

During this time, I had the opportunity to meet both of Ben's wives. Char, who lived in Las Vegas, was the mother of two of his children. Todd is now deceased. Vicky lives in Southern California with her husband and daughter. Russett was Ben's second wife and mother of his son, Austin Gypsy. They lived in upstate New York at that time.

We celebrated family reunions after almost 50 years of separation. The first was in New York with the five siblings and assorted spouses. This was held in Ben's apartment and was terrific fun. The next was held in Laguna Beach at Al's and my home. With 38 of us together for a week under one roof, it was like a huge slumber party. This gathering included our birth mother, Ellen, who was celebrating her 80th birthday. This was her first visit with her family in nearly a half-century.

Ben's passing left a void in our lives. I am so grateful for the years we had to reconnect. Even though we were very different in so many ways, I cherished the time we had together.

Love and miss you, Baby Brother,
Barbara

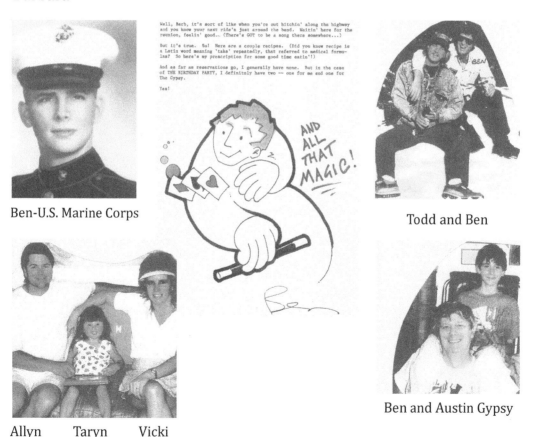

Ben-U.S. Marine Corps

Todd and Ben

Allyn   Taryn   Vicki

Ben and Austin Gypsy

Rogue's Gallery
Family and Friends

Chris Atkinson

Chuck and Barbara Arledge

Steve and Diane Andrews

Angel

Steve and Beth Brennan

Jill Atkinson   Brice Blanc

Mimi and John Bitzer

Janice and Greg Board

Albie Booth

Fred and Bettye Betts

Jane and Ed Blecksmith

Sylvie and Misael Castaneda

Woody and Lulu Clum

Mike and Sarah Cory

Phyllis and Fred Crosby

Dave and Grace Cashion

Jane and Jack De Gange

Jay and Lisa Dick

Louise and John Dorcak

Mary and Larry Epstein

Geno and Ann Louise Escarrega

Sally and Bill Farwell

Don and Judy Fickas

Sylvie and Roger Gertmenian

Melinda Gordon and
Sheila Doyle

Coyla and Dick Grumm

Tom and Sheila Hart

Paula and Dean Hawley

Pam and Dean Henderson

Charlie and Kaaren Hale

Jim Jennings

Ben Jennings

Elden and Priscilla (PJ) Jay

John and Barbara Jay

Jay Family

Maria and Berkeley Johnston   Barbara Kirmsse   Susan Lancaster

Jack and Sally MacLeod   George and Janet Miller   Bob and Kate Martin

Jan and Bob Meyerott

Al and Barbara Martindale

MaryElla and John Bitzer

Diane Mucillo

Kim and Larry Melin

Betsy and Gene McComber

Ben and Linda Massey

Robert and Ruby Mercado

Gloria and Lyman Newton

Bill Nurre

Sophie   Mike Nyeholt

Bill and Judy Opel

Jason and Rena Pilalas

Becky and Bill Poteet

Bob and Dee Olivari

Pam and Cameron Rueff

Chuck and Marion Rogers

Linda and Merle Robertson

Mara and Dan Redden

Sheila and Monte Ross

Mike and Dani Rueff

Dean and Dawn Stephens

Tom Spare

Steven, Ali, Mari,
Charlie and Matt Spare

David, Rosemary, and Sophie Spare

Judy and Bob Spare

Grandma Spare
(Lola)

Robert E. Spare

Amy, Wayne and Allene Sanders, Linda

John and Linda Seiter

Larry and Nancy Stone

Brad and Lynn Snowden

Stanley and Edwina Siu

Sue and Al Williams

Aunt Marge Wilde

Parker and Barbara Williams

Dad H. D. Windham

Mother Ellen Butler

Ray and Karen Tripp   Bob   Jim Jennings   Al and Barbara Martindale

CPSIA information can be obtained
at www.ICGtesting.com
Printed in the USA
LVHW070751040123
736424LV00016B/773

9 781733 729383